From Sophia to SWALEC

FROM SOPHIA TO SWALEC

A HISTORY OF CRICKET IN CARDIFF

ANDREW HIGNELL

SWALEC Sponsorship of the Stadium

SWALEC has been providing power to Welsh homes and businesses for decades and is one of the leading energy brands in the UK.

In March 2008, SWALEC and Glamorgan Cricket agreed a ten-year partnership which secured SWALEC naming rights for the stadium, as well as support for a range of community initiatives to benefit the sport of cricket across Wales.

SWALEC's sponsorship programme has been developed to support the communities it serves. It includes a partnership with The Welsh Rugby Union as National Community Partner and an association with golf at both competitive and development level.

First published 2009

The History Press Ltd.
The Mill, Brimscombe Port
Stroud, Gloucestershire, GL5 2QG
www.thehistorypress.co.uk

British Library Cataloguing in Publication Data.
A catalogue record for this book is available from the British Library.

ISBN 978 0 7524 4701 8

Typesetting and origination by The History Press Ltd.
Printed in Great Britain

Contents

Foreword

I'm really delighted by the ground developments that have recently happened at Glamorgan's headquarters in Cardiff, and it's been wonderful to see the new stadium take shape ahead of the Ashes Test in 2009. I would like to have played at the SWALEC Stadium – especially in front of a full house – and having been in the fantastic new changing rooms and other facilities at the Cardiff ground, I wish I was in my twenties again with many long years in front of me!

I began my Glamorgan career back in the mid-1980s and I can still remember the rather spartan facilities we had at our headquarters in Cardiff, augmented by the indoor school at Neath. At the time we were coached by Alan Jones and Don Shepherd, two of Glamorgan's true legends, whose practical advice and superb tutelage more than made up for the rather primitive facilities at our headquarters.

I've been fortunate that my career as a professional cricketer has allowed me to play on many fine grounds around the world and during my career, as both a player and coach with England, I was able to witness, at first-hand, some of the magnificent stadia that stage international cricket. There were occasions when I wished that I was fortunate enough to play in such wonderful surroundings all the time. All of that has now changed following the building work in the course of the past few years at Cardiff.

The SWALEC Stadium, after the multi-million-pound redevelopment, now compares with some of the finest Test-match grounds that I've visited throughout the world, and I have no doubt that it will soon be regarded by players, the media and spectators alike as one of the best – if not the best – medium-sized Test arena in the world.

I have many happy memories of playing for Glamorgan at the old Sophia Gardens. It was here where I scored my fifty-third century for Glamorgan, against Leicestershire in 2004, breaking the club record held by Alan Jones and Hugh Morris for the most number of hundreds in first-class cricket for the Welsh county. It was also at Cardiff, in 2000, where I scored another hundred in the semi-final of the Benson & Hedges Cup against Surrey, to help Glamorgan clinch a place – for only the second time in the club's history – in a showpiece one-day final at Lord's.

But I feel that the best is yet to come and I cannot wait to see England play Australia here in Cardiff – the capital city of Wales. Having been involved in several Ashes Tests, I know all about the special atmosphere that these matches generate and the fact that the game in 2009 will be the first-ever Test match in Wales will add extra spice to the greatest clash in international cricket.

Matthew Maynard
Glamorgan C.C.C. and England

ONE

Who was Sophia?

Like most things in nineteenth and early twentieth-century Cardiff, the history of the SWALEC Stadium, its original name and the development of cricket in the Welsh capital, are all intertwined with the affairs of the Butes, the aristocratic landowners whose extensive estate in South Wales focussed on the thriving port at the mouth of the Taff.

Without the actions of the Marquess and his agents, who oversaw the affairs of the estate, it is doubtful that Cardiff would have been transformed so quickly into the coal metropolis that, shortly before the First World War, exported more 'black gold' than any other port in the world. Without the actions of Sophia, the second Marquess's wife, Cardiff might not have had such beautiful pleasure gardens flanking the River Taff and Glamorgan Cricket would not have had the opportunity to develop such an impressive headquarters so close to the heart of the vibrant Welsh capital city.

John Crichton Stuart, the second Marquess of Bute, was the man who, in the 1830s, made the bold decision to open a dock adjacent to the mouth of the River Taff and the Glamorganshire Canal allowing coal and other minerals from the rapidly industrialising valleys to the north of the little market town to be exported to other parts of the United Kingdom, Europe and far flung parts of the British Empire.

It was a decision that earned the second Marquess the epithet 'the Maker of Modern Cardiff' and following the opening of the Bute Docks in 1839 the hitherto sleepy market town – lying literally in the shadow of Cardiff Castle – was transformed into a thriving industrial settlement.

In 1801 Cardiff had a population of just a couple of thousand, yet by 1851 it was home to 20,000 people. Despite this ten-fold increase in residents, the town's geographical boundaries had not dramatically expanded. The demand for labour in the booming docks had fuelled this population explosion, but there was a price to be paid as many of the workers were employed on a daily basis and they simply had to live as close as possible to their place of work.

The result was that the orchards, gardens and open spaces of the pre-industrial town were quickly built upon, producing overcrowded courtyards and population densities more akin to cities in the modern-day developing world. With chronic overcrowding came disease, illness and water shortages as the simple pumps extracting water from the river ran dry during the summer months, while wells sunk into the river's floodplain became contaminated as raw sewage seeped in from the open drains.

Living conditions were made even more unpleasant by the regular outpouring of foul and dirty floodwater from the River Taff, whose broad meanders scrolled the low-lying land to the west of High Street and St Mary Street. These areas were frequently flooded, leading to the outbreak of cholera and typhus. The outbreak of cholera in 1849 claimed 347 lives and the following year, William Rammell, the town's Health Inspector, made a report into the dreadful living conditions. During his inspection, he visited a dwelling in Stanley Street, which was run as a lodging house. Rammell counted the people residing there, and to his horror he found:

> Fifty-four persons, men, women and children, they live, eat and sleep all in one room. There are no bedsteads, but all the lodgers lie on the ground or floor. The children were sleeping in old orange-boxes and on shavings. Each party had with them all their stock, consisting of heaps of rags, bones, salt-fish, rotten potatoes and other things. The stench arising from this crowded house was hardly endurable, and there was stagnant water in the yard, with the privy midden running over and covered with filth of the most disgusting description.

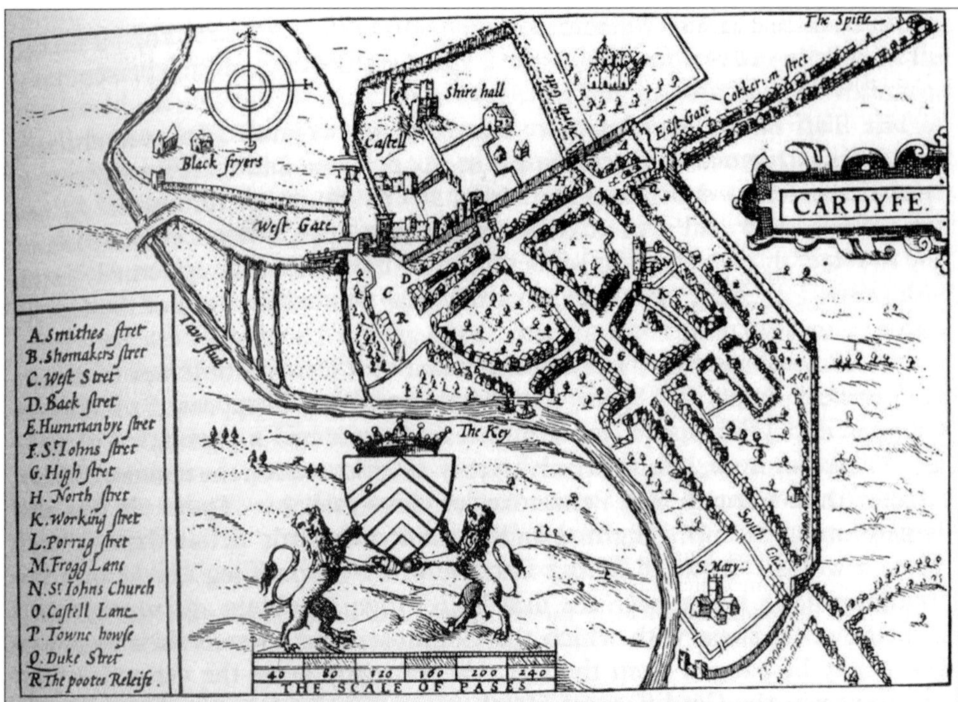

Cardiff in the 1700s, as shown on John Speed's early map of the small market town, adjacent to the River Taff.

This report into the putrid living conditions and bad health of Cardiff residents led to calls for schemes to improve the situation. The managers of the Bute Estate, who owned much of the land on which the housing was built, were naturally concerned and, like the many members of the landed gentry in other British cities, they felt a moral obligation as leaders of local society to improve matters.

As far as Cardiff was concerned, it was Sophia – the widow of the second Marquess – who in the early 1850s suggested a scheme to improve the living conditions of the town's residents. Sophia was the daughter of Francis, Marquis of Hastings, and in 1845 she became the Marquess's second wife, following the death four years earlier of his first wife, Lady Maria North, daughter of the third Earl of Guildford, whose life had been interspersed with bouts of illness, and who had failed to provide the Marquess with an heir.

Twenty-nine months after their marriage, Sophia duly provided the Marquess with a son, but within six months of his birth, she tragically became a widow. With her infant son, she spent considerable time in Cardiff Castle, and soon assumed the mantle of her late husband, acting as an aristocratic patroness of the town. In particular, she took great interest in the welfare of the townspeople; for instance, ensuring that the freighters who used the Bute Docks had ample accommodation.

Lady Bute also became acutely aware of the limited amount of open space in Cardiff, especially where she and the governesses could quietly wander with the young Marquess, who himself was quite a sickly child. In fact, his poor health may well have prompted her interest into the appalling living conditions in the town and the lack of open space.

The only green areas where the townspeople could roam were the castle grounds, but with the ten-fold increase in residents, they had also become crowded and there were reports of damage to the trees and shrubs in Cooper's Field by some of the more unruly townsfolk, leading to the closure to the public of parts of the castle grounds.

On a holiday to the continent Lady Bute, her son and their staff had enjoyed themselves promenading around various public parks. Upon their return from their European tour, Lady Bute suggested how nice it would be if Cardiff had something similar. The area that caught the attention of the land agents and Lady Bute were the fields on the west bank of the Taff to the south of Plasturton Farm – which the Marquess had purchased for her from the Homfray family of Penlline – and to the east of a small track running west of Canton Bridge towards Llandaff and its pretty cathedral.

The Bute officials welcomed her suggestions, as the creation of pleasure gardens helped to compensate for their decision to close the castle grounds to the general public on the opposite side of the river. But perhaps more importantly, they also appreciated how the creation of a public park would act as a catalyst in the creation of a high-class suburb on their land either side of the track leading to Llandaff. Once this was established they might profit further through the further lease of their property for housing.

With calls for new housing areas for the wealthier residents of the town, what better way to alleviate the situation than to create a desirable parkland which people would love to live near? Indeed, it was no coincidence that around the same time as the gardens were being planned, the Bute Estate announced that the road running north-west from Canton Bridge 'will be skirted by a long line of beautiful villa residences, and a new road will be formed, called the Cathedral Road.'

So in reality, the scheme to create the Sophia Gardens pleasure grounds owed as much to profit maximisation than it did to benevolent concern. The managers of the Bute Estate were quick to promote the scheme in the newspapers as another magnanimous and generous gesture by the family of the Marquess. But in all truth, the creation of Sophia Gardens was really a chance to further boost the Bute coffers, serving as the spark for a scheme that would provide, in the opulent villas lining Cathedral Road, a suitable and attractive home overlooking the pleasure gardens for the influential members of Cardiff's society, as well as the political supporters of the Butes, away from the dirt, depravity and dangers of the central areas.

In 1854 work began on the grand scheme, with the conversion of twenty-four acres of land belonging to Plasturton Farm into pleasure gardens, designed by the Bute Estate's architect Col. Alexander Roos. For several months in 1854 work took place levelling the land and laying out the pleasure gardens, with over £1,500 being spent on planting the lime trees which lined the main avenue, as well as the other flowers and shrubs. An offer to have a large Russian gun – captured during the Crimea War – as a focus point at the northern end of the avenue was rejected, with the designers instead opting for an ornamental lake.

The Designer of Sophia Gardens

The gardens and ornamental walks comprising Sophia Gardens were designed by Col. Alexander Roos, who had worked with Lady Sophia on several other projects, including the sailors' home in Butetown in 1853, and on the design of All Saints church in 1856. The young Marquess however was far less enamoured by the Colonel's designs than his mother and after his coming of age, the Marquess dispensed with Roos' services, though his work at Sophia Gardens is still regarded by many as his finest in the town.

In all, the work took three years, and during 1857 the first visitors used the gardens, with the *Cardiff and Merthyr Guardian* of 7 March saying:

> In no town in the Principality does such a pleasure ground exist. Cardiff therefore through the liberality of the Marchioness will set a noble example in the provision for the inhabitants of an arboretum, in which they may at pleasure, promenade amid fragrant flowers and shady trees, surrounded by beautiful natural scenery, and mingle with each other.

In 1858 the gardens were formally opened and named after Lady Bute, but right from the outset it was clear that the Butes had misgivings about allowing uncontrolled public access. Instead, they wanted to preserve the charm and quality of their new park, especially as any degeneration, as experienced in the castle grounds, would adversely affect the housing developments earmarked to happen in the future along Cathedral Road. Consequently, access was severely restricted – a move which upset many townspeople, especially the anti-Bute lobby, one of whom wrote to the *Cardiff Times* saying: 'Nursemaids and children – the scions of the noble houses of Cardiff – are to revel in these newly formed gardens, but they are not to be open to the public.'

A quite heated debate subsequently took place in the council chambers about the extent to which the gardens were in fact a public area. John Boyle, one of the Bute Trustees had been at great pains to announce this fact, both in the newspapers and in a grand speech when the Bath and West of England Agricultural Society held their annual show in Cardiff on the site of what is now the civic centre.

A lobby from Cardiff Corporation approached the Bute officials to offer instead Cathays Park as a public amenity, but the Trustees rejected the request and ended the disputes about public access, allowing people into the gardens shortly after dawn until dusk each day via two entrances – one next to Canton Bridge and the other from the newly created Cathedral Road. Two lodgekeepers were also employed to help keep a sense of decorum in what had become the first of the 2,000 or so acres of parks and recreation grounds in the city.

On 20 September 1859 Lady Bute, after a lengthy spell in Scotland and on the continent, visited the completed gardens for the first time and, before leaving, suggested that a large fountain should be erected in the ornamental lake. The Trustees agreed and soon afterwards Sophia Gardens had one of the first batch of water fountains that were being installed in the town as piped water replaced the foetid wells and inadequate pumps which had prompted the cholera outbreaks. Sadly, her Ladyship never saw the handsome fountain as she fell ill and died over the Christmas period in 1859, leaving her eleven year old son and the Bute Trustees to continue her good intentions.

The following summer, the next phase of improvements saw the start of early evening band performances by the Glamorgan Militia and the town's police band. They quickly drew crowds of several hundred, with people enjoying the promenading in the balmy summer evenings, and listening to the music in the tranquil gardens. The success of these evening concerts also led to a permanent bandstand being built in 1862.

For the first few years, cattle still grazed in the twelve acres of land to the north of the gardens, but as far as the history of sport in Cardiff, and cricket in particular, another important improvement took place in 1860 as, in the words of the Bute Estate, this field would be 'set apart for the purpose of athletic exercises.' Within a few years, several civic events were being held at the Sophia Gardens Field, including the annual review and inspection of the Glamorgan Militia and Artillery Volunteers, as well as the annual show held by the Glamorgan Horticultural Society.

A sketch of Sophia Gardens in 1878 showing the parkland on the west bank of the Taff.

It was here from the mid-1860s, at the Sophia Gardens Field (or Gala Field as some people called it) that the sons and daughters of the well-to-do and *nouveau riches* began to play a variety of sports. Indeed, the *Cardiff Times* on 11 May 1866 commented how:

> These delightful gardens are now in excellent order, and it is pleasant to observe the growing appreciation of them by the public. The garden is frequently crowded with visitors, while the field behind is occupied by a numerous lot of young men and boys, who engage in the healthy games of cricket, rounders, etc.

These early cricket matches were initially quite informal, but a greater degree of organisation steadily took place; so much so, that on 6 July 1866 the *Cardiff Times* carried a report which said: 'A juvenile cricket match was played on Saturday last in the field adjoining the Sophia Gardens between the Second XI of the Taff Vale club and the First XI of the Star Club.'

This game in July 1866 is the earliest known reference to a formal game of cricket at the Sophia Gardens Recreation Field. A hundred years later, Cardiff Cricket Club moved to the area as the Sophia Gardens became the focus of the club's activities.

Lady Sophia Bute and the young Marquess.

TWO

Cricket Comes to Cardiff

The first record of a cricket match being played in Cardiff came some fifty years before the creation of Sophia Gardens, with the *Carmarthen Journal* of 30 July 1819 reporting that a cricket club had been formed in Cardiff, and 'such is the rapid proficiency of the members that they bid fair to rival in a very short time any similar club in Glamorganshire.'

This was a time when a number of clubs were starting to be formed in the small ports, market towns and the other strategic points on the stagecoach routes and turnpike roads that weaved their way across the largely rural parts of South Wales. The earliest known club had been created in Swansea in 1785, and by the 1820s there were similar organisations in existence in Pontypool, Usk, Newport, Raglan, Maesteg, Carmarthen and Cardiff.

The activities of these clubs were, at first, quite limited. Unlike modern clubs with a plethora of teams and a crowded fixture list, these early organisations showed greater similarities to present-day golf clubs, where members gathered to practise and play competitions among themselves. Occasionally, fixtures took place with other clubs, but with quite limited public transport, these were the exception rather than the rule.

Some of these early clubs folded, as their founding members all got old together and failed to attract new blood. This is apparently what happened to the initial club in Cardiff, as nothing else was heard about any cricketing activity until in May 1846 the *Cardiff and Merthyr Guardian* announced that the Cardiff club had been reformed at a meeting on 5 May at the White Lion Inn. The new organisation seems to have been more go-ahead than its predecessors, as shortly after the meeting they secured the use of the cricket field laid out next to the Revd Sparks's academy at Longcross House to the east of the town, adjacent to the Newport Road.

It may have been no coincidence that the reformation of the club happened shortly after the opening of the Bute Docks in 1839. The increase in trade that followed prompted an influx of people to the town, with English-born migrants swelling the pool of cricketers, with the arrival of gentlemen who had already learnt the rudiments of the game, as well as being involved in matches of a decent standard.

The creation of the docks also led to improved transport facilities. In the winter of 1840/1, the Taff Vale Railway was built with a line running from Cardiff to Merthyr, while in the course of the next few years, construction work also took place on the South Wales Railway, with the opening of the line between Chepstow and Swansea taking place on 18 June 1850, followed the next year by an eastern extension to Gloucester.

This new form of public transport had three major effects – firstly, it allowed more people to travel and for clubs to consider away matches. A cheap day-return fare was within the scope of more working people, and following the passing of the 1847 Factory Act and Early Closure Movement, workers had more spare time to practise and play in matches. Secondly, the improved transport network also assisted the spread of information. News about cricket matches and players could be more easily disseminated throughout the region, with the *Penny Post* – inaugurated in 1840 – providing a cheap and rapid means for club officials to send reports to the newspapers, as well as making it easier to arrange games between clubs. Thirdly, the railway lines united the region and more clubs could aspire to challenging the 'crack' sides in neighbouring parts of England, and Severnside in particular. In short, the opening of these lines meant that South Wales was no longer isolated from England, or reliant on a few roads over the hills or a small ferry across the Severn for occasional contact.

A watercolour print of central Cardiff, *c.* 1845.

The reformed Cardiff club duly staged several fixtures against teams representing Tredegar, Merthyr and Newport, as well as various military teams. However, the club lagged behind others in the region, especially Newport and Swansea. Indeed, the *Cardiff and Merthyr Guardian* of 1 August 1846 proclaimed that 'We have seen the Swansea club play and from what we know of those gentlemen, we are inclined to the opinion that they would not have the slightest objection to meet the Newport Club at Bridgend and there stand for the honour of Glamorgan.'

One problem facing the Cardiff club was the rough state of the field at Longcross and for some matches, the club had to prepare a wicket on land at Splott Farm. Another difficulty appeared to be the day when they could use the facilities at Longcross and this resulted in a poor attendance of members. In July 1847 the *Cardiff and Merthyr Guardian* bemoaned how:

> It is barely possible to muster sufficient strength for a game of single wicket. We do not know to what cause to attribute this falling off. Some say the day (Thursday) appointed for playing is an inconvenient one, and that some day earlier in the week would suit the majority of members much better.

Both of these difficulties were quickly solved as a result of engineering work taking place just to the west of the town associated with the building of the South Wales Railway. A major problem facing the engineers was a suitable site for the town's main railway station, free from the danger of flooding by the Taff. Like many townsfolk, the Bute Estate was concerned by the proximity of the river, so in conjunction with Isambard Kingdom Brunel – then a young engineer working with the railway company – a plan was devised to create a straighter channel for the Taff, away from the town. Consequently, between 1848 and 1853 Brunel oversaw the diversion of the river away from the western edge of the town, thereby creating a larger and safer area on the south-west edge of the town where the railway station could be sited.

The straightening of the river significantly extended the area of meadowland at the rear of the Cardiff Arms, an impressive seventeenth-century townhouse, known originally as Ty Coch, which had been built for a wealthy family close to the West Gate into the small town. In 1787 the house and its garden running down to the Taff was sold and the property had been converted into an inn, known variously as the Cardiff Arms Hotel or Cardiff Arms Inn – the name 'Arms' being derived from a shield containing the red-and-yellow chevron crest of Cardiff, which hung above the doorway – and the garden at the rear became known as the Cardiff Arms Park.

The Cardiff Arms Hotel.

A view of central Cardiff in the early 1930s, showing the railway line, the Arms Park and the river which, before Brunel's work, had flooded the other side of the Arms Park complex.

The Cardiff Arms Hotel

The South Wales Daily News for 28 December 1911 contains the following snippet about the origins of the Cardiff Arms Hotel: 'It was a building not intended to be a hotel initially, but was the substantial three-storey townhouse of the wealthy Thomas family who built Wenvoe Castle. When they moved, it was taken over by a hotelier and run by a Miss Wood, who was the sister of the keeper of Cardiff Gaol. She was a superior type of woman and a high-class establishment was soon created.' The Cardiff Arms was demolished in 1882.

CARDIFF ARMS
ROYAL
Family & Commercial Hotel
AND POSTING HOUSE,
FACING THE CASTLE,
CARDIFF.
J. H. PERRY, Proprietor.

This Hotel is situate in the most pleasant part of the town, and the views of the River Taff and the surrounding country are not to be surpassed in the neighbourhood.

The Hotel is replete with every comfort both for Families and Commercial Gentlemen.

Carriages and Post Horses of a superior class.

Wedding Parties specially provided for.

The Pleasure Grounds attached to the Hotel are tastefully laid out, and the Cardiff Cricket Ground is within a minute's walk.

Omnibuses meet all trains.

b

A notice for the Cardiff Arms Hotel, *c.* 1874.

The hotel gained in importance and patronage as transport developed during the late-eighteenth and early nineteenth centuries, in particular with the evolution of stagecoach routes. The coaching inn became 'the place' to stay while stopping at the town and when King Edward, Prince of Wales, visited the town as a young boy he stayed at the Cardiff Arms.

In 1803 the Cardiff Arms and the park became the property of the Marquess, who allowed it to be used for recreation along with civic events, such as the town's celebrations in 1837 for the accession of Queen Victoria. Until the 1840s, however, the park was poorly drained and prone to flooding. The diversion of the Taff ended these difficulties and also enlarged the park to some eighteen acres.

With its improved drainage, the park started to become a popular place for recreation and in May 1848 the *Cardiff and Merthyr Guardian* reported how the members of the town's cricket club 'met in the field a little westward of the Cardiff Arms Hotel.' The club subsequently went from strength to strength and their switch in 1848 to the Cardiff Arms Park marked the start of a long and happy relationship between cricket in Cardiff and the Bute Estate.

The First Known Reference to Cardiff Arms Park

Up until the early 1800s, the area of open land and coppices at the rear of the Cardiff Arms was known as 'The Drying Hayes.' The word 'hayes' (or hays) was applied at the time to a small enclosure with a small woodland or copse. Several of these existed elsewhere in the areas, such as The Hayes near St John's Church, as well as Cathays (or Catt Hays as it was referred to in a document of 1715) to the north of the town.

The use of the word 'drying' in this early description related to the fact that the tanners working in the town and at the nearby slaughterhouses would use this area, especially the branches of its trees, for drying linen, cloth and hides.

The first known reference to Cardiff Arms Park dates from an advertisement in the *Cardiff and Merthyr Guardian* for 27 May 1837, with the advert referring to the use of Cardiff Arms Park by Batty's Amphitheatre.

THREE

The Visit of the All England XI

The 1850s were a boom period for the industrial town of Cardiff. The same could equally be applied to its cricket club, which thrived as a result of the switch to the Arms Park and the generosity of the Bute Estate, who allowed the club to use the area free of charge for their fixtures and practices. The influx of people to live in the town further swelled membership, as did the change in location to a more convenient ground, close to the heart of the thriving town and its welcoming taverns and hostelries.

Their list of opponents steadily rose as the public-transport facilities further improved, allowing regular matches against Newport, Abergavenny, Neath, Swansea, Llanelly and Aberdare, as well as the 'crack' Clifton club on the other side of the Severn Estuary. The membership roll also included sufficient numbers of young men and boys to allow a juveniles team to be formed in May 1849. Soon afterwards, the *Cardiff & Merthyr Guardian* was able to proclaim how:

> It affords us the greatest satisfaction to witness the growing interest which the young men of this town take in the game of cricket. Youngsters generally contrive to have periods of relaxation from business, and if they do not habituate themselves to employ their leisure hours usefully, or at least harmlessly, it is rather more than probable that the taproom, or even worse places will be frequented and a confirmed habit of smoking and tippling be induced.

There were, however, plenty of opportunities for the cricketers to socialise as the club's members were entertained in a large marquee, during both practice sessions and matches, erected on the edge of the boundary rope and adjacent to the entrance into the Arms Park from Westgate Street. The marquee was liberally supplied with ales and spirits from the adjacent coaching inn and a measure of the convivial atmosphere within the club's membership can be gauged from the fact that, at the end of the season, the club organised an annual outing to the nearby seaside town of Penarth.

With an increase in membership and playing activities,the Cardiff club decided in 1854 to copy the trend of other leading clubs in England by hiring the services of a professional cricketer, William Selby, who had played for Nottinghamshire in 1848. Contemporary reports described Selby as 'Cardiff's professional advisor' and 'a professional instructor', so like other professionals in England, he clearly undertook other duties, besides playing, including coaching the members and maintaining the wicket.

The England XIs of the Mid-Nineteenth Century

The mid-nineteenth century saw the emergence of wandering teams of star professionals playing exhibition matches against local XIs. The two most successful teams of professionals were the All-England XI and the United All-England XI. Besides being money-making ventures for their promoters, these exhibition games were also quite lucrative fixtures for the clubs with the opportunity of charging entrance fees so that the local residents could see these leading players in action.

Some of the contests with these itinerant XIs also involved financial challenges or were 'handicap' contests between the eleven stars and a team comprising of up to two-dozen or so local men, plus a few hired hands. There were also gambling tents on the ground, where spectators were able to place bets on how many runs each batsman might make.

Cardiff around 1850, as viewed from Leckwith Hill with the newly opened docks to the extreme right.

Fifty years later it was very different, as seen in this aerial view of Cardiff Docks in the early 1900s.

By 1855 most of the principal English towns and cities had staged matches involving the All-England XI or United England teams, with the games attracting decent crowds and the result viewed by locals as a measure of civic pride. With over 25,000 people now living in Cardiff and the Bute East Docks having opened, there was a growing sense of identity within the booming coal metropolis. Not surprisingly, the officials of Cardiff C.C. believed that they should also issue a challenge to the wandering England side, marking the coming of age for cricket in the town.

With the full support of the Bute Estate, discussions took place during June 1855 with William Clarke, the Nottingham-based entrepreneur, about staging a two-day match at the Arms Park between Clarke's All England XI and a combined twenty-two representing Cardiff and District. An agreement was quickly reached over a date in August, with notices advertising the match soon going up around the town. The local newspaper also proudly proclaimed how 'the event will prove an epoch from which we shall hereafter have to date the progress of South Wales to a higher elevation in the noble art of cricketing.'

Edgar Willsher, an early star who played for the All-England XI at Cardiff.

With a large crowd expected, a number of prominent townsmen agreed to take part, including Alfred Ollivant (the Bishop of Llandaff), the Revd Cyril Stacey who was curate of St John's and also Capt. Maher, who was in charge of the lightship in Cardiff Bay. Given the status of this game, the Cardiff officials were very keen to give the England side a decent run for their money, so a number of useful amateurs guested for the Cardiff team, including Wingfield and Cecil Fiennes, who played representative cricket for Herefordshire and Oxfordshire.

The Cardiff officials also covered the expenses of E.M.Grace and Alfred Pocock from the West Gloucestershire club, plus a second professional, Edmund Hinkley, a thirty-six year old fast-medium bowler who, while playing for Kent in 1848, had taken all ten wickets in the second innings of their match against England at Lord's. Hinkley had also played for Surrey, and with his professional appointments including spells with Watford, Weymouth and Manchester, he was typical of the journeyman professional who led a peripatetic existence in the mid-nineteenth century.

However, there was a significant cost to the Cardiff club in having all of these guests and professionals in addition to the considerable expense in staging the game, with Clarke having demanded a decent guarantee, as well as appearance money for his England players. The travel costs and, no doubt generous expenses claimed by Grace and Pocock, would have further added to the sizeable costs.

In the days leading up to the match, the *Cardiff and Merthyr Guardian* took great delight in reporting that 'our district players have within the last few weeks been assiduously engaged in testing sinew and muscle, by throwing the ball, plying the bat and practising the various rapid manoeuvres requisite for this vigorous and healthful game.' As it turned out, perhaps more practice was needed as the local team were dismissed for 64, with only Selby getting into double figures, as Edgar Willsher, the famous bowler from Kent, claimed ten wickets and William Clarke himself took eight.

Edmund Hinkley then earned his match fee by taking seven English wickets as the professionals were restricted to a first innings lead of just 72, with only George Parr playing with ease on the Arms Park wicket. Batting for a second time, the local men found runs slightly easier to acquire with both Francis Stacey, the son of Cyril Stacey, and Wingfield Fiennes able to show their talents with the bat as the Cardiff team mustered 105. This left the England team needing 98 to win, but with Parr in good form again and both Francis Tinley of Nottinghamshire and Willsher playing freely, the professionals cruised to their target with five wickets in hand.

Two-innings friendly
Cardiff and District XXII v. All-England XI
9, 10, 11 August 1855
Cardiff Arms Park

Result – All-England XI won by 5 wickets

Cardiff and District XXII		**first innings**			**second innings**	
T. Hodge	c Tinley	b W. Clarke	7		b Willsher	3
A. Watkins		b Bickely	0		not out	2
F.E. Stacey		run out	3		b Tinley	14
C. Worthington	c Stephenson	b W. Clarke	5		b Willsher	6
W. Selby	st Stephenson	b W. Clarke	11	c Caesar	b W. Clarke	4
Revd C. Stacey		b W. Clarke	3	c Anderson	b W. Clarke	0
G. Worthington		run out	6		run out	5
A.C. Bell		b W. Clarke	2		b Willsher	3
W.S. Fiennes		b Willsher	5		b Willsher	27
H. Grace		b Willsher	0		b Willsher	5
S. Fiennes		b Willsher	5		b Tinley	4
A. Pocock	c Marshall	b W. Clarke	2	c Stephenson	b W. Clarke	8
A. Thorogood		b Willsher	0	c Tinley	b W. Clarke	0
A. Ollivant		b Willsher	0		b Willsher	0
G. Williams		b Willsher	0		b Willsher	0
W. Bell		b Willsher	7		b Tinley	9
E. Hinkley		b Willsher	2		b Tinley	0
Jones	c Tinley	b Willsher	0		b W. Clarke	1
Dewdney		b Willsher	0		b Willsher	0
Capt. Maher		b W. Clarke	0		run out	0
S. Harks		not out	0		b W. Clarke	0
W. Ollivant		b W. Clarke	0		b W. Clarke	1
Extras	(b 2,lb 2, nb 2)		6	(b 8, lb 3, nb 2)		13
Total	(all out)		64	(all out)		105

Bowling	B	R	W		B	R	W
W. Clarke	153	32	8	W. Clarke	138	55	7
Bickley	92	12	1	Willsher	116	32	8
Willsher	60	14	10	Tinley	40	5	4

All-England XI		**first innings**			**second innings**	
R.C. Tinley		b W. Fiennes	9	c Selby	b Hinkley	25
H.W. Stephenson		b Hinkley	4			
G. Anderson		b W. Fiennes	9	c Selby	b Hinkley	8
G. Parr	c F. Stacey	b Hinkley	16		not out	27
J. Caesar	c Pocock	b Hinkley	7		b Hinkley	1
A. Clarke		b Hinkley	5			
S. Parr		b Hinkley	1		not out	10
J.A. Marshall		not out	7			
E. Willsher		b Hinkley	7	c F Stacey	b Hinkley	26
J. Bickley		b Hinkley	1			
W. Clarke		b W. Fiennes	1			
Extras	(b 5)		5	(w 1)		1
Total	(all out)		72	(for five wickets)		98

Bowling	B	R	W
Hinkley	208	23	7
Grace	28	16	0
W. Fiennes	175	28	3

	B	R	W
Hinkley	144	37	4
W. Fiennes	99	33	0
F. Stacey	16	14	0
Selby	24	11	0

Despite the defeat, the match had been a great success for the Cardiff club. A decent crowd had turned up and had thoroughly enjoyed themselves, either in the marquee erected to offer plenty of liquid refreshment or in the betting tent, where a number of hefty wagers were placed on the outcome of the game and the individual performances.

The Cardiff officials agreed to repeat the exercise, so in 1857 an approach was made to John Wisden who was overseeing the matches of the United All-England XI, an offshoot of Clarke's team. Terms were agreed with the Sussex professional and on 31 August, his team played a three-day match at Cardiff, once again against a XXII drawn from the local area, plus a few helping hands. Hinkley's services were acquired again by the Cardiff team, together with those of Capt. George Homfray, a leading figure with the rapidly expanding club at Newport.

Homfray was also a member of the local gentry with his Glenusk-based family being closely associated with many of the flourishing industrial centres in the South Wales valleys. His father Jeremiah had opened the Penydarren ironworks in Merthyr in 1805, followed by others in Ebbw Vale and Tredegar, and with the wealth that this generated, Jeremiah acquired Penlline Castle near Wenvoe in 1847.

George Homfray was not an outstanding cricketer, but what he lacked in talent he more than made up for in enthusiasm. He tirelessly promoted both Newport and Tredegar C.C., and if this wasn't enough, he also helped to found the South Wales Cricket Club in 1859 as a gentleman's XI playing matches against similar teams in the Home Counties and the West Country.

George Homfray, the founder of the South Wales C.C.

Two-innings friendly
Cardiff and District XXII v. United All-England XI
31 August, 1, 2 September 1857
Cardiff Arms Park
Result – United All-England XI won by 135 runs

United All-England XI		first innings			second innings	
F.P. Miller		b Jones	5	c C. Stacey	b Hinkley	6
J. Grundy		b Hinkley	22	c Nicholl	b Selby	2
T. Lockyer	c Hopkins	b Gibson	28	c C. Stacey	b Hinkley	6
W. Caffyn	c Selby	b Hinkley	1	c Wallace	b Hinkley	3
J. Wisden	c F. Stacey	b Hinkley	2		not out	35
W. Parry		b Gibson	5		b Hinkley	2
W. Mortlock		not out	11	st F. Stacey	b Hinkley	20
G. Griffith	c Gibson	b Hinkley	11	lbw	b Hinkley	0
F. Bell	c Gibson	b Hinkley	0		b Hinkley	22
J. Dean	c Cooper	b Gibson	0	c Kempson	b Hinckley	0
H. Wright		b Hinkley	0		b Selby	36
Extras	(b 3, lb 1, w 4)		5	(w 1)		12
Total	(all out)		93	(for five wickets)		144

Bowling	B	R	W		B	R	W
Jones	76	23	1	Jones	48	8	0
Hinkley	185	36	6	Hinkley	187	60	8
Gibson	112	26	3	Gibson	44	7	0
				Selby	156	57	2

Cardiff and District XXII		first innings			second innings	
Vigors		b Wisden	2		b Griffith	4
T Hodge		b Griffith	1		b Griffith	0
Jones	c and	b Wisden	2	c Caffyn	b Griffith	7
G. Worthington		b Griffith	1		b Dean	3
W. Selby	c and	b Wisden	3	c Wisden	b Griffith	0
W.J. Kempson	c Dean	b Griffith	15		b Griffith	0
Wallace		run out	6		b Griffith	5
F.E. Stacey	c Griffith	b Wisden	13		run out	4
Paine		b Wisden	0		b Griffith	3
Hammonds		b Griffith	0		b Griffith	0
C. Riches	c Lockyer	b Wisden	2		b Griffith	6
C. Worthington	st Lockyer	b Griffith	0		run out	0
Hopkins	c Parry	b Griffith	1	c Dean	b Caffyn	0
A.C. Bell		b Wisden	0		b Griffith	2
Capt. G. Homfray	c Caffyn	b Wisden	0	c Caffyn	b Dean	0
E. Nicholl		b Wisden	0		b Griffith	2
A. Ollivant	c Parry	b Wisden	0		not out	6
R. Gibson		b Griffith	0		absent	
Revd C. Stacey		b Griffith	0		b Griffith	0
Cooper		run out	0		b Caffyn	0
Marks	c Dean	b Griffith	0	c Griffith	b Dean	0
E. Hinkley		not out	1		b Griffith	5
Extras	(b 1)		1	(b2, lb3, w2)		7
Total	(all out)		48	(all out)		54

Bowling	B	R	W		B	R	W
Wisden	120	29	10	Griffith	92	14	13
Griffith	116	18	9	Caffyn	60	20	2
				Dean	32	15	3

Homfray did not score a run in either innings in the match against the United England team. He was not alone, however, as half of the forty-four innings of the Cardiff players ended in ducks as the England team ran out comfortable winners by the large margin of 135 runs. Wisden himself claimed ten wickets in the match, while the fast round-arm bowling of Surrey's George Griffith accounted for nine victims in the first innings and thirteen in the second. Francis Stacey and William Kempson, his friend from Cambridge University and fellow Blue, were the only men to get into double figures in the first innings. Nobody did so a second time around, as the England bowlers made merry progress though the local batting after John Wisden had given a fine display of strokes in making an unbeaten 35.

Subsequently, there was no return visit by Wisden's team, as the match drew heavily on the club's resources. With plenty of gambling also taking place, the defeat also left plenty of people, as well as the club, out of pocket. No coincidence that the local newspapers subsequently neglected to report on any inter-club matches of note, suggesting that the Cardiff club paid the price for their extravagance and were either forced to cut their fixture list or go out of existence.

When Julius Caesar Played Cricket at Cardiff

While Cardiff Castle has its links with the Roman invasion, it is known that Julius Caesar played cricket on the Arms Park. Not, however, the Emperor, but instead the Surrey professional who was one of the participants in the All-England match in 1855.

Caesar was a regular performer with the All-England side until 1863, when the onset of gout hastened the end of his playing career, suggesting that 'Julie' enjoyed the off-field revelry as much as the on-field activities. A carpenter and joiner by trade, Caesar was a strong man of medium height, who became one of the first players in the nineteenth century to regularly play the pull stroke to short, rising deliveries.

He also was a fine fielder, excelling at point as well as in the position of long-stop, which was frequently employed on the rough wickets in the nineteenth century, as the ball often flew past the wicketkeeper towards the boundary.

FOUR

A Permanent Home at the Arms Park

It had been very ambitious of the early Cardiff club to have staged fixtures with the professional England teams; this reflected the buoyant mood and go-ahead of the business community in Cardiff, rather than the standard of cricket and the skill level of the town's players. In fact, not everyone in the expanding town was in favour of cricket, especially games on the Arms Park on the Sabbath, and in 1859 the local newspaper was aghast to report how:

> A party of youngsters have, of late, taken to playing cricket in the Cardiff Arms Park on Sundays… On Sunday last, the hotel people fetched the police to them, whose appearance speedily had the effect of clearing the ground. It is hoped now that the matter has been brought to the cognisance of the police, that such flagrant desecration of the day will put a stop to it.

Such views were aligned closely to the Nonconformist attitudes which were prevalent at the time throughout several parts of South Wales. The religious disapproval had been prompted as much by the heavy drinking and after-match socialising as people deciding to play ball games on Sundays. In some parts of the region the religious leaders spoke vehemently about these issues. Indeed, the Revd P.M. Proctor of Monmouth went as far as issuing a pamphlet in which he described the activities of a young miner called Morgan, who was, he affirmed:

> Normally first on the ground, yet the last to return home. But one Sunday he decided to refrain from his heathen tendencies and drinking habits by going to church instead. He was immediately converted and never went near a cricket ground again. He died deeply penitent and Heaven gained a very good batsman.

As far as Cardiff was concerned, there was a sizeable Nonconformist lobby as reflected in the 1852 town elections where Walter Coffin, a staunch Liberal and Nonconformist, beat John Nicholl, the aristocratic Conservative candidate, who lived at Merthyr Mawr and avidly promoted cricket matches in the grounds of his country home.

The waves of immigrants to Cardiff from large industrial centres in England steadily led to a decline in this Nonconformist antipathy towards sports of all kinds. Their arrival in Cardiff during the second half of the nineteenth century also coincided with the spread of the ethic of Muscular Christianity and in particular, the views of Charles Kingsley. He was a vocal advocate of healthy recreation, writing:

> Through sport, boys acquire virtues which no books can give them; not merely daring and endurance, but better still, temper, self-restraint, fairness, honour, unenvious approbation of another's success, and all that give and take of life which stands a man in good stead when he goes forth into the world and without which, indeed, his success is always maimed and partial.

The arrival of people, well versed in the writings of Kingsley, not only led to a decline in Nonconformist views but also led to Cardiff's cricket club being reformed in 1861. The new club, with its fresh blood, took great pains to learn from the experience of the earlier organisation, carefully building on its achievements and its greatest legacy, namely the trend for major cricket matches, along with principal sporting events at the Arms Park.

Fixtures resumed in 1861 with other leading clubs in the region, including Newport and Bridgend, as well as regular visits across the Severn to play at Durdham Down against the Clifton club. From 1863, Cardiff's fixture list also included matches against the Cadoxton club near Neath, which had been founded by J.T.D. Llewelyn, the squire of Penllegaer. His input and support helped both the Cardiff club and the South Wales C.C., with the officials of the latter club also selecting several Cardiff players for their two-day and three-day fixtures against leading clubs and county sides in England. These matches in London and the south-east of England, plus the support of Llewelyn, all helped the new club in Cardiff to acquire a useful series of contacts.

In fact, it may have been no coincidence that around this time, the new Cardiff club also hired the services of a professional from Surrey called Clarence Walter, a twenty-five-year-old all-rounder, who had been employed on the groundstaff at The Oval. His employment at the London ground had primarily been as a net bowler, so perhaps he impressed some of the Cardiff gentlemen when they were uptown playing for the South Wales side.

Walter had also made a couple of first-class appearances with Surrey and this experience proved invaluable for his new employers. Having an energetic young professional was also highly beneficial for the Cardiff club, and Walter's move to South Wales proved to be a very happy experience for all concerned, as he remained in Cardiff until his death in 1918. During the course of his career as both a professional and a coach with the town club, he saw a significant upswing in membership, playing standards and facilities.

An indication of his efforts came in March 1865 when the *Cardiff and Merthyr Guardian* proclaimed, 'The Cardiff club of late has not been in a very flourishing condition and exertions are now being made to establish the club upon an improved footing by increasing the number of members and creating greater interest.'

In addition to coaching the members of the Cardiff club, Walter was also hired out to the schools and academies in the local area, where the young boys were no doubt eager to become model examples of Muscular Christians. He also held sessions at smaller clubs in the area, including Penarth and Roath, who helped to cover his expenses by organising a benefit match for him.

The teenage Marquess, who was now at school at Harrow, was also caught up in the mood of the age and in 1865 he readily agreed to become the patron of the Cardiff club. His support was a major coup for the club as it signified a new era with a much closer relationship between the cricket club and the Butes. This link became increasingly important as a number of other clubs had come into existence and were also using the Arms Park for their games. Reports in the *Cardiff Times* for 1866 refer to nine other clubs playing in the town: Prince of Wales (Canton), Windsor, Canton, Taff Vale, Star, Loudon Square, Mount Stuart, Roath and Longcross. Several used the Arms Park for their matches and in 1867 the newspaper carried reports of matches on the park between company teams representing ironmongers, drapers and grocers.

The increased use of the Arms Park worried the influential members of the town club who desperately wanted to have a pristine wicket on which they could challenge the leading players of other premier clubs. They also wanted a base where they could express their commercial and political standing. The latter was an important consideration at a time when the town council was dominated by Liberals, and the influential Conservatives within the town's cricket team realised that they could use the club as a means of consolidating their identity in the increasingly cosmopolitan town.

This was a time of growing agitation with 'the Castle', especially their money-making activities, and in 1866 the Bute Estate was approached by the town council about the Arms Park being donated as the site for the new cattle market. After the outbreak of various diseases and a rapid increase in the number of townsfolk, there was certainly a need for a market reasonably close to the growing town and there were many who felt that if the Bute Estate were really benevolent to Cardiffians, they would donate the land for the badly needed facility.

One could also speculate as to whether the ruling-Liberal influence on the Council saw the approach to the Bute Estate for the Arms Park as a means of quelling the Tory power via the town's cricket club. But the young Marquess and the other Bute officials showed their true-blue colours and rejected the approach from the Council for the use of the Arms Park. Shortly afterwards, in 1867, an agreement was reached between the Bute Estate and Cardiff C.C. whereby the club could acquire, at a peppercorn rate, a plot of land on the Park that they could develop into their permanent home. This was a decision entirely in keeping with the Marquess's sympathy to Tory causes and one that gave a massive boost to both the Cardiff club, as well as the early Glamorganshire club that was subsequently created in 1869.

FIVE

County Cricket at the Arms Park

An important development in Welsh cricket from the middle of the nineteenth century onwards was the emergence of county sides. One of the first so-called County XIs was the Monmouthshire club, who from 1824 played at Raglan. However, they were very much a gentleman's XI and were not representative of the county as whole. Similar teams represented Glamorgan from the 1850s, with members of the Cardiff club including John Wallis and Ernest Worthington being invited to participate.

During the 1860s a more representative Glamorgan side was assembled, with John Nicholl, the Conservative MP for Cardiff organising a two-day match in June 1868 at his home at Merthyr Mawr between teams representing the West and East of the county. The East XI, comprising players from Cardiff and Bridgend, duly won by six wickets, as the contest showcased the pool of talent in the premier clubs and confirmed the potential for the creation of a county side.

Flushed with the success of these games, Nicholl also approached the All-England XI to see if an exhibition match could be arranged against a Glamorgan XXII, which would help to raise funds to start a county club. Negotiations however broke down over the financial terms and no dates were agreed.

Another Old Etonian then took centre-stage in the creation of a Glamorgan club, as, through the efforts of J.T.D. Llewelyn, a meeting was called in March 1869 at the Castle Hotel in Neath to establish a formal county club. It didn't take very long for a Glamorganshire club to be formally inaugurated and during the Spring a number of inter-county fixtures were secured. The Bute Estate also lent their support and agreed that the new county organisation could use the Arms Park for their inaugural match against Monmouthshire in mid-June 1869.

The two-day contest saw the Glamorganshire side, containing several Cardiff players, perform with great credit against the men from Monmouth, but the game ended in a draw with Glamorganshire well on top. The visitors had to return home on the 6 p.m. train from Cardiff General, so stumps had to be drawn early at 5.30 p.m. with the visitors on 11-3 in their second innings.

J.T.D. Llewelyn – the Father of Glamorgan Cricket

John Talbot Dillwyn Llewelyn was the undisputed father of Glamorgan cricket. The Old Etonian was a useful all-rounder in his own right and could claim to have dismissed W.G. Grace in an exhibition match when the good doctor was comprehensively beaten by Llewelyn's pace.

'J.T.D.' was one of the most active promoters of the cricket in South Wales and he reinvested some of the money he had made in industry by promoting both cricket and rugby. He lived at Penllegaer to the west of Swansea and was a leading member of the Cadoxton club. He was also very supportive of events in the south-east of the region and was a leading figure with the early Glamorganshire club, as well as the Welsh Rugby Union (W.R.U.).

His son Willie followed in his illustrious father's footsteps and played for Glamorgan in friendly matches in the late 1880s. In the early 1890s Willie led the county side but he committed suicide within the grounds of his family's home in 1893, just weeks before his proposed marriage to the daughter of Lord Dynevor.

Two-day friendly
Glamorganshire v. Monmouthshire
Cardiff Arms Park

14, 15 June 1869

Result – Match Drawn

Glamorganshire		**first innings**		**second innings**		
W.P. Whittington		b Davies	2		b Davies	5
W. Bennett		b Waterfall	3		b Waterfall	5
Capt. S.G. Homfray		b Davies	0		b Waterfall	0
D.E. Watson		b Davies	7		b Waterfall	1
F.E. Stacey		b Davies	3	c sub	b Davies	23
E.W. Jones		b Evans	55	c Evans	b Davies	24
W. Richards		b Davies	8		b Davies	14
J.T.D. Llewelyn		b Waterfall	20	c Cartwright	b Evans	7
Revd C. Stacey		b Davies	1		b Davies	1
Capt. Maxwell	c Cartwright	b Jackson	0		not out	6
C. Milsom		not out	11		b Evans	75
Extras	(b16, lb3, w12)		31	(b7, lb 5, w 4)		16
Total	(all out)		141	(all out)		177

Bowling	B	M	R	W		B	M	R	W
Davies	128	8	57	6	Davies	99	5	64	5
Waterfall	80	10	21	2	Waterfall	120	9	54	3
Evans	56	3	26	1	Evans	56	5	26	2
Jackson	8	1	6	1	Jackson	24	0	13	0

Monmouthshire		**first innings**		**second innings**		
F. Lewis					b Bennett	4
J. Evans	c Bennett	b Llewelyn	9		b Llewelyn	0
B. Williams		b Bennett	7			
F. Allfray		b Llewelyn	7		b Llewelyn	0
D.C. Davies		b Llewelyn	9		b Bennett	6
H. Lloyd	c Watson	b Bennett	8			
Capt. Jackson		b Bennett	2		b Bennett	1
Capt. Pearson		not out	15		not out	2
T.A. Middleton	c Watson	b Llewelyn	4			
W.E. Waterfall		run out	7			
W. Cartwright		b Watson	11			
Extras	(b18, lb6)		24	(b1, lb1)		2
Total	(all out)		107	(for 4 wickets)		11

Bowling	B	M	R	W		B	M	R	W
Bennett	152	14	41	4	Llewelyn	28	5	3	2
Llewelyn	148	19	40	4	Bennett	26	4	6	2
Watson	8	1	2	1					

With Cardiff C.C. having established themselves as one of the premier clubs in the region, and the Arms Park now being used for county matches, the Bute Estate decided to make further improvements at the Cardiff ground in 1870, with the Marquess financing the erection of a small pavilion in the south-west corner of the ground 'for the convenience of the Cardiff C.C.

The Cardiff C.C. team that played Newport C.C. on 23 July 1875. *Back row, left to right*: A. Thackeray, D.E. Watson, W. Graves, W.C. Gould, E.W. Jones, J.G. Thomas. *Front row, left to right*: A.S. Morris, W. Bennett, J. Walker, C.N. Alexander and J.W. Morris. Lying on the ground, J.A. Corbett.

scorers, etc. The elevation is bold, with a pretty verandah in rustic work, designed on the model of a Swiss chalet.'

Perhaps to gain support from the other town clubs using the ground – and to quell some of the anti-Bute feeling – it was subsequently agreed that the other clubs using the park could also use the new pavilion, but whenever Cardiff C.C. had a home fixture, they still had first call on the facilities, including the central wicket which their enthusiastic professionals had taken steps to develop.

Not everyone was happy with this arrangement, however, as shown in a letter to the *Western Mail* on 8 July 1871 by a member of the Science & Arts Club who had been granted permission by the Marquess to play on the Arms Park. The correspondent wrote:

> I do not believe that Lord Bute would, if he was aware of it, permit one club to monopolise whenever they chose the whole of the park field. This assumption is borne out by the fact that for some years other clubs have – with his Lordship's permission – used the field as their cricket ground. Even they, however, are compelled to 'stump' whenever the Cardiff club plays what they may consider a grand match.

The outcome was that when Cardiff did not have a prestigious First XI fixture, a myriad of other matches took place on the Arms Park, with games often sharing overlapping boundaries. But this was far from ideal, as mentioned in a report from June 1874, when the keenly fought annual encounter between the teams representing the Rhymney Railway and the Taff Vale Companies took place alongside a far more social and relaxed contest involving the members of staff of the *Western Mail*, as a Married XI challenged a Single XI.

The increased usage of the park for such informal and social games also led to damage being caused, with the *Cardiff Times* reporting 'repeated acts of mischief and injury being done to trees and fences.' It was a situation that clearly could not continue and with increasing numbers of cricket clubs being formed each year, the Bute Estate decided in April 1875 to restrict access to the Arms Park solely to Cardiff C.C. and only to other bona fide clubs if space permitted.

This decision, like those taken over the creation and usage of Sophia Gardens, showed elements of social control on the part of the Bute Estate. You clearly had to be a gentleman and, better still, a Tory supporter in order to be guaranteed the use of the Arms Park. Additionally, the initial decision over access into Sophia Gardens and the exclusion of the masses preserved the high status of the Arms Park, duly reinforcing Cardiff C.C. as the premier club in the town. It might also have been no coincidence that the Bute Estate were permanently in the market during the 1860s and 1870s for plots of land – either freehold or leasehold – in the area adjoining the Arms Park and the centre of the town. Their subsequent sale or lease would have been significantly enhanced by the creation of a well-tended cricket ground.

The decision by the Marquess in 1867 for Cardiff C.C. to develop their base at the Arms Park also had a wider significance, as during the 1870s various influential members of the cricket club so enjoyed their comradeship and camaraderie that they decided to form a rugby team, the reason being that they could continue playing healthy recreation during the winter months.

A postcard of Sophia Gardens in the early 1900s.

In the spring of 1868 newspapers carried reports of 'football' matches being staged on the Arms Park between members of the Cardiff club, plus a few guests from the Canton cricket club, against a team representing the 23rd Royal Welsh Fusiliers, who were based in Newport. So that damage was not caused to the wicket, these matches took place on the southern part of the Arms Park on rougher land which was less well drained than the northern side, and had been part of the course of the River Taff before Brunel's grand scheme to straighten the meanders.

Whether these were rugby matches as we know them today, or a hybrid form of association football and rugby football is not clear, but it is apparent that these games quickly grew in popularity and during the winter of 1873/74, the Glamorgan Football Club was formed with S. Campbell Cory, from the influential shipowning family, being its prime mover. Practices were organised on the southern part of the park, with the cricket pavilion being used as a place where the gentlemen could leave their coats – at the time there was no kit and players turned out in their ordinary attire. By November 1874 the rugby club had sixty-six members and an away match was played against Cowbridge Grammar School, whose headmaster and teaching staff were advocates of Muscular Christianity.

Around the same time, several other rugby teams emerged in the town, including the Tredegarville club, which was formed in the early 1870s. They used the Recreation Field at Sophia Gardens and comprised a group of old boys from Monkton House school who, being good Muscular Christians, had so much enjoyed their summers playing cricket that they were now looking for suitable winter exercise. The headmaster of the school, Henry Shewbrook, was also a keen supporter of rugby and through his involvement, and that of another master, C.E. Pryor, the Tredegarville rugby club went from strength to strength.

Around the same time, another club called the Wanderers was formed and in November 1874 they challenged the 2nd XV of the Glamorgan club on the new rugby pitch in the Arms Park. The *South Wales Daily News* took great delight in reporting that, 'cricket was out, and football was in, as between thirty and forty muscular young men met for a trial of skill and strength.'

Rugby football was also increasing in popularity in other South Walian towns, especially Newport and Swansea. Their teams frequently defeated the Cardiff clubs, much to the disgust of the town's sporting gentlemen who believed that Cardiff should also have a crack team. The solution was agreed at a meeting in the Swiss Hall in Queen Street on 22 September 1876, at which it was agreed that the Wanderers and Glamorgan clubs would merge, thereby forming Cardiff Football Club.

The Marquess agreed to a request from the newly formed club – who in their first year wore black jerseys with a white skull and crossbones – to have their first practice the Arms Park on 14 October 1876, but when it came to fixtures it was a different matter. The Bute Estate were perfectly happy for the new rugby club to play at Sophia Gardens, but there was, at first, a reluctance on the behalf of the Bute Estate for the club to play on the Arms Park.

Their cautious stance might have been the result of the damage caused to the park by a rather unruly element of so-called sporting supporters. Indeed, in April 1875 the *Western Mail* announced that:

> The Marquess of Bute has been compelled to take the step of requiring that special permission should be obtained for the use of Cardiff Arms Park – in consequence of the repeated acts of damage in the Cardiff Arms Park, no person will be allowed to enter it without special permission.

A letter from 'Ye Goal Post' in the same newspaper later that year summarises the disappointments felt by the rugby enthusiasts at being deprived of the use of the Arms Park. In it, the correspondent wrote:

> Unfortunately, on applying for the use of the Cardiff Arms Park it was refused, notwithstanding the expressed intention of the club to maintain a man to look after the ground. Mr Corbett (the Bute Trustee) very kindly offered, and indeed put himself to considerable trouble, to find a suitable field elsewhere, but without success. Thus, for want of a convenient ground, this club – a real boon to the town – must collapse. Although we have no doubt that Mr Corbett had his reasons for refusing the Cardiff Arms Park, still we firmly believe that if the Marquess of Bute fully understood, not only the disappointment, but the great injury that this refusal will cause to so many young men in Cardiff, he would, with his usual generosity and desire to further the interests of the town, immediately give the required permission.

The Marquess and his advisors were also still keen to promote the exclusivity of the Arms Park and the land adjacent to it. It may have been no coincidence that J.A. Corbett was also a leading member of the Cardiff Cricket Club (see the photograph on p.27). The hurly-burly of rugby and its rising popularity among working men may not have matched their lofty ideals, and this might have been the reason for putting the rugby players 'on probation' away from the Arms Park.

For the first three years of their existence, Cardiff Rugby Club used the Sophia Gardens Recreation Field. By the autumn of 1879 their relationship with the Bute Estate had improved – based no doubt, on trouble-free and successful matches in Sophia Gardens – and that season Cardiff R.F.C. began their long and hugely profitable association with the Arms Park. It swiftly grew in importance as the focal centre for the sporting activities of Cardiff's premier sporting teams – an association that owed its origin to the approach to the Marquess by the cricket club in 1867. Had he not agreed, Cardiff Arms Park might not have become the fortress stronghold of so many great Welsh rugby teams.

SIX

The Bute Household XI

By the 1870s cricket – both nationally and at the local scale – was being played by an ever-broadening cross-section of the population. No longer was it the preserve of well-heeled gentlemen, as the cricket field on the Arms Park saw games being played by teams of drapers, ironmongers and grocers. But this spread had an important knock-on effect as the wealthier elements of the town's society, just like their counterparts in England, took action to preserve their identity and importance.

Previously, the leaders of Cardiffian society had been perfectly happy to play alongside less affluent individuals, as well as professionals and other paid 'guests'. But everything changed, reflecting trends on a wider scale with increased social awareness and class consciousness. The result was that the well-to-do townsfolk and members of the gentry increasingly sought opportunities to distance themselves from the paid ranks and those who they perceived as having an inferior standing.

This was reflected in other aspects of town life, as residential segregation took place with affluent suburbs such as Llanishen, Lisvane and Whitchurch developing to the north of the town. Sporting segregation saw the emergence of 'country-house cricket', as members of the cricketing and social elite met up at the homes and estates of the upper class for a jolly old time, during which they could enjoy a good game with their social equals before retiring to the banqueting hall or ballroom for an evening of conviviality.

On occasions, participation in these matches owed more to the lure of the ballroom and the champagne corks rather than prowess with leather and willow, but as far as the game's development in South Wales was concerned, these country-house matches played an important role in cricket's evolution. Indeed, it was at Merthyr Mawr, the palatial home of John Nicholl, where the embryonic Glamorgan XI was first assembled for matches against gentlemen's teams representing Carmarthenshire and Breconshire.

By the end of the 1860s, most of the leading families had their own teams, with the Morgans of Tredegar Park, the Fox-Talbots of Margam, as well as the Earls of Plymouth and Dunraven all staging lavish matches on their estates. With many keen cricketers working for the Bute Estate, it wasn't long before the Marquess had his team as well, as in 1870 he agreed to a suggestion by William Churchman, the forty year old 'house steward', that a household cricket team should be formed.

Contact was soon made with the town club and in July 1870 a game was staged in the castle grounds between a Bute Household XI and the Second XI from the town club, with a return fixture a few weeks later on the Arms Park. In fact, there was sufficient interest within the Bute staff for a Second XI to be raised and in August 1873 they played a match against a St Fagans side. On the Marquess' twenty-sixth birthday in September, a match took place in Cooper's Field between the Bute Household First XI and Second XI with Lord Bute and his wife, plus their many friends among the spectators who attended the game. Entertainment was also provided by the Royal Glamorgan Militia's brass band and following the match, a grand dinner was held in the Angel Hotel.

However, the creation of a Bute Household team may not have been entirely for social reasons, as in the mid-1860s, a Bute Cricket Club had also been formed, using the Arms Park for their matches. The motive behind the formation of this team – at a time when Cardiff was being run by a Liberal council – may well have been political, with the participants in the matches being staunch Conservatives or Tory sympathizers.

After the refusal by the Butes to allow the Town Council to use the Arms Park for the town's cattle market, the creation of a cricket club, chock-full of young Conservatives and playing

Cardiff Castle and the Lawn, as seen around the turn of the century.

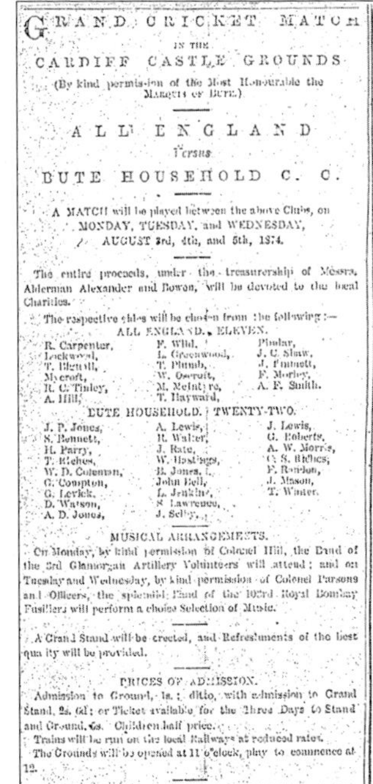

GRAND CRICKET MATCH

IN THE

CARDIFF CASTLE GROUNDS

(By kind permission of the Most Honourable the Marquis of Bute.)

ALL ENGLAND

versus

BUTE HOUSEHOLD C. C.

A MATCH will be played between the above Clubs, on MONDAY, TUESDAY, and WEDNESDAY, AUGUST 3rd, 4th, and 5th, 1874.

The entire proceeds, under the treasurership of Messrs. Alderman Alexander and Bowen, will be devoted to the local Charities.

The respective sides will be chosen from the following:—

ALL ENGLAND ELEVEN.

R. Carpenter,	F. Wild,	Pinder,
Lockwood,	L. Greenwood,	J. C. Shaw,
T. Bignall,	T. Plumb,	J. Emmett,
Mycroft,	W. Oscroft,	F. Morley,
R. C. Tinley,	M. McIntyre,	A. F. Smith.
A. Hill,	T. Hayward,	

BUTE HOUSEHOLD TWENTY-TWO.

J. P. Jones,	A. Lewis,	J. Lewis,
S. Bennett,	R. Walter,	G. Roberts,
H. Parry,	J. Rate,	A. W. Morris,
T. Riches,	W. Hastings,	C. S. Riches,
W. D. Coleman,	B. Jones,	F. Rendon,
G. Compton,	John Bell,	J. Mason,
G. Levick,	L. Jenkins,	T. Winter.
D. Watson,	S. Lawrence,	
A. D. Jones,	J. Selby,	

MUSICAL ARRANGEMENTS.

On Monday, by kind permission of Colonel Hill, the Band of the 3rd Glamorgan Artillery Volunteers will attend; and on Tuesday and Wednesday, by kind permission of Colonel Parsons and Officers, the splendid Band of the 103rd Royal Bombay Fusiliers will perform a choice Selection of Music.

A Grand Stand will be erected, and Refreshments of the best quality will be provided.

PRICES OF ADMISSION.

Admission to Ground, 1s.; ditto, with admission to Grand Stand, 2s. 6d; or Ticket available for the Three Days to Stand and Ground, 6s. Children half price.

Trains will be run on the local Railways at reduced rates.

The Grounds will be opened at 11 o'clock, play to commence at 12.

377 Entrance by West Lodge, near Cardiff Bridge. 3713

An advertisement from *The Cardiff Times* for the match in 1874 between the All-England XI and the Bute Household Cricket Club.

regular fixtures on the park, blew a loud raspberry in the face of the Liberal councillors. Indeed, with several Liberals playing for the Cardiff club, the creation of the Bute club was another example of segregation, with the Bute club only open to those who supported the Conservative cause.

In July 1870 there was an all-Bute match on the Arms Park as the Bute Castle Household XI played the Bute club in a two-innings match, while during the intervals the band of the Royal Glamorgan Militia entertained the many spectators who turned up – several of whom were no doubt eager to show their allegiance to the Tory and Bute cause.

The Household XI went from strength to strength in the mid-1870s, adopting its own badge and colours – 'a dark-blue cap, with the initials B.H.C.C., and a belt made of the Stuart plaid.' However, the biggest move forward came in June 1874 when, as a means of displaying their high social standing and political stature, the Bute Household C.C. agreed terms with the promoters of the All-England XI for a three-day game between the two teams in Cooper's Field.

Friendly match
Bute Household C.C. v. All-England XI
3, 4, 5 August 1874
Cooper's Field, Bute Park, Cardiff

Result: Match Drawn

Bute Household C.C.		**first innings**			**second innings**	
J.P. Jones	c Fairbank	b Greenwood	1	c Shaw	b Greenwood	12
S.S. Lawrence		b Greenwood	7		b Greenwood	5
D.E. Watson		b Greenwood	14			
J. Mason		run out	0		b Greenwood	0
C. Walter		b Shaw	1		b Greenwood	1
H. Parry	c Pryor	b Shaw	3		b Fairbank	0
A.D. Jones	c Tinley	b Shaw	2		b Greenwood	0
A.W. Morris		b Greenwood	1		b Fairbank	3
G. Roberts		b Greenwood	1		not out	0
G. Levick		b Shaw	0	c Shaw	b Fairbank	0
J. Bell	c Tinley	b Shaw	2		b Greenwood	4
T. Riches		b Shaw	6			
C. Riches		b Shaw	0		b Greenwood	0
J. Selby		retired hurt	3			
F. Randon		b Greenwood	8	lbw	b Greenwood	7
L. Jenkins	c Pryor	b Shaw	17			
A. Lewis		b Howitt	15			
J. Lewis		b Howitt	2		b Fairbank	0
S. Bennett		b Shaw	1			
E. Clarke		not out	0			
W.D. Coleman		b Howitt	0			
B. Jones	c Tinley	b Howitt	4			
Extras	(b1)		1	(b 1, w 1)		2
Total	(all out)		89	(for 12 wickets)		34

Bowling	B	R	W
Shaw	184	49	9
Greenwood	116	15	6
Howitt	40	13	4
Tinley	28	10	0

	B	R	W
Greenwood	76	20	8
Shaw	32	8	0
Fairbank	44	4	4

All-England XI

T. Bignall		b Randon	0
F. Wild	c Lawrence	b Jenkins	15
M. McIntyre		b Randon	23
R. Carpenter		b Randon	9
F. Mills		b Randon	0
F. Pryor		b Randon	0
L. Greenwood		b Jenkins	3
J.T. Fairbank		b Randon	5
R.C. Tinley		not out	14
J.C. Shaw	c sub	b Randon	1
G. Howitt		run out	5
Extras	(b5)		5
Total	(all out)		80

Bowling	B	R	W
Randon	152	47	7
Walter	52	14	0
Jenkins	92	11	2

Aware of the financial difficulties faced by the Cardiff C.C. the last time an England team visited the town, the Bute Estate were very careful about the monetary arrangements for the contest. Having agreed to cover the entire costs incurred by the All-England XI, they decided to levy admission charges of sixpence by foot, 2*s* 6*d* for every carriage drawn by one horse, and 5*s* for two-horse carriages. To quell any suggestions – especially from the Liberals – that this was another money-making exercise with the Bute Estate profiting from the rising interest in cricket, it was also agreed that some of the admission charges would go to local charities, but only once all the costs had been covered, including the payments to the two Cardiff professionals, Randon and Selby, who turned out for the Bute Household XXII, as well as the expenses of the guest players such as Lewis Jenkins, the talented opening batsman from the Cadoxton club near Neath, who was drafted in to strengthen the Bute ranks.

The chance to see some the finest cricketers in England taking on the cream of local talent predictably drew a large crowd to Cardiff Castle for the first day's play on 3 August. *The Western Mail* described:

> How the beautiful grounds, which have been the scene of many a vigorous contest by the Bute Household club presented a gay and animated picture as the afternoon drew on and people began to arrive... Nature has hemmed in the cricket ground by a group of ornate trees and their umbrageous shade enabled hundreds of spectators to view the match unmolested by the dazzling light of the sun. A marquee erected for the accommodation of members and their friends, a long refreshment tent and two or three smaller ones used by the respective clubs, completed a scene of vivacity but seldom excelled, even in the grounds of Cardiff Castle.

Unfortunately, William Selby dislocated his thumb during the pre-match practice and had to withdraw from the contest. However, his colleagues performed with great credit, amassing a decent total of 89. Lewis Jenkins top-scored with a fluent 17, before the All-England team were dismissed for 80, with Carlton Riches taking the bowling honours by claiming seven wickets. Thoughts of a dramatic defeat for the English side were literally dampened by heavy rain on the second day, followed by showery outbursts on the third day, and in what little play was possible, the local side moved on to 35-11 when stumps were drawn with honours even.

The match also saw the Bute Household, with the assistance of the *Western Mail* – the town's newspaper which supported Conservative causes – setting up a printing press on the ground so that up-to-date scorecards could be made available for the spectators. Their innovation met with great approval, but sadly not everything associated with the match went according to plan, as a rather loud and unruly element were present, and let it be known to all and sundry in rather vehement tones that they wanted to see the Englishmen beaten. Consequently, Major Bond of the Glamorganshire Militia had to summon all of his night-duty men from the docks to quell the rumpus.

Despite these disturbances, the Bute Household club continued their activities; in the course of the next eighteen months they played the Tredegar Park side, raised by Colonel Morgan, as well as home and away fixtures with the Cadoxton and Swansea club teams. Indeed, the *Western Mail* described the game with the Swansea men in Cooper's Field as 'a match between the two strongest clubs in Glamorgan.'

The Bute Estate were also very keen to promote the Cooper's Field wicket and the venue of the Bute Household club, as in August 1874 a fixture took place between the Gentlemen of South Wales and the Players of South Wales 'in the grounds adjacent to Cardiff Castle.' Unlike the match with the All-England XI, there was free admission to this match and rather than seeing the match as a money-making venture, the Bute authorities viewed this Gentlemen *v.* Players match as more of a social fixture, replicating the famous fixture in England.

Other teams were allowed to use Cooper's Field, but these were mainly teams with strong ties with Bute and Tory causes. One of these was the cricket club representing the Taff Vale Railway, whose line from Merthyr to Cardiff had been opened in 1841, thereby starting an association that allowed both the docks and the town to flourish.

There were many fine cricketers, and staunch Conservatives, working for the railway company, including Cuthbert Riches, an engineer who had starred with the ball in the match with All-England, and his cousin Tom Hurry Riches, a railway superintendents and works manager to the Bute Docks Trustees.

However, their best player was F.E. Stacey, the son of the curate of St John's, and a director of the company. In fact, Francis Stacey was regarded by many as the finest player in the whole of Glamorgan, with the wicketkeeper-batsman having shown his talents appearing in Cardiff's matches against the All-England XI in 1855 and the United All-England XI in 1857, while still a student at Cambridge University. The Law student was also a regular in both the Glamorganshire team and in various M.C.C. sides, and he was a good enough player to have also been invited to appeared at the Canterbury Festival for the Gentlemen of England in a special exhibition match. Having acted as his tutor, Stacey was a close friend of the Marquess and one of the leading barristers on the South Wales circuit, as well as legal advisor to the Bute Estate. So with such prominent Conservatives and cricketing luminaries working for the Taff Vale Railway, it was no surprise that the Taff Vale club played regularly on Cooper's Field, with their fixture list also including an annual challenge with the Great Western Railway at Swindon.

Strauss' debut at the Arms Park

Andrew Strauss, the Middlesex batsman and England captain may have appeared several times at Sophia Gardens recently, but it is not the first time that the efforts of a Strauss have been warmly applauded at a cricket match in Cardiff.

Indeed, the melodies of Johann Strauss – the great Austrian composer – were among the specialities of a band who were regularly invited to play during the intervals of major matches at the Arms Park and in Cooper's Fields. 'The Hungarian Band ' were resplendent in their blue uniforms and peaked caps and were a familiar sight at other bandstands around the town, as well as in Sophia Gardens.

When major matches were staged at the Arms Park, the Hungarian Band always set up adjacent to the pavilion with their playing entertaining the crowd and the players. In fact, the band were so popular that their encores often continued when play resumed after the intervals and there were many instances when incoming batsmen danced or even waltzed out to the wicket!

A postcard showing people strolling through Sophia Gardens shortly before the First World War, with the bandstand in the distance.

SEVEN

Glamorgan County Cricket Club is Formed

By the summers of the early 1880s, the Sophia Gardens Recreation Field was teeming with young men, and many ladies as well, all of whom were enjoying the air outdoors. In the gardens themselves, the great and the good of Cardiff society promenaded around in the summer sun, basking in their own wealth and the success of the city and its docks.

A few hundred yards away at the Arms Park, the town's leading cricketers staged their premier fixtures, while in the castle grounds, many Tory sympathizers enjoyed the use of the Bute Household's wicket in Cooper's Field. At many other sites across the city and its thriving suburbs, workingmen also enjoyed their ball games, while during the winter months these locations, together with Sophia Gardens and the Arms Park, played host to rugby and football as Cardiff R.F.C. rapidly became one of the leading clubs in South Wales.

Their players also won international honours with the Welsh rugby team, who played their first games in 1881 following the creation of the W.R.U. at the Castle Hotel in Neath. After staging home games at Newport and Swansea, the union officials chose, for the first time, the Arms Park as the venue for the match against Ireland on 12 April 1884. On a chilly and overcast spring day 4,000 people thronged into the ground, but the fine running play of the Welsh backs warmed their hearts as the home team won the first of many internationals at the Cardiff ground.

Sailor's Games at the Arms Park

In addition to staging prestigious cricket and rugby matches, the Arms Park was also used for a number of friendly cricket games held by companies based in the town, as well as teams from various businesses based in the Bute Docks.

The cricket field was also used by teams comprising the crew from visiting boats, and the names of the vessels added an exotic element to the match reports published in the local newspaper, as in the case of the contest in July 1890 between *Empire* and *New Mazeppa.*

Like the economy as a whole, sport in the region was on the up, but one thing was missing – a representative cricket team. It must have greatly hurt the many supporters of the summer game, and sporting enthusiasts as a whole, to see the following letter in the *South Wales Daily News* on 29 August 1881

> It must be admitted that cricket in South Wales is in a backward state, and at the present time, there is very little chance of any marked improvement taking place, and the old adage 'that the nearer you get to London, the better the cricket' has recently been verified.

Sadly, the Glamorganshire club had folded after staging only a handful of matches in the mid-1870s. The South Wales Cricket Club had also run out of steam, going through both 1880 and 1881 without a single victory. With such a modest run of results, doubts started to grow over the very existence of the South Wales club, with hefty criticism of the way the club was dominated by a clique of gentlemen who clung onto old-fashioned ideals, selecting time and again ever-aging players because of their past reputations, rather than their recent, very modest performances.

These parochial and elitist attitudes meant that many of the emerging middle-class players – especially those who performed with credit for the clubs using Sophia Gardens and the Arms Park – viewed the activities of South Wales C.C. as little more than a form of social entertainment, and a jolly gathering of old boys.

'Old Stager' of the *South Wales Daily News* spoke for many of the town's cricketers when he wrote in April 1886:

> When, oh when, shall we be able to put in the field an XI sufficiently strong to oppose, with some prospect of success, a really first-class team? Not I fancy until the miserable cliqueism that at present marks the management of some of our leading clubs is swept away, and men are played simply because they know how to play and not because their names are Jones, Brown, Robinson and so on.

As a newspaper which supported the Liberal, rather than the Tory, cause in the town, it was no surprise to see Old Stager having a swipe at some of the town's clubs and their snobbishness, as well as the South Wales C.C. The 1886 season saw the club lose all of their fixtures yet again, and their was an air of resignation when the club's officials met up in December 1886 in a room at the Angel Hotel. Unanimously, they decided to discontinue the club's activities, yet within eighteen months Glamorgan County Cricket Club was formed, and across the way in the Arms Park they staged their inaugural fixture in the summer of 1889.

The man who turned the situation around so quickly was J.T.D. Llewelyn, the energetic patron of sport in the region, who was also in the vanguard of the W.R.U. Indeed, the creation of the W.R.U. was part of a clamour of nationalistic feeling that had swept like a tidal wave across the booming industrial centres of the region during the 1880s – an era which saw the National Eisteddfod Society become inaugurated to co-ordinate cultural and artistic affairs, as well as a University College of South Wales and Monmouthshire being established in Cardiff in 1883. The latter had also seen the Marquess of Bute contribute £10,000 out of the £50,000 needed to create this new seat of learning, but he refused an approach to purchase the Arms Park as a site for the new university. Instead, the estate's Trustees said, 'Lord Bute is not disposed to give the Arms Park as a site for the new University College as he desired to reserve it as an open space for recreational purposes.'

Having reaffirmed his intention to preserve the area for healthy recreation, he offered instead a plot of land on Cathedral Road, no doubt aware that the presence of the university would give a further boost to the development of a high-class suburb, close to the attractive Sophia Gardens. In the end, the university was located on land to the north of the town centre at Cathays Park, and the Marquess turned instead to the clergy as a means of promoting the Pontcanna suburb, with numbers 41–43 Cathedral Road becoming the Archbishop of Llandaff's residence.

The success of the W.R.U. – for whom J.T.D. Llewelyn acted as president between 1885 and 1906 – fuelled Llewellyn's ambition for a representative cricket team being formed, and a proper side which would carry forward and promote the name of the economic and industrial heartland of South Wales. The demise of the South Wales C.C. had clearly demonstrated the pitfalls of relying on aged amateurs, but Llewelyn and the many officials of the region's leading clubs knew that there was a pool of sufficient talent to create a decent team.

One of these enthusiastic individuals was John Price Jones, the captain and secretary of Cardiff C.C., who was a prominent architect having designed several buildings in the town. Among his creations were several distinctive properties on Bute-owned land, especially to the western side of the town in the emerging suburb of Canton. 'J.P.' also came from a family with a strong cricketing pedigree – his father Daniel Jones had been heavily involved with the reformation of Cardiff C.C. in 1861, and had twice been mayor of the town. His brothers Daniel Elias Jones and William Price Jones were also useful players for both the Cardiff and the Bute Household clubs, with William acting as a shipbroker in the docks; Daniel also served as an architect for the Bute Estate.

J.P., together with many of the other leading members of the Cardiff club, had taken part in a fixture between a XXII from the town club and the South of England XI during June 1880. The *Western Mail* hailed the game as a being, 'indicative of a revival in the interest in cricket... and

Following the Joneses

Besides being one of the town's leading cricketers, the architect J.P. Jones was a leading figure in the social and political life of the town. From the mid-1880s he gained a number of high-profile commissions, including the design of the market buildings and both the High Street and Wyndham Arcades, now famed for their glass roof and slender iron arches, as well as extensions to Howell's department store in St Mary Street, plus the Royal Hotel and the Queen's Hotel.

'J.P.' was also a great supporter of rugby football, acting as treasurer of Cardiff R.F.C. and in later life serving as a vice-president of Cardiff Harlequins. He clearly was a very popular and energetic man around town, indeed, his obituary referred to him as being, 'unselfish, true and generous – the friend of every athlete and the perfect gentleman who carried sunshine and good fellowship wherever he went.'

proving convincingly that cricket is looking up in Cardiff – three years ago it would not have been possible to put such a good twenty-two in the field.' The three-day game against the England XI ended in a draw, but it was evidence of the strength of the clubs in South Wales and it gave J.P. the confidence to pursue the creation of a Glamorgan side. He was also a member of the South Wales C.C. and served on their Glamorganshire sub-committee that, among other things, oversaw the arrangements by club teams based within the county when taking part in the South Wales Challenge Cup. It also gave him an opportunity to run his keen eye over some of the emerging talent within the county, and based on his experience with the Cardiff club, make judgements about how clubs and players were moving forward.

The parochial nature of the South Wales C.C. and its old-fashioned values clearly irked J.P. who held a much more go-ahead and forward-thinking approach. He also didn't see eye-to-eye with some of the strong Tory sympathisers within the club's hierarchy, and at their A.G.M. in 1886, J.P. proposed dissolving the club and forming a completely new county side which selected the best players within the area, regardless of their social standing or aspirations.

The club's officials decided they would not vote on the topic at that time, but Jones was clearly not a man to be put off by stuffy intransigence as he announced that he had already made arrangements for a series of matches at Newport, the Arms Park and Llanelly between a Glamorgan side and the Rest of South Wales, which would help to showcase the talent in the area.

Nothing eventually came of the games at Cardiff or Llanelly, but J.P. was able to lead a Glamorgan XI into the field at Newport against an XVIII of South Wales. During 1886 he was also the chief instigator in the formation of a 'Cardiff United' side, which drew upon the top players from the junior and workingmen's teams that played at Sophia Gardens and elsewhere in the town, with the United team playing a fixture against the Second XI of the Cardiff club.

A few cynics argued that his prime motive was talent spotting for Cardiff C.C. and by forming a United team, he could lure players to the town club. A few years later, his motives were questioned again when the issue of suitable professionals joining the Glamorgan club was discussed and the county committee were trying to work out how to finance their acquisition – Jones said at the time that he would be happy to cover the costs of such a player turning out for Glamorgan himself, providing that the professional was able to play for the Cardiff club.

However, Jones' motives in 1886 appeared to be honourable enough and were genuine attempts at nurturing the grass roots of the game, both within the town of Cardiff and across the county. Indeed, the following year T. Page Wood, who owned the town's leading sports outfitters, instigated the creation of the Cardiff and District Cricket Union, as well as a knockout challenge cup.

Sir Edward Read, the town's M.P., also lent his support to the initiative, as during June 1888 the first games in the Cardiff and District Challenge Cup took place; to the delight of the Tory sympathisers, the final saw the Taff Vale club play St Paul's. Besides organising the knockout competition among the junior clubs, the new union also co-ordinated the inter-club fixtures, so that the use of the best facilities on the Arms Park was maximised. At the end of the season, the union also selected an XVIII, which challenged the Cardiff club.

But having a co-ordinated structure of games in Cardiff, plus blossoming junior clubs would not automatically allow a Glamorgan side to flourish. Gaining the support of other areas, especially in the west, was essential and during 1887 Jones also canvassed the support of other leading club officials, and most important of all, secured the backing of the Swansea Cricket and Football club. Initially, they had been a little bit sceptical of showing too close an allegiance to a scheme that

Cardiff C.C. assembled in front of the early wooden pavilion at the Arms Park in 1889. J.P. Jones is the gentleman third from the right in the back row, wearing a bowler hat.

would reinforce Cardiff, along with the Arms Park ground, as the cricketing centre of the county. With J.T.D. Llewelyn's close association with the St Helen's club, however, it did not take Jones too long to persuade William Bryant, the Swansea secretary, that the formation of Glamorgan would be good for both east and west, with county matches taking place at the St Helen's ground as well as at the Arms Park.

Soon after their meeting, Llewelyn was able to write the following letter to all of the leading clubs in the region:

> I have much pleasure in convening a meeting at the Angel Hotel, Cardiff, on Friday 6 July at six o'clock in the evening to consider the advisability of forming a county cricket club. I need scarcely say that it is essential that the meeting should be thoroughly representative of cricket in the county, and shall be glad therefore if you will do your utmost to attend.

Over thirty representatives attended the meeting at which Glamorgan C.C.C. came into being. Fittingly, J.P. Jones was elected chairman of the new club, with his teammate William Yorath, the town's coroner and a leading solicitor, being appointed secretary. Llewelyn agreed to act as honorary treasurer, while other leading figures from clubs in the west joined their counterparts from the east on the committee. After an approach from J.P., the Marquess of Bute also agreed to act as the club's president, but his role with Glamorgan was not just a passive one. The Marquess immediately showed his support of the fledgling county by agreeing to let them use the Arms Park for their fixtures and trial matches, in addition to providing financial support to cover the cost of travel and hiring of professional players.

The support of so many leading figures in the social and business world of South Wales meant that others quickly followed and Glamorgan's finances were healthy enough for a series of trials to be staged on the Arms Park, along with a practice match in August 1888 against the Llwynypia club.

A *carte de visite* for the Angel Hotel in the 1880s. Note the refreshment tent on the cricket ground to the right of the picture.

On the day of the match, three amateurs who had originally been selected belatedly withdrew, and three members from the Llwynypia club were drafted in as late replacements. What followed was even worse as Emmett and Peate, the guest professionals from Yorkshire, dismissed the new county side for 20, as they slumped to a dramatic eight-wicket defeat.

However, none of the Glamorgan officials lost heart and contact was made with Herefordshire, Somerset, Worcestershire and Staffordshire for potential fixtures in 1889. All said no, but an affirmative reply came from the M.C.C., Surrey Club and Ground, and also Warwickshire although only after the Birmingham-based club had received a guarantee of £40, paid for by Jones and Llewelyn out of their own pockets.

Glamorgan's long-awaited inaugural fixture came about on 21-22 June against Warwickshire at the Arms Park. It ended in a resounding defeat for the Welsh club, but once again the new county were unable to field their strongest side as three of their key players were injured in the weeks leading up to the game. In contrast, Warwickshire fielded a strong side, led by Ludford Docker, who had toured Australia with Arthur Shrewsbury's team in 1887/88. The opposition also included Arthur Lilley, one of the country's finest wicketkeepers and John Shilton, an accomplished fast bowler.

Edmund David of St Fagan's C.C. captained the predominantly amateur Glamorgan XI and, given the strength of the visiting side, it was almost a case of David against Goliath. However, David won the first blow, and after winning the toss he opted to take first use of the Arms Park wicket. It did not prove to be a fairytale start; Lewis Jenkins was dismissed from the second delivery, and despite some firm blows from Billy Bancroft of Swansea C.C. and Theo Robinson from the home club, the vastly experienced Warwickshire bowlers dominated proceedings in the pre-lunch session. With the scoreboard reading 81-9, it looked as if the Welsh county would make a rather embarrassing start, but their faces were saved by a rather jaunty last wicket partnership between Astley Samuel, an estate agent from Pontardawe, and Dan Thissen, the wicketkeeper from Morriston. They started

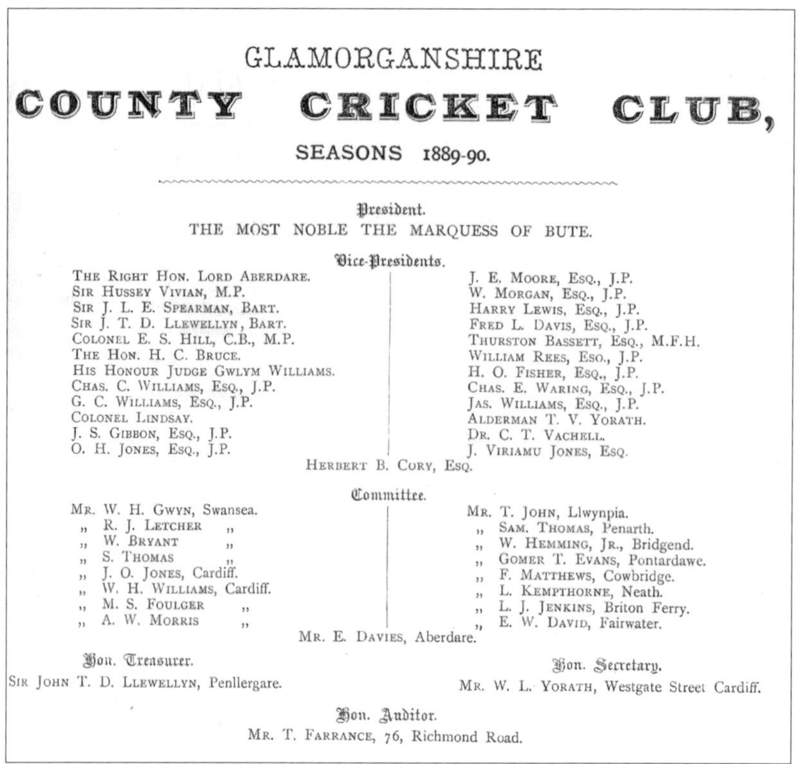

GLAMORGANSHIRE

COUNTY CRICKET CLUB,

SEASONS 1889-90.

President.

THE MOST NOBLE THE MARQUESS OF BUTE.

Vice-Presidents.

THE RIGHT HON. LORD ABERDARE.
SIR HUSSEY VIVIAN, M.P.
SIR J. L. E. SPEARMAN, BART.
SIR J. T. D. LLEWELLYN, BART.
COLONEL E. S. HILL, C.B., M.P.
THE HON. H. C. BRUCE.
HIS HONOUR JUDGE GWLYM WILLIAMS.
CHAS. C. WILLIAMS, ESQ., J.P.
G. C. WILLIAMS, ESQ., J.P.
COLONEL LINDSAY.
J. S. GIBBON, ESQ., J.P.
O. H. JONES, ESQ., J.P.
J. E. MOORE, ESQ., J.P.
W. MORGAN, ESQ., J.P.
HARRY LEWIS, ESQ., J.P.
FRED L. DAVIS, ESQ., J.P.
THURSTON BASSETT, ESQ., M.F.H.
WILLIAM REES, ESQ., J.P.
H. O. FISHER, ESQ., J.P.
CHAS. E. WARING, ESQ., J.P.
JAS. WILLIAMS, ESQ., J.P.
ALDERMAN T. V. YORATH.
DR. C. T. VACHELL.
J. VIRIAMU JONES, ESQ.
HERBERT B. CORY, ESQ.

Committee.

MR. W. H. GWYN, Swansea.
" R. J. LETCHER "
" W. BRYANT "
" S. THOMAS "
" J. O. JONES, Cardiff.
" W. H. WILLIAMS, Cardiff.
" M. S. FOULGER "
" A. W. MORRIS "
MR. T. JOHN, Llwynpia.
" SAM. THOMAS, Penarth.
" W. HEMMING, JR., Bridgend.
" GOMER T. EVANS, Pontardawe.
" F. MATTHEWS, Cowbridge.
" L. KEMPTHORNE, Neath.
" L. J. JENKINS, Briton Ferry.
" E. W. DAVID, Fairwater.
MR. E. DAVIES, Aberdare.

Hon. Treasurer.

SIR JOHN T. D. LLEWELLYN, Penllergare.

Hon. Secretary.

MR. W. L. YORATH, Westgate Street Cardiff.

Hon. Auditor.

MR. T. FARRANCE, 76, Richmond Road.

The Glamorgan annual report for 1889.

to prosper against the tiring bowlers and also confused the Warwickshire fielders by calling to each other in Welsh. This gallant partnership took the total to 136 and lifted their morale as David led his team onto the field.

James Lindley, the Cardiff professional, immediately struck by removing Docker and he picked up a further four victims as the visitors found run-scoring difficult against the accurate Glamorgan attack and lively fielding. It was a measure of their tenacity that Warwickshire only secured a first innings lead of two runs, but the Glamorgan batsmen failed to consolidate when they batted again. Shilton took seven wickets and only Gowan Clarke, a railway engineer who played for the Cardiff club, offered any resistance.

This left the English county needing just 79 to win, which they comfortably reached in mid-afternoon for the loss of two wickets. A large crowd had assembled in the hope of seeing another spirited fightback by the Glamorgan side, so with a couple of hours remaining, Warwickshire continued batting for exhibition purposes, to entertain the keen spectators.

It was not the start that anybody wanted, but the fact that the club survived and kept going through many rocky periods – unlike the South Wales club and the earlier Glamorganshire side – was a testament to the hard work of the Glamorgan officials, especially J.P. Jones. Having such a prominent Cardiffian as figurehead meant that the new club attracted greater support and was not just reliant on Tory sympathisers. Like the Cardiff United club that Jones had encouraged in 1886, the town of Cardiff was now united behind the new Glamorgan club.

Friendly Match
Glamorgan v. Warwickshire
Cardiff Arms Park,
21, 22 June 1889
Toss: Glamorgan won and elected to bat
Result: Warwickshire won by 8 wickets

Glamorgan		first innings			second innings	
L. Jenkins	c Richards	b Shilton	0	c Lilley	b Whitehead	7
D.E. Jones	c Lilley	b Bird	12	st Lilley	b Whitehead	12
A.W. Morris	c Bird	b Leake	9		b Shilton	8
W.J. Bancroft		b Shilton	13	c Leake	b Whitehead	1
T. Robinson	c Leake	b Shilton	19	lbw	b Shilton	15
*E.U. David	c Lilley	b Bird	0		b Shilton	2
J.G. Clarke	c D. Docker	b Bird	2		b Shilton	20
J.V. Lindley	lbw	b Shilton	7		b Shilton	3
W.E. Lewis	st Lilley	b Shilton	10		not out	9
A.W. Samuel		not out	28	c Richards	b Shilton	1
+D.E. Thissen	c Leake	b Whitehead	33	lbw	b Shilton	0
Extras			3			2
Total	(all out)		136	(all out)		80

Fall of wickets: 1-0, 2-11, 3-37, 4-52, 5-52, 6-54, 7-60, 8-66, 9-81, 10-136 | 1-1, 2-2, 3-11, 4-37, 5-39, 6-42, 7-42, 8-53, 9-74, 10-80

Bowling	O	M	R	W		O	M	R	W
Shilton	36	16	49	5	Shilton	28.4	13	42	7
Leake	17	2	38	3	Bird	7	5	4	0
Bird	29	11	44	1	Whitehead	21	9	32	3
Whitehead	1.1	0	2	1					

Warwickshire		first innings			second innings	
D. Docker	c David	b Lindley	8		b Samuel	0
A. Law		b Lindley	24		not out	26
W. Richards	st Thissen	b Samuel	0	lbw	b Robinson	21
*L.C. Docker	c Thissen	b Lindley	41		not out	25
C.F. Hunt		b Samuel	11			
W.F. Collishaw		retired hurt	0			
J.E. Shilton	c Bancroft	b Lindley	18			
A. Bird	c Thissen	b Lindley	1			
*A.F.A. Lilley		run out	8			
J. Leake		not out	8			
S.J. Whitehead		b Samuel	3			
Extras			16			7
Total	(all out)		138		(for 2 wickets)	79

Fall of wickets: 1-11, 2-16, 3-52, 4-88, 5-108 6-110, 7-121, 8-133, 9-138 | 1-0, 2-35

Bowling	O	M	R	W		O	M	R	W
Lindley	26	7	51	5	Lindley	13	6	17	0
Samuel	21	7	56	3	Samuel	10.3	1	37	1
Robinson	6	1	15	0	Robinson	7	0	18	1

EIGHT

Rugby Gains a Foothold at Sophia Gardens

By the time Glamorgan staged their inaugural fixture at the Arms Park, there had been significant changes a mile or so away at Sophia Gardens within the vicinity of Cathedral Road, which was now lined by elegant rows of detached and semi-detached houses. Those on the eastern side of the road also had their own private access into the gardens, while most of the impressive townhouses also had coach houses and stables at the rear. A couple of churches had also been built and consecrated, to provide for the spiritual needs of the rapidly expanding, and well-to-do, population living in this inner suburb.

A decade or so before, the road had been flanked by just a few detached villas, chiefly in the southern section, but during the late 1870s and into the 1880s construction work saw the addition of many other impressive properties along the 2km-stretch of roadway, with a mix of three-storey and four-storey semi-detached and detached properties, with steep gables and other features of Gothic architecture. So popular were these new properties that the Bute officials also planned a series of roads running at right angles to Cathedral Road, with the Marquess – who had undergone a Catholic conversion while a student at Oxford – deciding that it would be most appropriate if the new roads were named after some of the leading religious figures in Wales.

With a seemingly insatiable demand for decent housing, the Bute officials also planned a major extension of the housing areas to the north of the Sophia Gardens Recreation Field onto the fields of Pontcanna Farm, with a grand avenue leading all the way towards the cathedral at Llandaff. Nothing came of this elaborate plan and despite other plans drawn up after the Second World War by the City Council for a hospital or a racecourse, Pontcanna Fields have remained as part of the open green spaces in the Welsh capital.

The houses along Cathedral Road soon became the home for many of the prominent figures in Cardiff society, with the 1881 *Census* listing the occupations of the heads of household in one row of villas as civil engineer, architect, master printer, surgeon, solicitor, land agent, colliery proprietor, timber merchant, steamship owner and master brewer.

Indeed, this first batch of well-heeled residents contained several leading figures with both Cardiff C.C., and the early Glamorganshire team, including George Robinson – a Lincolnshire-born architect and surveyor – who kept wicket both for the town club and county. Just up the road was the home of Dominic Watson, the locally born brewer who was a leading batsman with Cardiff and Glamorganshire, as well as Charles Young, a shipbroker, who had moved from his birthplace in North Shields to Cardiff during the 1860s following the expansion in trade at the Bute Docks. He too played cricket for both town and county, and his son George followed in his father's footsteps, playing for Glamorgan in 1892 and 1893, as well as winning two Welsh rugby caps.

Another prominent sporting family to move to Cathedral Road in the early 1880s were the Ingledews, with John Ingledew moving his rapidly expanding family from their previous home in Windsor Place. Ingledew was a highly influential figure in the legal world of Cardiff, acting as the solicitor for the Taff Vale Railway, as well as being a Tory sympathiser. His second son, Hugh, also led a legal career after reading Law at Oxford, returning to work in Cardiff and playing cricket for Glamorgan in 1891, besides winning three Welsh rugby caps.

A sketch of Sophia Gardens in the late 1890s, showing the Bowls Club and the Recreation Field to the north.

Given the close proximity of their family homes to the Sophia Gardens Recreation Field, no doubt Young and Ingledew first honed their ball-skills through participating in the many informal games of rugby and cricket that were taking place. Indeed, since the 1870s, rugby football had been increasingly staged on the Recreation Field, with many clubs taking advantage of the freely available public facilities. Cardiff Rugby Club still used the pitches at Sophia Gardens for their Second XV fixtures, and when conditions became too muddy at the Arms Park, several of Cardiff's First XV matches were also transferred to Sophia Gardens.

A number of schools also used the pitches at Sophia Gardens. Chief among these was Monkton House, who were based in The Parade, on the north-eastern side of the town, and from 1870 acted as a private school for young gentlemen. It's founder was Henry Shewbrook, a twenty-five year old schoolmaster, who had been born in Taunton and educated at the University of London. Shewbrook was himself a keen sportsman, acting as a referee for some of the early matches played by the Cardiff rugby team.

Monkton House had opened on 25 January 1870 with an advert placed in the town's newspaper proclaiming 'The course of instruction will include all of the subjects of a thorough English education, including French, Classics and Mathematics.' What wasn't said, but was equally important to Mr Shewbrook and his staff, was that there would also be plenty of time for sport. Indeed, just six months after their opening, the young scholars from Monkton House used the Recreation Field for

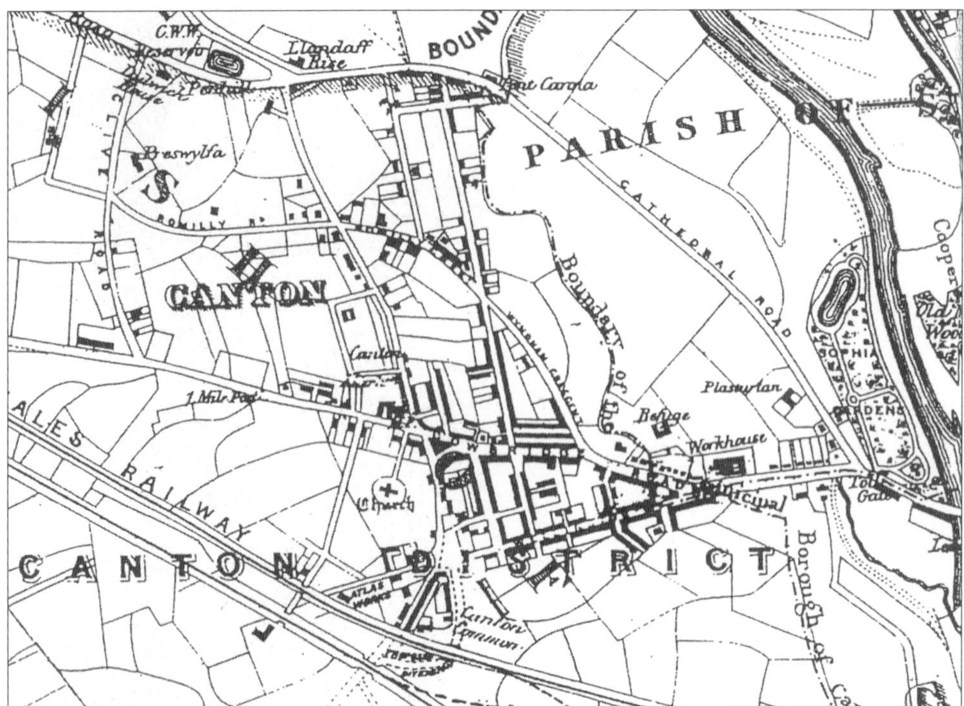

A map of Pontcanna after the opening of Sophia Gardens in 1869, prior to the construction of houses along Cathedral Road.

a cricket match against the Revd Green's Classical and Commercial School, a well-established rival, based in Charles Street.

Perhaps Shewbrook was being a bit too ambitious in staging this contest so soon after the school's opening, as the *Cardiff Times* reported how, 'The XIs appear to have been very unequally matched, for while Mr Shoebrook's (sic) scholars only made 31 runs in two innings, their opponents scored 153 in a single innings.' But at least it was a start, and he took several steps in the course of the next year or so to further boost the playing of ball games at his academy. The first came through his rugby contacts, as he persuaded J.A. Bush, the father of Welsh rugby legend Percy, to mix his duties as head of the Arts and Science School to teach art at Monkton House, and to help out with some games coaching.

The second line of assistance came from John Ingledew, who was one of the first governors of Shewbrook's school. Through his encouragement, Sophia Gardens quickly became the school's regular base for their summer and winter games, with Ingledew often wandering across from his home in Cathedral Road, either socialising with the parents who were watching fixtures, or lending a hand with practices.

In February 1872 Monkton House played their inaugural rugby match at the Sophia Gardens Field, against a XV from Bridgend School. The field quickly grew in popularity for their fixtures, so much so that a group of Old Monktonians formed their own club which played regular fixtures at Sophia Gardens until after the First World War, before moving to other sites in Cardiff, and then establishing a permanent base in 1951 as Glamorgan Wanderers R.F.C. at the Memorial Ground in Ely.

The pupils at Henry Shewbrook's school included many of the sons of the mercantile elite and other well-to-do people in the town. The school roll in the 1890s included Norman Riches, the man who went on to lead Glamorgan in their inaugural Championship match in 1921. His father, Carlton, was a keen cricketer with the Cardiff club, as was his uncle Cuthbert, an engineer with the Taff Vale Railway, who had played with distinction for the town club, the Bute Household side and the Glamorganshire team.

Another family member was John Gowan Clarke, a prominent batsman with the Cardiff, Bute and Glamorgan teams, so it was no surprise that young Norman, surrounded by so many sports-mad

Henry Shewbrook standing in civvies and surrounded by some of Cardiff's early rugby players.

relatives, should be sent to a school run by a fervent disciple of Muscular Christianity. Norman's love of ball games was quickly nurtured and, as he later recalled during a talk to the pupils in July 1925, he and the other pupils thoroughly enjoyed playing ball games at Sophia Gardens, under the influence of Henry Shewbrook:

> …or daddy as we used to call him… he used to play (rugby) football with us, and he played a very vigorous game. He was too heavy for us smaller fry to tackle, so we didn't try, but he suffered severely on many occasions from more than vigorous 'hacks' on the shins!

By the late 1870s the rugby pitches at Sophia Gardens had reached such a standing that they were used for some of the season's leading fixtures, including the matches organised by the South Wales Football Club. Formed in 1875, several of their officials were also prominent figures in cricketing circles, including Major T. Conway Lloyd and C.C. Chambers, who were leading lights with the Brecon and Swansea clubs respectively. Both had also been leading figures with the South Wales Cricket Club, so this 'sister' organisation gave the region's top players exposure against some of the leading English clubs, as well as XVs representing neighbouring Welsh and English counties.

With interest in the oval-ball game on the up, these fixtures also attracted large crowds, so when the South Wales club challenged Monmouthshire at the Sophia Gardens Field in November 1875, the Bute Estate – never ones to miss out on an opportunity to make a few bob – decided to charge 6*d* admission for gentlemen, with ladies allowed in free to watch the hurly-burly game and to admire the muscular prowess of the participants.

Their actions generated sufficient returns that they levied an entrance fee again in the spring of 1879, when the Sophia Gardens Field played host to the final of the South Wales Challenge Cup – the premier inter-club competition – with Cardiff playing the crack Newport club. This allowed the pitch to be roped off by the Bute staff and their efforts raised the sum of £72, but not everyone

Cathedral Road at the turn of the century, showing trams which ran from the inner suburb into the bustling city centre.

was happy, with the local newspaper subsequently carrying letters from people upset at parting with their hard-earned money, especially at a so-called public park.

With the Bute Estate wary of allowing too much rugby on the Arms Park, the Glamorganshire side also used the Sophia Gardens pitch for some of their matches, including the game against the Rest of South Wales on 24 November 1877. The weather though, was particularly foul, with the *Cardiff Times* describing how 'the rain fell in torrents, the field was half under water, and the game was played under the most untoward circumstances.' In 1879 the Bute Estate allowed Cardiff R.F.C. to play on the Arms Park on a regular basis. In practice, it also meant that most of the other representative matches also moved to the Arms Park and the upshot was that the Sophia Gardens Recreation Field became the sole preserve of the ever-expanding number of junior clubs and school teams.

The demand for the use of the field remained high, simply because so few of the rugby clubs in the Cardiff area were fortunate enough to have their own ground. The chance to acquire a lease of their own ground, enclose the playing area and charge admission for games was out of the question for the vast majority of rugby clubs in Victorian and Edwardian Cardiff. As a result, practices and fixtures were staged on public parkland, or on wasteland awaiting development on the fringes of the built-up area The latter, though, was the least favoured option, as it gave little continuity and as a consequence, the Sophia Gardens Field grew in popularity as alternative venues were quickly swallowed up by urban sprawl.

The Sophia Gardens Recreation Field had other advantages; for a start, it was easily accessible by public transport, with a frequent service of horse-drawn trams running from the city centre over Cardiff Bridge and down Cathedral Road. Secondly, the field was not too far away from the pubs and taverns where teams could change, and then either drown their post-match sorrows or celebrate victory.

No surprise then that Sophia Gardens became the place where an ever-increasing number of the townsfolk learned and developed their sporting skills. By the late 1880s, hundreds of young men and boys played in matches at Sophia Gardens throughout Saturdays. In the words of local rugby historian Gwyn Prescott, 'Without this large and accessible facility, it is questionable whether rugby would have expanded quite as it did in Cardiff, with well over 200 teams in the district by the end of the 1880s.'

Over time, several clubs secured, albeit in an *ad hoc* way, their regular patch of land on the Recreation Field. Their posts – much lighter and smaller than the ones used today – were carried over from the side of the field, or from the local pub, and erected on their patch for their training and matches. There were few other facilities for the players and if somebody wanted to wash after a game, it was a case of a quick dip in the Taff to wash away the mud and sweat after their manly exertions!

The Harlequins ground, off Newport Road, in the early 1900s. A similar scene would have been seen on the Sophia Gardens Recreation Field, full of young men and boys engaged in healthy recreation.

The lack of decent facilities was also commented upon by a report in *The South Wales Daily News* for 10 February 1885, with the correspondent writing how:

> There is a lack of a proper place… for the players' clothes, bags, etc. The dressing rooms pertaining to public houses in the neighbourhood of the Sophia Gardens Field are quite inadequate for the number of our local clubs which play… there every Saturday and Wednesday – players have to deposit their clothes in a wash-house… which might accommodate four persons at the most, and on the open field… pilfering goes on at an alarming rate. A few weeks ago the members of one club alone lost £2… Such trifling articles as a spare football, hats and mufflers disappear with annoying frequency. One player recently had his bag and contents 'lifted' owing to the nuisance of either having to come to the field dressed and go back dirty, or to dress on the field and have your things stolen. Many men will not turn up… what is wanted is a good large erection in the Sophia Gardens Field with conveniences for washing….This would be an incalculable boom to the football community.

For the clubs that were unable to use Sophia Gardens, the threat of eviction at short notice, or the loss of land to building were real threats to their very existence, so these spartan conditions and petty thefts were a small price to pay for the security and stability that playing on the Recreation Field offered.

There were other hindrances that were also tolerated, such as the need to cancel games or practices when the field was used for other events and civic shows. This was the case in September 1891 when Col. W. Cody (or Buffalo Bill as he was popularly known) turned up with his Wild West show and, with the blessing of the Bute officials, took over the Recreation Field. Some of the rugby teams, however, found a few unoccupied stretches of land in between the tents and sideshows where they could have a kick around.

Four years later, when the players turned up one Saturday afternoon to get ready for their matches, they found that the Band of Hope had occupied the field for a meeting to preach the virtues of the Temperance Movement. The fixtures had to be hastily cancelled, but many of the rugby players happily retaliated by heading off to the nearest pub to enjoy a free afternoon!

Cathedral Road, Cardiff, in the years before the First World War.

The Gardens and Recreation Field were used for a variety of activities and camps prior to the First World War.

Rounders at Sophia Gardens

From the late 1860s rounders was another one of the sports staged on the Sophia Gardens Recreation Field, with the *Cardiff Times* for 11 May 1866 saying 'how pleasing it is to observe the growing appreciation of the gardens, while the field behind is occupied by a numerous lot of young men and boys, who engage in the healthy games of cricket, rounders, etc.'

The games staged at Sophia Gardens often coincided with social gatherings, such as those played on Good Friday 1870, when matches took place between apprentice engineers and their shipwright counterparts, followed a few weeks later by a game between the Bute Engineers and a team representing Hearts of Oak.

The entrance into Sophia Gardens adjacent to Cardiff Bridge, as seen around the time of the First World War, with a circus tent visible in the background at the end of the tree-lined avenue.

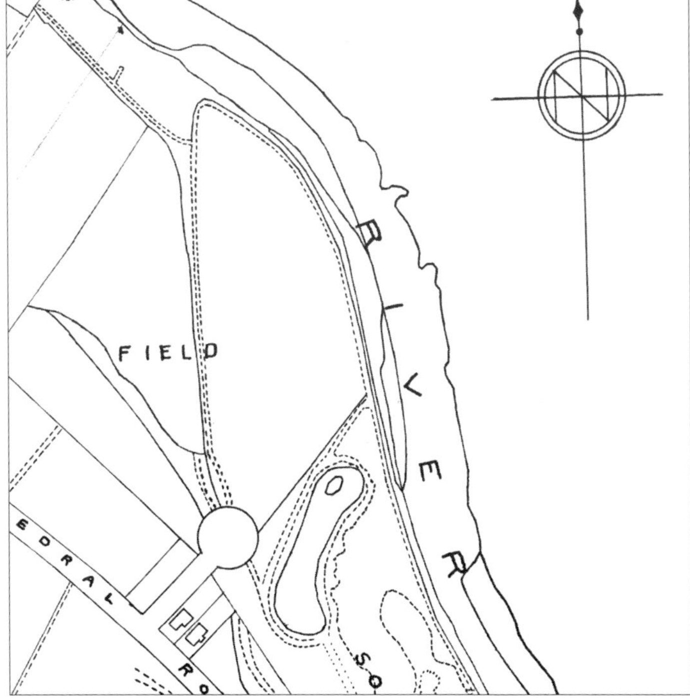

A sketch of the Sophia Gardens area in the 1880s by H.H. Pettigrew, showing the footpath around the perimeter of the Recreation Field as well as the ornamental lake.

NINE

The Brains Behind Glamorgan

27 May 1890 was a red-letter day both for Glamorgan and the Cardiff C.C., as it was on that day that the Welsh county recorded its first win at the Arms Park. The game, against neighbours Monmouthshire, also saw nineteen year old Herbie Morgan record the first-ever century for Glamorgan, with the young farmer from Llandough coming in at number seven and flaying the visitor's bowling to all parts of the Cardiff ground.

Ironically, Herbie was only playing because on the eve of the game Daniel Jones withdrew from the side through illness. The young batsman from Penarth C.C. duly celebrated his late call-up by smashing 4 sixes and 15 fours until being run out for 147 as Glamorgan rattled up 420, before forcing Monmouthshire to follow-on as the visitors were dismissed for a paltry 76. They faired little better a second time around, with Morgan also claiming a wicket with his occasional spin bowling as Monmouthshire lost by an innings.

Glamorgan's first home victory thrilled the correspondent of the *Western Mail* who wrote how 'lovers of the game are in hope that this is a good augury for local county cricket in the future.' Sadly, it did not prove to be the case as the early 1890s proved to be quite difficult years for Glamorgan, with the new county side only managing two wins in its first dozen matches. With the selectors still choosing some of the old members of the South Wales C.C., a few cynics wryly suggested that the new county club would go the way of the old Glamorganshire side. But J.T.D. Llewelyn was determined that the club would survive and, on occasions, he even dipped into his own pockets in order to cover the expenses of playing several professionals, especially in away fixtures. Having a paternalistic figurehead was one thing, but Glamorgan badly needed a dynamic leader on the field and who, through their efforts with bat and ball, could lead the side with success. To J.T.D.'s delight, that person arrived in South Wales during 1890 as Joseph Brain, the young Gloucestershire and Oxford University batsman, moved across the Severn Estuary to oversee the running of the Old Brewery in Cardiff, which his uncle, Samuel, himself an enthusiastic cricketer, had acquired in 1882.

The brewery had previously belonged to Samuel's wife Frances Thomas, but in 1882 Samuel, together with his brother, J.B. Brain, the chairman of the West of England Bank in Bristol, acquired the business. Samuel Brain initially managed the day-to-day affairs of the new business venture, before handing over the reins in 1890 to his nephew Joseph Brain after he had completed his studies at Oxford and gained some experience in the business world.

J.H. Brain

J.H. Brain was educated at Clifton College, where he led the school XI in 1883. In his final year at school, the talented batsman made his debut for Gloucestershire, before going up to Oxford, where he won four Blues and led the university side in 1887.

As a Freshman, he was in the Oxford XI that defeated the 1884 Australians and later in the summer, he hit an attractive 108 for Gloucestershire against the tourists – an innings which led some judges to regard Brain as one of the brightest prospects in the county.

Many regarded Brain as a possible successor to W.G. Grace as captain of the Gloucestershire side, but in the 1890s he crossed the Severn Estuary and devoted his energies to the affairs of the family's brewery and Glamorgan C.C.C.

The Old Brewery in Cardiff.

Herbie Morgan, Glamorgan's first centurion.

Joseph Brain, seen here as an undergraduate at Oxford.

Joseph Brain played his final match for Gloucestershire in August 1889, fittingly at Clifton College against Kent and then moved from Bristol to Cardiff that winter. The officials of Glamorgan were delighted to have such an illustrious cricketer in residence in Cardiff, and it was a great coup for the fledging county side when Brain agreed to take over the captaincy in 1891, followed by the secretary's duties in 1893. He remained in these roles until 1908, during which time the county went from strength to strength, joining the Minor County Championship in 1897. By the first decade of the twentieth century, Glamorgan C.C.C. were establishing themselves as one of the strongest sides below first-class level.

This transformation from being a third-class county to joint-Minor County champions in 1900 was entirely down to the acumen and skill of Brain. His first positive act was to use his contacts to organise a fund-raising match at the Arms Park in May 1891 between Glamorgan and Gloucestershire, plus a return fixture at Bristol. The match at Cardiff was chiefly a publicity stunt; with the legendary W.G. Grace in the visitor's line-up, it was designed to swell the coffers of the Welsh side, thereby enabling them to draw on the services of more professionals, thus not relying solely on so many kind benefactors such as J.T.D. Llewelyn.

After discussions with J.P. Jones and other influential officials, Brain also contacted all of the clubs in the region, asking them for the names of their promising young players who could take part in a Colts trial over the Whitsun Bank Holiday. So great was the response that a decent XXII was raised to play a County XI and the success of the fixture in 1891 led to its repeat in the next two years.

Brain also used his contacts within the West Country to secure the services of several talented amateur batsmen, while he also dipped into his own pocket to hire a couple of professionals. Besides turning out for the county, the professionals could help coach the emerging talent and work as labourers in the Old Brewery during the winter months. His younger brother, William Brain, who had played regularly for both Oxford University and Gloucestershire, also moved across to the Welsh side of the Severn Estuary in 1893 and became Glamorgan's regular wicketkeeper.

With a stronger side taking the field on a more regular basis, Glamorgan's results improved, with his side winning six of their nine games in 1892, including four-successive victories in May and

William Brain.

June over the M.C.C., Wiltshire and twice against Monmouthshire. Glamorgan also won at Lord's in late August, with William Morgan of Llwynypia C.C. scoring 91 and 61, besides taking 13-143 as the Welsh county won for the second successive year at cricket's H.Q.

To further boost public interest, Brain also used his extensive contacts to secure a fixture in 1894 with the South Africans. The match – Glamorgan's first against a touring side – proved to be something of a flop, as the tourists comfortably won by ten wickets, while the gate receipts did not prove to be as high as Brain and his colleagues had anticipated. Ralph Sweet-Escott, the rugby-playing batsman from Cardiff, was the only batsman to offer any resistance against the visiting bowlers, with the twenty-five year old scoring an unbeaten half-century as Glamorgan mustered a modest 139 in their first innings.

Despite some accurate seam bowling from Cardiff professional Alfred Eldridge and his clubmate Selwyn Biggs, who also won nine rugby caps for Wales, the Springboks amassed a decent 99-run lead on first innings. The clatter of early wickets then took place as Glamorgan batted again. After Gowan Clark and Billy Bancroft had shared a half-century partnership for the fifth wicket, the visiting bowlers made short work of the Welsh tail. This was one of five defeats for Brain's team in 1894 and in his end-of-season review, the captain highlighted the need for a greater professional atmosphere about all aspects of the club's play. He had been appalled at what he described as 'an air of apathy and indifference' shown by some of the amateurs and highlighted by the away match with Wiltshire, when two of the amateurs chosen in the Glamorgan party simply failed to turn up at Cardiff General to catch the train to Swindon. Quite rightly, he felt that such a casual approach had no place in a team that had aspirations of playing at a higher level and with this in mind, he persuaded the other officials to appoint Billy Bancroft, the twenty-four year old all-rounder from Swansea – who was also an outstanding rugby player, winning thirty-three Welsh caps – as a full-time professional.

Bancoft's appointment led to a dramatic rise in the club's fortunes as they went through 1895 without defeat, before recording a series of comprehensive victories during 1896, including innings wins over Herefordshire and the M.C.C. The match with Monmouthshire at Newport epitomized the new spirit in Glamorgan's ranks as they chased a target of 210, only to lose five quick wickets.

William Pullen of Somerset, Gloucestershire and Glamorgan.

Vernon Hill, the former Somerset batsman who helped organise fund-raising matches at the Arms Park.

It seemed a hopeless position, but Bancroft got his head down, and with the support of the lower order, they turned the game around, winning by two wickets, the Glamorgan professional scoring a fine century.

Brain was also fortunate enough to be able to draw on the services of a couple of talented amateurs with fine track records for West Country sides in William Pullen and Vernon Hill. Pullen had appeared during the 1880s for both Somerset and Gloucestershire, striking 161 for the latter when only eighteen-years old. In the early 1890s Pullen became a lecturer at Cardiff University and he willingly mixed his academic commitments with appearances for the Glamorgan side.

Vernon Hill was the son of Sir Edward Hill of Llandaff, who was the Conservative M.P. for Bristol. Hill had been a contemporary of William Brain at Oxford University, making 114 in the Varsity Match and playing as a free-scoring batsman for Somerset. His business interests brought him to Cardiff, and the Brain brothers were delighted when their friend helped to organise an All-England XI for a special fund-raising game at the Arms Park in 1895. Hill persuaded a number of his former Somerset colleagues to play in the exhibition match, together with C.B. Fry, one of England's most illustrious all-round sportsmen, plus Ranjitsinhji, the Sussex and England batsman. Their presence drew a large crowd, and even though the Indian 'prince' was late arriving, the crowd were treated to a regal display as Fry made a graceful 71, before Sammy Woods struck a fine century.

With healthier finances, Brain was able to secure the services of Sam Lowe, the former Nottinghamshire bowler for the 1896 season; Lowe proved to be a fine acquisition as he claimed 35 wickets at just 12 runs apiece as Glamorgan recorded a further string of victories. These successes somewhat vindicated Brain's belief that the Welsh county would be able to hold their own by playing at a higher standard in the Minor County Championship.

Brain had been a leading figure behind the formation of this competition, serving as chairman of the Minor County Cricket Association between 1896 and 1898. With an air of confidence still permeating the committee room, it did not take the chairman of Brain's Brewery too long in persuading the other Glamorgan officials that they should apply to join the second-class competition. A formal letter was duly sent and a few weeks later, the M.C.C. endorsed their application, admitting Glamorgan to the Minor County competition for 1897.

Their inaugural Minor County Championship fixture took place in the first week of June against Surrey Second XI at The Oval. It ended in a draw, as the Welsh side performed with much credit against a Surrey team containing nine players with first-class experience. Glamorgan's first win as a minor county came at Swansea in July as they defeated Monmouthshire by four wickets. Brain's team were brought down to earth in their next match, at the Arms Park, as Worcestershire recorded an innings victory, but they returned to winning ways in their following match at St Helen's as they defeated Cornwall by 241 runs, with Sam Lowe becoming the first Glamorgan bowler to claim a hat-trick. Cornwall were dismissed for just 25 as the Cardiff professional returned the remarkable figures of 6-2-9-5.

Glamorgan's first victory as a minor county at the Arms Park came in the last week of July, as they defeated Wiltshire by ten wickets, with Sam Lowe claiming ten wickets in the match, as the English county followed-on against some fiery Welsh bowling. It was a victory that helped Brain's team secure second place in the competition – much to the delight of all the Glamorgan officials – behind Worcestershire who were crowned the Minor County Champions for 1897.

They had smiles on their faces again the following year, as Glamorgan recorded four further victories to maintain a position in the top part of the table, finishing in fourth place behind Worcestershire, Berkshire and Northamptonshire. They improved their position by one place in 1899 as they won a further six games, including a 53-run victory over Surrey Second XI at The Oval, with Herbie Morgan hitting a forthright 110 and William Brain an unbeaten 99. In the return fixture at Swansea, Billy Bancroft recorded the rare feat of a century and a hat-trick but the visitors secured victory by 194 runs as Glamorgan went down to their only defeat of the summer.

Brain's request for a fixture with the 1900 South Africans was turned down as Glamorgan were unable to meet the financial guarantees set down by the M.C.C. But at the end of the season, the Glamorgan captain had a broad, beaming smile on his face as Glamorgan became joint-Minor County Champions, sharing the title with Durham and Northamptonshire having recorded six victories. The bowling of William Russell, the professional with the Cowbridge club, was one of the key factors behind Glamorgan's success. He took 10-83 as Wiltshire were defeated by eight wickets, followed by 9-86 in the innings victory over Surrey Second XI, finishing with 9-68 as Berkshire were beaten by seven wickets.

Brain himself had a successful summer in 1900, making 88 against Surrey Second XI at The Oval and then 102 in the return match at the Arms Park, his side recording another innings victory. Home

The Glamorgan team of 1901. *Back row*: H. Creber, R. Lowe, S. Lowe, W. Russell, W.J. Bancroft. *Front row*: N.V.H. Riches, H.E. Morgan, J.H. Brain, W.H. Brain, A.J. Osbourne and A.W. Cameron

and away victories against Berkshire, followed by draws with Wiltshire and Northamptonshire allowed Glamorgan to maintain their position at the top of the table and, much to the delight of the Glamorgan officials, share the title.

At the end of the summer, a series of celebratory dinners were held to toast the success of the Glamorgan side and to recognise Brain's leadership skills and business acumen in transforming Glamorgan from a third-class county into one of the top minor-county outfits. Such tributes were richly deserved, as J.H. Brain had been a natural leader who helped to fill the vacuum that was present within cricketing circles in South Wales during the early 1890s.

His active involvement, however, begs one final, but quite important question: why did an English gentleman act so strenuously in the promotion of cricket in Cardiff and a Welsh county side? Both were areas in which J.H. Brain had previously spent so little time and to which initially he held no affiliation.

One reason may have been personal betterment, as leading Glamorgan allowed Brain to fulfil several personal ambitions, no doubt fuelled by his leadership of teams at Clifton and Oxford, and his experience of county cricket with Gloucestershire. The promotion of the family business must have also played a contributory role. A measure of his business skills can be gauged from the fact that in 1882, Brains supplied just eleven pubs in the Cardiff area; by 1900 they either owned or leased eighty, as output had increased from around 100 barrels a week to in excess of 1,000. His involvement with the county side helped to nurture valuable contacts and supporters within the business community. In turn, the staging of matches at the Arms Park that would attract a large crowd no doubt helped to swell the demand for Brain's beer in the city's taverns.

With J.H. Brain as their energetic manager, the company expanded the Old Brewery, transforming it into the largest brewery in South Wales. Under his leadership, the company introduced ideas and production methods from other parts of England. This willingness to innovate and introduce new personnel from outside Wales were lessons that Brain put into practice with the cricket team. Indeed, one factor that did not play a role was the question of Welsh identity, as the desire to create a successful team was at the top of Brain's priorities.

Indeed, in his early years as Glamorgan captain, the number of Welsh-born players actually dropped. Around seventy per cent of his team in 1892 had been born in the Principality, yet by 1896 this figure had fallen to around forty-six per cent, as more English-born gentlemen and cricketing acquaintances turned out for the Glamorgan club. This reliance on players because of their cricketing prowess – rather than because of social reasons or native loyalty – allowed Glamorgan to survive rather than fold, as with the earlier Glamorganshire side and the South Wales C.C.

There were other factors as well, not least the fact that with J.H.Brain as secretary, the club steadily became more businesslike in its approach, and left behind for good the rather relaxed and easy-going atmosphere of the old South Wales club. The fact that he was a fresh face, untainted by the failure of previous organisations, was another huge plus in Brain's favour. Another determinant was that he had an ever-growing network of contacts within the English cricket world; being a member of the M.C.C. and a graduate from the dreaming spires of Oxford, he had an established channel of communication with those in the higher echelons of English cricket.

After having been in Cardiff for a relatively short period of time, Brain was able to weld onto this very impressive cricketing information field a whole network of contacts from within the business and Conservative community of South Wales. Indeed, he may have seen promoting Glamorgan as a means of supporting Tory causes, rather than what J.T.D. Llewelyn was eager to do, ostensibly creating a Welsh cricket team and promoting South Wales in the sporting world.

A measure of the family's high standing within the local community can be gauged from the fact that S.A. Brain, who had arrived in the region in 1882, was appointed the Mayor of Cardiff in 1899/1900. How fitting it was, therefore, that during his period in office, his energetic nephew should lead Glamorgan to the minor county title and lay the foundations for an even larger goal – Test cricket in Cardiff.

TEN

Soccer Kicks-Off at Sophia Gardens

The success of Glamorgan as a minor county saw an upswing in the number of junior clubs using the Sophia Gardens Recreation Field in the late Victorian era. One of the teams using the facilities during the summer months was Riverside C.C. – a team comprising a group of young men of quite humble means who lived in the inner suburbs of Canton and Riverside.

Despite the limited facilities at Sophia Gardens, the men of the Riverside club so enjoyed their summer exertions that they started to consider ways of maintaining their sporting camaraderie over the winter months. One of the possibilities was to play association football, which had grown in popularity in South Wales during the last two decades of the nineteenth century. It proved to be an astute choice as Riverside C.C. metamorphosed into Cardiff City Football Club, the Welsh capital's premier football team, and the side who, at Wembley in 1927, became the first and, so far, only Welsh side to win the F.A. Cup Final.

The first inkling that the members of the cricket club should diversify their activities came in the late summer of 1899 when a meeting was held to discuss the formation of a football club. After protracted discussions, Riverside A.F.C. came into being with Bartley Wilson, a lithographic artist from Bristol, acting as the new club's secretary. In fact, Bart Wilson had been the instigator of the meeting and through his influence, eight committee members were appointed, with membership fees set at half a crown and a strip of chocolate-and-amber quarters.

By the time they came into being in 1899/1900, Riverside AFC were too late to join the recently formed Cardiff and District League, which included some of the other football teams that used Sophia Gardens. Nevertheless, they were able to secure a series of friendly fixtures, with the first taking place on Saturday, 7 October 1899 as they played Barry West End F.C. It proved to be an inauspicious start, as the newly formed club were trounced 9-1, but at least it was a start.

Through the energetic efforts of Wilson and the other committee members, fixtures were subsequently secured against other junior teams outside Cardiff, including Barry District Juniors and Penarth Parish Church F.C. Indeed, there was sufficient interest for the Riverside club to raise a reserve team later in the season, and as a result of Bart Wilson's initiative, the reserve team also entered the Junior Medal Cup of the South Wales and Monmouthshire Football Association. Their first round contest against Roath Road Wesleyans, however, ended in both defeat and acrimony, as the Riverside officials lodged a complaint about the eligibility of some of the Wesleyan team. Despite losing their appeal, the Riverside officials remained very optimistic and energetic, with team officials regularly walking around the touchline at Sophia Gardens with small collecting boxes to accept donations from the growing number of spectators who travelled to watch Riverside's home fixtures.

In 1900/01 the club entered the Cardiff and District League, and following further success, they amalgamated with another local club, the Riverside Albions in 1902/03, so that they could join the South Wales Amateur League, and also take part in the various knock-out competitions sanctioned by the South Wales and Monmouthshire Football Association.

In 1905 the Riverside team won the Bevan Shield, one of the local cup competitions, and with rising aspirations in the city, Bart Wilson led a campaign for Riverside A.F.C. to be called Cardiff City A.F.C. The ruling authorities rejected their application, ostensibly on the grounds that they did

The members of Riverside C.C.

The Cardiff City football team in the early 1900s with Bartley Wilson standing at the right behind the back row.

not play in a sufficiently high enough competition. They recommended to Bart Wilson and his fellow officials that they join the South Wales League instead. Wilson and his colleagues followed this advice, but Riverside struggled against their new and stronger opponents. Plenty of people still turned up for the league games at Sophia Gardens but, by and large, Riverside continued to lose more games than they won. Undeterred, the club's officials continued their campaign that they be known as Cardiff City. On 5 September 1908 Wilson won a huge moral victory as the South Wales and Monmouthshire Football Association resolved 'that permission be given on the condition that if a professional team should be started in Cardiff in the near future, they would relinquish the name.'

After many years of hard work, not least trudging around the touchline at Sophia Gardens with a collecting box, this was a huge triumph for Bart Wilson and the Riverside club, who had grown from a local park side, playing in a rugby stronghold, to an organisation that could lay claim to be the representatives on the football field of both the 'Coal Metropolis' and the fastest-growing area of the Principality.

The late 1900s saw a huge upswing in public interest in football. Each Saturday morning the foyer of Cardiff General Railway Station was full of football enthusiasts, eagerly buying tickets so that they

Bartley Wilson in later life, and seen below standing second from left.

Cardiff City F.C. in 1906/07, in front of the Lodge at Sophia Gardens (now the Mochyn Du).

could travel to watch a League game. Many went to Aberdare, Merthyr or Treharris to watch those teams in their fixtures in the second division of the Southern League, while many others travelled to the other side of the Severn to Ashton Gate in Bristol to watch the city's football team in action in Division One of the Football League.

Sandwiched in between the hotbed of football in the valleys and the thriving clubs in Bristol, the time seemed ripe for the newly named Cardiff A.F.C. to join the Southern League. This decision was held up by the league requirement of an enclosed ground and, with Sophia Gardens serving as a public recreation area, a permanent home in the Recreation Field was completely out of the question.

Using the Arms Park rugby ground was a completely different matter, especially as requests for using the pitch for exhibition soccer matches would allow the Bute officials to charge an entrance fee, thus cashing in on the growing demand to watch association football. An agreement over the share

A working-men's football team (note the ordinary shirts) at Sophia Gardens in the early 1900s.

Lord Ninian Crichton Stuart.

of gate receipts was duly drawn up and, on 5 October 1909, Cardiff City A.F.C. played out a highly creditable 3-3 draw against Crystal Palace, the Southern League team, on the rugby ground.

Six weeks later, the Cardiff club, augmented by various amateurs from other local sides, returned to the Arms Park to play Bristol City. Despite a 7-1 drubbing, the game continued to fuel the aspirations of Bart Wilson and his colleagues. A decent crowd had also turned up to the Mecca of rugby to watch a game of association football and in the course of the next few months, the Cardiff City officials approached the Bute Estate for a plot of land away from both Sophia Gardens and the Arms Park that they could develop into their home ground, and, at long last, turn professional.

Sites at Leckwith Common and off Sloper Road in Grangetown were discussed and after protracted discussions, the latter was secured. It was duly named after Lord Ninian Crichton-Stuart, the son of the third Marquess, who had done so much to broker the deal.

An aerial view of Ninian Park in the 1920s showing the main Swansea to London railway line to the north.

The newly incorporated Cardiff City Association Football Club Limited played their inaugural professional match on 1 September 1st, 1910 against Aston Villa, the Division One Champions. 7,000 spectators thronged into Ninian Park, with the handsome crowd including many of the diehards who had spent countless hours watching Bart's boys play at Sophia Gardens.

Their move to their new ground in Grangetown marked a new era, not just for the club, but for the history of professional sport in South Wales as a whole. Their debt of gratitude to the previous Riverside club, and to the many smaller clubs – whose cricketers had enjoyed themselves on the Sophia Gardens Recreation Field – had not been forgotten.

International Football at the Arms Park

In the years before the creation of Ninian Park, the Marquess of Bute gave permission for international football to be held at the Arms Park rugby ground. In all, six games took place against Scotland, Ireland and England:

1896	Wales *v.* England	1903	Wales *v.* Scotland
1900	Wales *v.* England	1906	Wales *v.* England
1902	Wales *v.* Ireland	1910	Wales *v.* England

ELEVEN

1905 and All That

By the start of the second decade of the twentieth century, the newly instigated city of Cardiff could boast its own professional football team. Had events taken their expected course, the city might also by this time have staged Test-match cricket. This would, of course, have been a major coup for the Glamorgan club, who at the time were a minor county, but after becoming joint champions of the Minor County Championship in 1900, they held a couple of lofty and most laudable ambitions – to be admitted to the first-class County Championship and to stage a Test match at the Arms Park.

Glamorgan were fortunate to still have J.H. Brain as their captain, by now the energetic chairman of Brain's Brewery and a highly powerful figure within the corridors of power at Lord's and the M.C.C. He had also become an extremely influential figure within Tory circles in Cardiff and, having shared his aspirations of bringing major matches to the Arms Park with the Bute Estate, the Marquess's advisors and fellow Conservatives agreed to make the Cardiff ground available for these lucrative fixtures, knowing full well of the many benefits for both Cardiff, and the estate.

Through Brain's influence, the M.C.C. agreed to allocate a showcase fixture in 1902 to the Arms Park, with Glamorgan combining forces with Wiltshire – another strong minor county – to play the Australians. It was the first time the Aussies had ever played in Cardiff, so it was no surprise that the contest attracted an enormous crowd. Around 12,000 people attended the game, far surpassing the previous ground record and each day, trains packed with excited cricket supporters travelled to Cardiff from as far away as Milford Haven in the west and Swindon in the east.

By a happy coincidence, the three-day match was arranged by the Glamorgan committee – chock full of Conservative supporters – at the same time as the civic celebrations were taking place in Cardiff to celebrate the coming-of-age of John Crichton Stuart, the fourth Marquess. A week of special events were held, including a garden party in the castle grounds at the end of the second day's play. The famous Australian cricketers, together with leading members and officials of the Glamorgan club, were all able to mix with the great and good of South Walian society and Tory politics.

The combined side batted first and made 121, albeit in 52 overs after some doughty resistance from the minor county batsmen, especially William Brain who made a dogged 32* and defied the Australian attack for over two hours. William Overton, the Wiltshire slow bowler, and Glamorgan's Harry Creber were soon among the wickets with the Swansea professional dismissing the first three Australian batsmen as the tourists also struggled in the face of some spirited bowling.

Ernie Jones and Bert Hopkins staged a late fightback to guide the Australians to a twenty-seven-run lead on first innings. Herbie Morgan then unfurled some aggressive strokes and to the delight of the local supporters, he made a fine fifty, while Walter Medlicott, Wiltshire's Oxford Blue, also made an unbeaten half-century as the combined side set the tourists a target of 155.

Second time around, the Australians found runs easier to come by, and after a platform had been carefully laid by openers James Kelly and Clem Hill, the tourists eased to a six-wicket victory.

The twenty-one year old Marquess was one of the special guests at this prestigious match and he also arranged for the tourists to have a special tour around the Bute Docks. The tourists thoroughly enjoyed their visit to the Cardiff ground, and on departing by train from Cardiff General for their next match in Hampshire, their captain, Syd Gregory said:

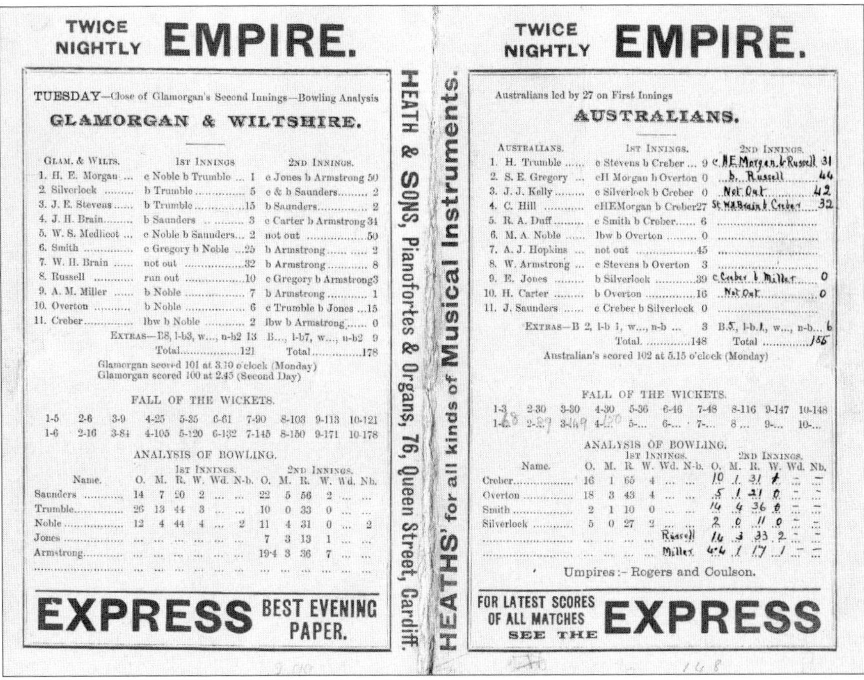

TWICE NIGHTLY **EMPIRE.**

TUESDAY—Close of Glamorgan's Second Innings—Bowling Analysis

GLAMORGAN & WILTSHIRE.

Glam. & Wilts.	1st Innings		2nd Innings	
1. H. E. Morgan	c Noble b Trumble	1	c Jones b Armstrong	50
2. Silverlock	b Trumble	5	c & b Saunders	2
3. J. E. Stevens	b Trumble	15	b Saunders	2
4. J. H. Brain	b Saunders	3	c Carter b Armstrong	34
5. W. S. Medlicot	c Noble b Saunders	2	not out	50
6. Smith	c Gregory b Noble	25	b Armstrong	2
7. W. H. Brain	not out	32	b Armstrong	8
8. Russell	run out	10	c Gregory b Armstrong	3
9. A. M. Miller	b Noble	7	b Armstrong	1
10. Overton	b Noble	6	c Trumble b Jones	15
11. Creber	lbw b Noble	2	lbw b Armstrong	0
	Extras—B8, l-b3, w..., n-b2	13	B..., l-b7, w..., n-b2	9
	Total	121	Total	178

Glamorgan scored 101 at 3.10 o'clock (Monday)
Glamorgan scored 100 at 2.45 (Second Day)

FALL OF THE WICKETS.

1-5	2-6	3-9	4-25	5-35	6-61	7-90	8-103	9-113	10-121
1-6	2-16	3-84	4-105	5-120	6-132	7-145	8-150	9-171	10-178

ANALYSIS OF BOWLING.

Name.	1st Innings O.	M.	R.	W.	Wd.	N-b.	2nd Innings O.	M.	R.	W.	Wd.	Nb.
Saunders	14	7	20	2	...	...	22	5	56	2	...	...
Trumble	26	13	44	3	...	...	10	0	33	0	...	...
Noble	12	4	44	4	...	2	11	4	31	0	...	2
Jones	...	...	...	...	...	...	7	3	13	1	...	...
Armstrong	...	...	...	...	...	...	19·4	3	36	7	...	...

EXPRESS BEST EVENING PAPER.

HEATH & SONS, Pianofortes & Organs, 76, Queen Street, Cardiff.

HEATHS' for all kinds of Musical Instruments.

TWICE NIGHTLY **EMPIRE.**

Australians led by 27 on First Innings

AUSTRALIANS.

Australians.	1st Innings.		2nd Innings.	
1. H. Trumble	c Stevens b Creber	9	c H.E. Morgan b Russell	31
2. S. E. Gregory	cH Morgan b Overton	0	b. Russell	44
3. J. J. Kelly	c Silverlock b Creber	0	Not Out	42
4. C. Hill	cHEMorgan b Creber	27	St W.H.Brain b Creber	32
5. R. A. Duff	c Smith b Creber	6		
6. M. A. Noble	lbw b Overton	0		
7. A. J. Hopkins	not out	45		
8. W. Armstrong	c Stevens b Overton	3		
9. E. Jones	b Silverlock	39	c Creber b Miller	0
10. H. Carter	b Overton	16	Not Out	0
11. J. Saunders	c Creber b Silverlock	0		
	Extras—B 2, l-b 1, w..., n-b ...	3	B.5, l-b.1, w..., n-b...	6
	Total	148	Total	155

Australian's scored 102 at 5.15 o'clock (Monday)

FALL OF THE WICKETS.

1-3	2-30	3-30	4-30	5-36	6-46	7-48	8-116	9-147	10-148
1-68	2-89	3-149	4-150	5-...	6-...	7-...	8 ...	9-...	10-...

ANALYSIS OF BOWLING.

Name.	1st Innings O.	M.	R.	W.	Wd.	N-b.	2nd Innings O.	M.	R.	W.	Wd.	Nb.
Creber	16	1	65	4	...	...	10	1	31	1	-	-
Overton	18	3	43	4	...	...	5	1	21	0	-	-
Smith	2	1	10	0	...	...	14	4	36	0	-	-
Silverlock	5	0	27	2	...	...	2	0	11	0	-	-
Russell	...	...	...	...			14	3	33	2	-	-
Miller	...	...	...	...			4·4	1	17	1	-	-

Umpires :- Rogers and Coulson.

FOR LATEST SCORES OF ALL MATCHES SEE THE **EXPRESS**

The scorecard for the match between a combined Glamorgan and Wiltshire XI against the 1902 Australians.

> You have a thorough sporting crowd in Cardiff and they evidently know the game of cricket, judging by the way they cheered every bit of good play. We are tired of playing the same counties year after year, and we enjoy a break such as this visit to Cardiff.

The kind words of the tourists, plus the record-breaking crowd, gave a huge fillip to the Glamorgan officials and their campaign for both first-class and Test cricket at Cardiff. But there was still one problem – the rather modest pavilion at the Arms Park, and its cramped accommodation for both cricketers and supporters. For the visit of the Australians, a series of spacious marquees had been erected around the boundary edge and adjacent to the rugby field, but Brain and his advisors knew that much more would need to be done if international cricket was going to be successfully staged at the Arms Park.

In the course of the next few months, the Glamorgan officials started to rectify the situation by drawing up plans for a much larger and grander pavilion, with facilities that would be truly worthy of a Test-match venue. Once again, the Bute Estate gave their full support to the proposals and tenders were gathered for the erection of the new structure.

With estimated costs exceeding £3,000, a series of fund-raising events were held with members of both Glamorgan and Cardiff C.C. working tirelessly with the civic authorities in organising a grand bazaar at the Park Hall in Queen Street (the ground floor of the present Park Hotel) for four days in early May. The function – which encompassed a wide range of money-raising activities and other entertainments – was masterminded by Arthur Gibson, the Cardiff and Glamorgan cricketer, and W.J. Board, the deputy town clerk. Through their efforts, a host of civic dignitaries and leading politicians attended the bazaar, as well as leading personalities from the cricket world and other Tory sympathizers, eager to lend their weight to that of the Brains and the Butes.

Fittingly, it was J.H. Brain who opened the bazaar and, as a true-blue Tory, he ensured his speech paid a fulsome tribute to the Marquess and his supporters, with the Glamorgan captain speaking warmly about the Cardiff ground and the kindness of the Bute Estate in supporting county cricket, 'We have in Cardiff what I consider to be the finest natural cricket ground in the country, and through the kindness of the Marquess of Bute and his late father, we have enjoyed the privilege for many years of playing upon that ground.'

EVENING EXPRESS AND EVENING MAIL. MONDAY. AUGUST 4. 1902.

THE CORNSTALKS AT CARDIFF.

Match with Men of Glamorgan and Wilts.

PHOTOS AND BIOGRAPHIES OF THE CONTENDING TEAMS.

A cartoon from the *Evening Express* showing the Australian, Glamorgan and Wiltshire players who took part in the special match at Cardiff in 1902.

A photo montage celebrating the visit of the 1902 Australians to Cardiff.

The plans for the building of the new pavilion were further evidence that the Glamorgan club was rapidly moving forward and in their preview of the 1903 season, the *Western Mail* were able to proudly say that:

> There are indications which cannot be mistaken that the present season will be one without parallel. It is fitting that Cardiff should be leading the way. The erection of the new pavilion on the Arms Park will mark a new era, not only in town, but in Glamorgan county cricket.

Further fund-raising took place during the 1903 season, with Glamorgan's minor county fixture list augmented by a game with the touring Philadelphians. The famous American cricketers were also the special guests of the Mayor of Cardiff, together with members of the county side, at a special function in the Mansion House. Later that year, the Butes also allowed a couple of rugby matches to be staged on the Arms Park ground between a team representing East Wales and another side representing the West, all to raise cash for the new pavilion.

These games, together with the proceeds from the bazaar, raised over £2,000 and after the receipt of other donations, including a sizeable contribution from the Bute Estate, work was able to commence on the building of the new pavilion in the south-west corner of the Arms Park – a position which the Marquess could view from the castle.

Joseph Brain (right) leads out the Glamorgan team from the old wooden pavilion at the Arms Park in 1902, he is accompanied by William Russell, William Brain, Harry Creber and Norman Riches.

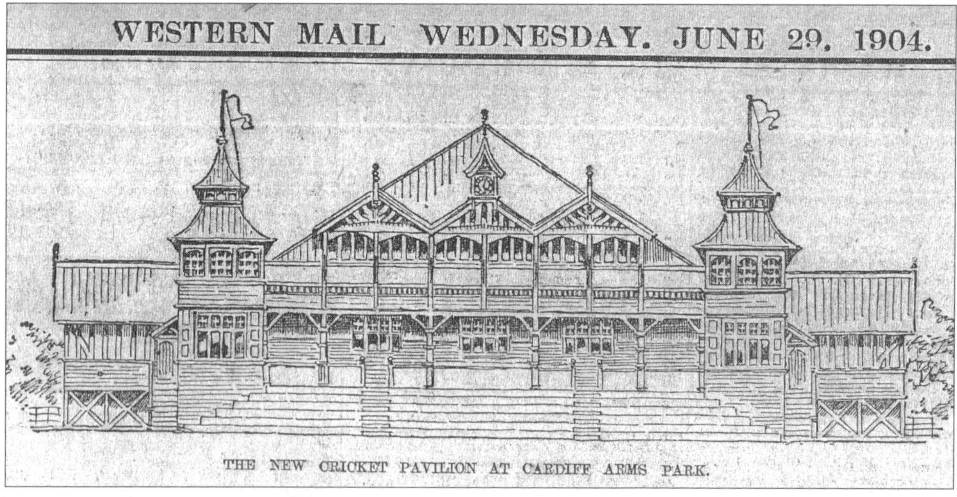

WESTERN MAIL WEDNESDAY. JUNE 29. 1904.

THE NEW CRICKET PAVILION AT CARDIFF ARMS PARK.

The original design of the Arms Park pavilion, as published in the *Western Mail* in June 1904. As the photgraph opposite shows, some of the more elaborate elements were dispensed with during the building phase.

The elaborate design for the new pavilion matched the grandiose dreams of the county club and its urbane supporters, with the building containing two turrets, as well as other castellated effects, flanking a raised balcony and with a seating area below. Also incorporated was a spacious gymnasium – frequented presumably by the burly rugby players rather than the gentlemen cricketers – while at the rear there was a stable area for the groundsmen's horse.

The seating area in front of the new structure was used for the first time in June 1904 when Cardiff C.C. played host to E.M. Grace's XI and later in the summer, the new pavilion was formally opened, with many more tributes being paid to the Marquess of Bute for his kindness in providing the playing facilities in the first place. Other speeches were made outlining the aspirations of Glamorgan in securing both first-class status and playing host to Test cricket at the Cardiff ground.

The Glamorgan committee were naturally delighted that the first step towards these dreams had been successfully achieved, so at the end of the 1904 season, they asked J.H.Brain to formally contact the M.C.C. and register Glamorgan's application for Cardiff Arms Park being chosen as one of the venues for the five-Test series against Australia planned for 1905. The Welsh county were duly invited to send a delegation to address the M.C.C. committee at their meeting in December 1904, when the administrators at Lord's would finalise the arrangements for the Australians and make a decision about allocating the First Test either to the Arms Park or Trent Bridge.

For several weeks before the important meeting, Brain and his advisors carefully planned their presentation to the M.C.C. officials. They had the support of Sammy Woods, the famous England and Somerset amateur, who was a good friend of J.H. Brain and had first-hand experience of the excellent facilities and the splendid wicket at the Arms Park. Woods, whose brother worked in Cardiff, also knew of the progressive attitude of the Glamorgan club and the valiant support of both the Bute Estate and the city's business and political community. At the meeting in December, Woods addressed the M.C.C. committee for around a quarter of an hour about the suitability of the Cardiff ground as a Test venue.

There were several people on the M.C.C. committee who believed that the traditional venues should continue to host the Tests against Australia, but there were precedents, as the M.C.C. had previously allocated Test matches to a fledgling county. In 1902 they had allocated Test cricket for the first time to the Edgbaston ground – the home of Warwickshire – who had only been awarded first-class status in 1895. By coincidence, they had the support of another leading brewery, Ansells.

The words of the Glamorgan officials, and Sammy Woods in particular, were very persuasive and they gathered a decent share of the votes. But at the end of the day, they were just not quite

The pavilion at the Arms Park, as seen in a postcard, *c.* 1910.

Sammy Woods.

enough to win the prize for Cardiff. It was by the slender margin of a single vote that the Trent Bridge ground in Nottingham won the election to join Old Trafford, Headingley, Lord's and The Oval as the venues for the five Tests against the 1905 Australians. Nevertheless, the M.C.C. had been impressed by Glamorgan's claims of higher recognition, and they decided to allocate a fixture to Cardiff during the August Bank Holiday, with the Australians playing a combined South Wales XI, drawn from the leading players of Glamorgan and Monmouthshire.

Once again, a crowd in excess of 10,000 turned up to see some of the finest Welsh cricketers pit their skills against the famous Australians. Monmouthshire provided Arthur Silverlock, the vastly experienced batsman from Newport and Edward Phillips, the Cambridge Blue, as well as Dick Steeples, the former Derbyshire seam bowler, plus Edwin Diver, the Surrey and Warwickshire all-rounder. But even so, the Australian bowlers still proved too strong for the local batsmen, albeit after some spirited defence, especially from Billy Bancroft. When Steeples was dismissed in the seventy-second over, the South Wales innings ended on 132.

The Australian batsmen then put the Welsh bowling to the sword, as Charlie McLeod struck a vibrant century and both Warwick Armstrong and Bert Hopkins made half-centuries as the tourists amassed a mammoth 229-run lead. McLeod then took a couple of early wickets, as the South Wales side ended the second day on 80-3. The locals were saved from defeat by a heavy storm that washed out much of the play on the final day.

Every raincloud, however, has a silver lining and the Australian cricketers, while taking shelter from the weather, had a chance to more fully appreciate the new facilities at the Arms Park ground. Overall, they were mightily impressed with the new pavilion and to the delight of J.H. Brain, Monty Noble – the famous Australian cricketer who was leading the touring team – spoke to the throng of journalists after the contest, calling for Test matches to be allocated to Cardiff. Noble said:

> We have enjoyed our visit to Cardiff immensely, and we shall urge the claims of Cardiff upon the M.C.C. at Lord's. I know that all of our men are keen on playing a Test match at Cardiff. We could not have played before a fairer or more enthusiastic crowd of spectators and the arrangements made by the officials of the Glamorgan club were excellent.

MR. GWYN NICHOLLS.

International Football Match.

NEW ZEALAND v. WALES,

AT CARDIFF, DEC. 16, 1905,

Kick-off at 2.30.

NAMES AND POSITIONS.

The programme for the rugby match between New Zealand and Wales at the Arms Park in December 1905, perhaps the greatest-ever rugby match staged on the Cardiff ground which saw Wales defeat the All Blacks. Had the voting been slightly different within the M.C.C. committee room earlier in the year, the summer of 1905 might also have witnessed Test cricket in Cardiff.

However, there was no opportunity for the Glamorgan authorities to immediately capitalise on this support, as no Tests were planned in 1906, and then when the South Africans visited in 1907 only three Tests were arranged at the traditional venues of Lord's, The Oval and Headingley. No international games were held again in 1908, and then for the five-Test series against Australia in 1909, Edgbaston got the nod over Trent Bridge as one of the venues.

By this time, J.H. Brain had retired from playing and a host of financial worries prevented the Welsh county, along with their Tory supporters, from making a further application to the M.C.C. for a Test match in Cardiff. Neither could they consider Glamorgan's elevation into the County Championship, but they were not to be disappointed for too much longer, thanks to the stringent efforts of Norman Riches, another leading figure in Cardiff cricket, who had honed his skills at Sophia Gardens and the Arms Park.

The South Wales Team which met the 1905 Australians, with N.V.H. Riches sitting on the far left of the front row.

The South Wales opening batsmen walking out to bat against the 1905 Australians at the Arms Park.

TWELVE

From Rags to Riches

Norman Riches was the leading figure in Cardiff cricket circles either side of the First World War. Norman made his Glamorgan debut – at the tender age of seventeen – in 1900, recording his maiden century for the county four years later.

Norman Riches

A member of the well-known Cardiff family, whose numbers included some of the town's leading dentists, engineers and amateur sportsmen, Riches had been born in Cardiff in 1883 and educated initially at Monkton House, before studying at Abingdon School, Cardiff University and Guy's Hospital, where he gained the necessary qualifications that allowed him to join his father's dental practice in Dumfries Place. His father, though, was always generous enough to give him sufficient time off so that he could play plenty of county and representative cricket.

He was one of seven children, with his sister Beryl later becoming a famous stage actress, living close to Lord's cricket ground in St John's Wood.

By the mid-1900s, Norman developed into a prolific opening batsman, showing a liking in particular for the Northumberland attack, striking them for 109 in 1905 and 178* the following year. His success was built upon a sound technique and temperament, plus a wide range of strokes, particularly off his legs. Norman was also a very shrewd reader of the game, and often employed the tactic of cleverly placed singles to force opposing captains into making a fielding change. He would then gleefully smash the ball to the boundary through the gap which he had deftly instigated.

Not surprisingly, he became the mainstay of the Glamorgan batting as the club showed fine form in the reorganised Minor County Championship, which now saw its participants divided into four regional groupings before an end-of-season knockout competition involving the group winners. Glamorgan, under the captaincy of J.H. Brain, topped the western group in 1907, winning all its zonal games with Riches finishing the summer as their leading run scorer with 613 runs at a healthy average of 51.

After winning their zone, Glamorgan also secured home advantage for the semi-final as Surrey Second XI travelled to the Arms Park. The visitors secured a first innings lead, before collapsing against Glamorgan's two professional bowlers – Harry Creber of Swansea and Jack Nash of Cardiff – who shared nine wickets between them. Glamorgan were left with a target of 155, but they began poorly with Riches departing for a rare duck and Brain making just 3, but Billy Bancroft steadied the ship with an innings of 86 that saw Glamorgan home by four wickets and a place in the Minor Counties Championship final.

The following day there was further good news when it was confirmed that the Arms Park ground would stage the final, with Lancashire Second XI travelling to Cardiff. A large and patriotic crowd turned up for the contest between 9–11 September, but their hopes of cheering Glamorgan on to their first title were dashed, largely by the all-round skills of James Heap, who initially top scored with 81 as Lancashire amassed 243. Then his left-arm spin had Glamorgan in complete disarray by the close of play on the first day as they slumped to 56-8, with Heap claiming six victims. Fred Preedy, one of Cardiff's professionals, then put the brake on the visitors when they

Fred Preedy demonstrates his bowling action at the Arms Park.

tried to extend their healthy first-innings lead. On the final day, the home team never looked like scoring the 291 runs they needed to lift the title and despite a stubborn 80 from Joseph Brain, Lancashire won by 108 runs.

1908 saw Glamorgan finish level with Monmouthshire at the top of the western zone again, necessitating a play-off at the Arms Park in the last week of August. Rain washed out the contest and it was left to Sir Francis Lacey, the M.C.C. secretary, to decide who should progress to the semi-finals. After some deliberation, it was Glamorgan who progressed, with Lacey basing his decision on the rather dubious grounds that Glamorgan had won the group the year before – much to the ire of the Newport men, who felt that he had ignored the fact that Monmouthshire had enjoyed by far the better of the drawn game with Glamorgan the previous week at the Arms Park with Arthur Silverlock having scored 187*.

With lady luck seemingly on their side, Brain and his men had high hopes of lifting the title. Their hopes were initially dampened when they travelled to Chippenham to play Wiltshire in the semi-final, only to see the first two days of the contest washed out. But Creber then produced a magnificent performance with the ball, taking 8-18 as Wiltshire were bundled out for 41 on the drying wicket. After securing a first-innings lead, Glamorgan secured a place in the final against Staffordshire at Stoke-on-Trent in the first week of September.

Staffordshire had the legendary Sydney Barnes in their ranks – rightly regarded as one of the finest bowlers in the country – and a man who could alter his bowling to suit all types of wickets. His mix of brisk seam and clever cutters proved far too good for the Glamorgan line-up, with Barnes returning match figures of 15-54, as Staffordshire wrapped up a nine-wicket victory inside two days.

It was not the greatest of ways for the Brain brothers to bow out of county cricket, as both Joseph and William retired at the end of the summer after fantastic service to both the county club and the Cardiff side. In their absence in 1909, Riches took over behind the stumps, and Tom Whittington – the twenty-seven year old solicitor from Neath – was appointed as the new captain and secretary.

Tom Whittington.

The new regime were eager to build on the success from the previous two seasons and, with talk of Glamorgan pressing for first-class status, they knew it was important to have another good summer. Results went their way once again in the first part of the 1909 season, as Carmarthenshire and Cornwall were each beaten by an innings, both at home and away, with Riches scoring commanding centuries against each opponent. Monmouthshire were also defeated by an innings at the Arms Park, then Devon were comprehensively beaten at the Cardiff ground to give Glamorgan a place in the semi-finals for the third successive year.

There was further good news a few days later when it was confirmed that the match – against Nottinghamshire Second XI – would take place at the Arms Park, but once again, the semi-final was ravaged by bad weather and the first day was completely washed out. However, Riches prospered on his home wicket, scoring a workmanlike half-century as Glamorgan made 136 in difficult conditions, before Jack Nash, another Cardiff man, took 6-30 as the Welsh county secured a match-winning first-innings lead.

The Glamorgan officials were delighted when news came through shortly afterwards that Glamorgan would have home advantage again for the final against Wiltshire. With talk of it being third time lucky for Glamorgan, events seemed to be going Glamorgan's way as Nash immediately took a wicket when the visitors batted. James Maxwell, from Swansea C.C., took 7-43 as Wiltshire were dismissed for 122. But any thoughts of a Welsh title were quickly dashed as the visitors struck back and dismissed Glamorgan for 96. Then, in their second innings, they built up a decent lead to set Glamorgan a target on the final day of 324. Despite having Riches, Whittington and the veteran Bancroft in their top order, the target was well beyond the Glamorgan batsmen and Wiltshire ran out victors by 164 runs.

For the third successive year, Riches and his colleagues sat in the changing rooms at the Arms Park, contemplating how they had lost the final. There were several glum faces among their supporters, who offered a few sympathetic words as the Glamorgan side left the ground. But it

Cardiff Arms Park, *c.* 1909, with a minor county match in progress.

A pair of advertisements for the National Pageant in 1909, held at the Sophia Gardens Recreation Field.

was not all gloom and despondency within the committee, as the fact that the club had reached the final again – and with several new faces in their ranks – was evidence that Glamorgan were still among the best minor counties, and had every reason to hold lofty aspirations about bidding for first-class status.

Ever since 1905 and the visit of the Australians to Cardiff, the Glamorgan hierarchy had been planning their campaign for first-class status. Staging high-profile matches against touring teams and other exhibition games at the Arms Park were prominent in their strategy, promoting both the playing resources in South Wales and the excellent facilities and wicket at the Cardiff ground.

1906 saw the visit of both Yorkshire and the West Indies to the Arms Park, followed in 1907 by the South Africans and in 1908 by the Philadelphians. Then in 1909 Riches and Whittington used their contacts within the M.C.C. to secure a plum fixture with the Australians. The county's officials assembled a strong South Wales side containing the cream of amateur and professional talent, in an attempt to further showcase Glamorgan's talents. The fixture caught the imagination of the local Press as during the week leading up to the game in August 1909, they published detailed descriptions about the Australian squad, as well as the local players.

The first day saw over 10,000 spectators thronging into the Arms Park, with hundreds more left outside in Westgate Street, peering over the walls that surrounded the ground. To their delight, the South Wales batsmen made a decent start with Silverlock and Riches adding 74 for the first wicket, and by early afternoon, the Welsh side had reached 150-3 with both Bancroft and Edward Sweet-Escott, another talented batsman from Cardiff C.C., scoring freely against the visiting bowlers.

There were broad smiles in the Glamorgan committee room as it looked as if the Australians were going to be given a good run for their money, but in mid-afternoon, a collapse took place as the South Wales side was dismissed for 228. Creber, Maxwell and Nash then made the visiting batsmen work hard for their runs as Australia, slowly but surely, built up a first-innings lead of 43. Their bowlers then produced a fiery new-ball spell in the final hour as the Welsh side batted again, with both Riches and Silverlock sent back to the half-timbered pavilion before their total had reached double figures.

Whittington and Bancroft resisted stoutly on the final morning, but once they had been removed, there was little resistance from the remaining batsmen, leaving the Aussies a modest target of 65. They reached it after less than an hour at the crease, for the loss of just two wickets, before – to the delight of the 5,000 people inside the ground – the tourists continued batting for another hour and half before stumps were drawn.

It wasn't just the Arms Park into which thousands of people were heading in August 1909, as over at Sophia Gardens, the Recreation Field hosted the lavish National Pageant of Wales. During July, teams of workmen had erected enormous grandstands with thousands of seats around the edge

Performers in the National Pageant assemble on the Sophia Gardens Recreation Field. The cycle track can be seen in front of the trees in the top left-hand corner of the image, which is looking north from where the Welsh Institute of Sport currently stands.

The South African touring team at the Arms Park in 1912.

of the field, with enough seats to accommodate 30,000 people, as great scenes from Welsh history were re-enacted by various members of South Walian Society.

In order to accommodate the vast number of spectators at Sophia Gardens, some of the wooden grandstands at the Arms Park rugby ground were temporarily transferred to the Recreation Field so that there was adequate seating for the people who were eager to watch the pageant. The event had taken many months to prepare, and the Marquess was very happy to provide facilities for the event, held between 26 July and 7 August, although it meant a certain amount of disruption to the many junior clubs who were planning to use the Recreation Field for their cricket matches and other sporting activities. The pageant was further evidence of the heightening of national consciousness that pervaded Welsh society at the time, and it gave a further lift to the Glamorgan officials who were desperately seeking first-class status for the Welsh county.

Despite the result of the game with Australia, the match had been a success for the Glamorgan club and, coupled with their fine form in the Minor County Championship, once again the committee discussed their campaign for first-class recognition. Worcestershire had successfully applied to the M.C.C. in 1899 after winning the Minor County Champioship title, while Northamptonshire had also been elevated in 1905 after several good years in the Minor County Championship. After their own success on the field in 1909, the Glamorgan committee therefore instructed the secretary to write to the authorities at Lord's.

The M.C.C. duly replied that Glamorgan would have to secure eight home and eight away fixtures with existing first-class teams. Their pleasure at not being rebuked soon evaporated as Hugh Ingledew, now the club's treasurer, started to estimate the costs involved, plus the guarantees that would be required and all of the other expenses of staging regular county cricket. Ingledew had been one of the many amateur sportsmen to enjoy cricket at the Arms Park and Sophia Gardens, and he knew of the further benefits that regular first-class cricket would bring to Cardiff. But there were financial realities to be faced up to and without vast capital reserves, it was clear that the major stumbling block to Glamorgan's aspirations was a financial one.

During the winter of 1909/10, a fund-raising campaign began, headed by the Earl of Plymouth who lived at St Fagans Castle. The Earl, who was the county's president, also issued a circular saying, 'A strong attempt will be made to justify the county's claim to promotion to the first-class ranks. To succeed in this, however, a substantial increase in the club's membership and in subscriptions and donations are necessary and an appeal is made for assistance in these directions.' To assist with the fund-raising, another series of exhibition games were staged at the Arms Park in 1910, with games against Worcestershire, Somerset and Sussex Second XI, while the Cardiff club also hosted a cricket week which included a match against the M.C.C.

However, the highlight of the season was a three-day contest between an East of England XI and a West of England side. Players from Essex and Hampshire made up the East side, while leading amateurs from Somerset and Gloucestershire, plus Whittington and Bancroft comprised the West XI. A decent-sized crowd turned up and were treated to some batting fireworks on the final afternoon by Gloucestershire's Gilbert Jessop, as the West successfully chased their target of 208.

As far as the minor county games were concerned, the competition had been restructured yet again with the introduction of a northern and a southern section, the latter including Glamorgan. A decent performance was imperative but 1910 was a disappointing season, especially as Riches – the club's finest batsman – was laid low with enteric fever, causing him to miss several weeks. Without him, Glamorgan struggled in a number of games, including their matches against Worcestershire and Somerset which ended up in comfortable victories for the first-class sides.

Glamorgan were also handicapped by the loss of several days' play through bad weather, so given these factors, they did quite well to finish in second place behind Berkshire. However, the rain and modest results meant at the end of the year Glamorgan's overdraft had risen to £574, and rather than contacting the M.C.C. with confirmation of sufficient fixtures for first-class status, the Glamorgan secretary wrote to members and others in the business community seeking further financial support so that the club could fulfil its fixtures in 1911.

A shilling fund was also opened, while a public meeting was held at the City Hall in Cardiff and attended by many leading figures in the political and social world of South Wales. There was plenty of goodwill and cash started to come in, albeit slowly, but there was still not enough to contemplate a first-class campaign. On the field, the results were once again disappointing in 1911 and with Glamorgan unable to field as many professionals as in previous years, they ended up in fifth place, suffering a couple of heavy defeats against Staffordshire.

1911: an annus mirabilis for Norman Riches

1911 was a record-breaking summer for Norman Riches as he struck 1,015 runs at an average of 92. He struck two centuries against Monmouthshire, plus 150 against Carmarthenshire, before rounding off a wonderful summer with 194 against Buckinghamshire at Neath to become the first man to amass over 1,000 runs in a season for any minor county side. His achievement met with rich praise and in describing his innings at Neath, the *Western Mail*'s correspondent wrote, 'When the loose ball comes along, he revels in putting the full face of the bat hard against it. Perfect footwork, perfect timing, an elegant flash of the bat and the score-box is ringing up another four!'

Riches was highly regarded at Lord's and was viewed as one of the finest amateur batsmen in the country. When available, he turned out for the M.C.C. against touring teams and other first-class sides. A few discrete enquiries were made about his availability for the winter tour to the West Indies in 1912. But rather than speaking directly to the Cardiff dentist, the M.C.C. officials spoke to another leading figure with the Glamorgan club who, in an off-the-cuff remark, suggested that he doubted Riches would get time off to tour abroad in the winter. In truth, his father would have been only too pleased to grant his son leave of absence, but sadly no invitation ever came his way from Lord's.

During 1912 further improvements had taken place to the facilities at the Arms Park, with the prospect of top-class cricket being staged one day, as well as international rugby, right in the heart of the city. Cardiff C.C. invested in some improved seating areas, while the W.R.U. helped to fund the construction of a new south stand, plus temporary stands on the northern side of the rugby ground and new terraces to the east and west. They were officially opened by Lord Ninian Crichton-Stuart, who kicked off in the match between Cardiff and Newport in October 1912, as the Arms Park became the finest rugby ground in the Principality.

Norman Riches, seen here in the 1960s when president of Cardiff Athletic Club.

Cardiff R.F. C., 1909/10. Sitting second-from-left on the front row is Billy Spiller, who in 1921 scored Glamorgan's first-ever Championship hundred. The inset to the left shows Percy Bush who played rugby and cricket for Cardiff, beside winning several Welsh rugby caps.

The crowd in the grandstand at the Arms Park rugby ground in 1912 for the match between Cardiff and London Welsh.

It was beneficial to Glamorgan C.C.C. that the official capacity of the Arms Park rugby ground had now risen to 43,000 as the W.R.U. lent their support to the county's frantic fund-raising, as a special East *v.* West rugby match was staged at the newly expanded ground, with Glamorgan taking the gate receipts. With two touring teams in the UK in 1912, the Glamorgan committee were also able to arrange an extra tourist match between South Wales and the South Africans at Swansea, but the highly lucrative match at the Arms Park between South Wales and the Australians was washed out. The loss of revenue from this match at Cardiff was not offset by income from the touring game at St Helen's, so by the start of the 1913 season, Glamorgan's debts had risen to £450 while the bank overdraft stood at £323.

In an attempt to turn things around on the field, Norman Riches was appointed the county's captain for 1913, and the change did the trick as he led Glamorgan to the top of the southern section. His side recorded home and away victories over Kent Second XI, as well as an innings win against Wiltshire, plus victories at the Arms Park over both Monmouthshire and Surrey Second XI. Their reward was a match in the first week of September against Norfolk at Lakenham to decide the destiny of the title. Norfolk batted first, but only Reg Popham was at ease against the accurate Glamorgan bowlers led by Creber and the former Gloucestershire seamer Stamford Hacker, who had joined Cardiff C.C. The home team eventually ended on 244, before Riches and 'Jock' Tait shared a half-century stand. But once Riches departed, wickets fell at regular intervals and despite some hefty blows by Edgar Billings, the Swansea wicketkeeper, Norfolk secured a decisive first innings lead of 36 runs.

Heavy overnight rain delayed the start on the final day and when play resumed in the afternoon, the drying wicket was fully exploited by Creber, who reverted to cut and spin on the damp surface. The Swansea left-armer proved to be almost unplayable, as Norfolk were dismissed for 61, leaving Glamorgan a target of 98 to clinch, at long last, the Minor County Championship title outright. But soon after Norman Riches had led his team off, the rainclouds had gathered again and, as Riches and Tait buckled on their pads, steady rain started to fall. It gradually got worse, preventing any more play. Under the competition's regulations, the outcome of the title was decided by the first-innings totals. Norfolk were therefore adjudged champions, and the Glamorgan team made their long return journey by train, ruing their luck with the weather

This, however, had been Glamorgan's most successful season for several years and with further fund-raising having reduced the deficit to just £42, it looked as if the Welsh county had turned the corner, allowing a reinvigorated push for first-class status. When the Glamorgan officials met up in the spring of 1914, there was a mood of great optimism within their ranks, as they discussed how to consolidate on the progress they had been made under Riches' astute leadership.

Contemporary events, both at home and on the global scale, brought everyone down to earth with a bump. Firstly, Joseph Brain – who had done so much in recent years behind the scenes in supporting the fund-raising schemes – was taken gravely ill and died in June 1914. A host of tributes were paid to the county's former captain with the *Western Mail* summing up his immense

A ladies football team pose in front of the Arms Park pavilion with military personnel before a fund-raising game for the war effort in 1915.

contribution, both on and off the field, by saying, 'His prowess at the wicket won him celebrity; his sportsmanship won him friendship; his generous patronage of the game won him gratitude.'

Soon after his passing, a second hammer blow was delivered as war was declared, and the closing fixtures of the 1914 season were cancelled as the young men, and the attention of the nation, turned to the conflict with Germany. It was another setback for the Glamorgan club, especially as they seemed poised to mount a successful bid for first-class status. Their campaign did, however, achieve its goal, but only after six bloody years had passed, with the loss in the First World War of several promising players and many hundreds of people who had supported the county club, and cricket in Cardiff, through thick and thin.

THIRTEEN

First-Class at Last!

As the First World War drew to a close during the autumn of 1918, life slowly returned to normal. Minds turned back towards cricket and resuming the pursuit of first-class status for Glamorgan. A county committee was reformed with interests in the east and west married by the appointment of Tom Whittington of Neath C.C., and Billy Bowden of Cardiff C.C., as joint secretaries. The latter also oversaw at the Arms Park a full programme of First XI fixtures for the town's premier club. Despite losing four summers to the First World War, Norman Riches was still in prime form and in 1919 he created a new club record by amassing 760 runs for Cardiff's First XI, surpassing the previous best of 730 made by the late J.H. Brain

Several regular faces though were sadly missing – a pattern repeated across South Wales as cricket clubs swung back into action. No county matches were held during 1919, but several trials and exhibition matches were organised so that the county's selectors could assess the talent that was available. The bowling resources were something of a concern as both Bancroft and Creber had decided to retire, while Bill Bestwick, the burly Derbyshire seamer who had been qualifying for the Welsh county, decided to return north

Given the question marks over playing resources, Glamorgan's fixture list for 1920 included a full compliment of minor county matches, plus exhibition games against the M.C.C. and other scratch XIs with a view both of raising capital and assessing the abilities of certain players. While the foundations of a new Glamorgan were being built on the field, off the field work began to further boost the club's finances, while Whittington made preparations for approaching the M.C.C. and other county officials to secure sufficient fixtures to support their application for first-class status.

Riches' commitments at the family's dental practice prevented him from accepting an offer to lead the county side on a regular basis in 1920, but he pledged his support to Whittington and made himself available for all of the key fixtures, including the showcase fixture with the M.C.C. at the Arms Park. Aware of the importance of the game, Riches and Whittington shared a century partnership as Glamorgan made 217. The M.C.C. replied with just 80, as Percy Morris, the Swansea amateur, took 9-28 with his right-arm seam bowling.

Following-on, the M.C.C. made 170 in their second innings, leaving Glamorgan with a target of 34. Whittington re-jigged the batting order, giving two other promising amateurs a chance to steer Glamorgan to victory and to show their talents. The cosmopolitan pairing of Col. Arthur O'Bree, an Indian-born Army officer who was now based in Cardiff, and New Caledonian-born Willie Gemmill of Swansea C.C. duly saw the Welsh county to an emphatic ten-wicket win, which further boosted Glamorgan's lofty aspirations. Two victories over Surrey Second XI also showed the depth of talent in Glamorgan's new squad – in the first match at The Oval, the Welsh county successfully chased a target of 371, with David Reason of Neath C.C. making a highly impressive 90*. In the return fixture at the Arms Park in August, the new generation of bowlers, plus the veteran Nash, saw Glamorgan complete an innings victory.

With the local economy booming, there was a feel-good factor in these immediate post-war years. Sport was on the up with the Football League having been expanded to include teams from Aberdare, Cardiff, Merthyr, Newport and Swansea. Add to this Glamorgan doing well on the cricket field and there was excited chatter in and around Cardiff about their bid for first-class status.

The stumbling block before the war had been a financial one, but Whittington and Dyson Williams, another prominent solicitor in Swansea, secured the backing of the business community in West Glamorgan, while Bowden and Riches, plus William and Pat Brain, courted the support

Cardiff C.C. of 1920. *Back row, left to right*: Billy Bowden, Cross (professional), Arthur O'Bree, Bert Tayler, unknown, Arthur Gibson, Jack Nash, scorer. *Front row, left to right*: Cec Spiller, James Horspool, Norman Riches, Henry Symonds, John Chandless, George Cording, Tom Morgan.

of leading businessmen in Cardiff, including Sir Sidney Byass, who gave the club a £1,000 loan over a ten-year period.

Their support meant that at the end of the 1920 season, the committee instructed Whittington to make contact with a dozen English counties and to secure home and away fixtures with at least eight. Somerset quickly agreed, followed by Gloucestershire, Worcestershire, Derbyshire, Leicestershire, Northamptonshire and Lancashire, although in a couple of cases Whittington was forced to agree that the Welsh county would guarantee a sum of £200 towards the fixture. The enthusiastic secretary duly reported back to the committee in November that he had secured the support of seven first-class counties. Jubilant at the news, the committee told him to 'obtain the eighth at any cost whatsoever.'

However, strong persuasion was not needed, as both Sussex and Hampshire readily agreed to Whittington's approach. At the next committee meeting, in December 1920, the Neath solicitor was able to confirm that the requisite number of fixtures had now been secured. There was, however, one bit of gloomy news, as the club's debt at the end of the 1919/20 financial year had risen to £350. A few committee members duly expressed reservations about whether the club would in fact be able to honour their commitments in 1921.

After all of his hard work, and travel, in the autumn months, Whittington was not going to be defeated and further assurances were secured from businessmen in both Cardiff and Swansea who agreed that they would write off the club's debt if they were elevated to first-class status by the M.C.C. in the New Year. With handsome pledges from Daniel Radcliffe and J.T.D. Llewelyn, the committee duly instructed Whittington to contact Lord's.

A few weeks later, the news that everyone had been waiting for came through, as the M.C.C. endorsed Glamorgan's application. Messages of good luck were soon flooding the club's small offices in High Street, and there were tears in the eyes of J.T.D. Llewelyn – the 'grand old man' of Glamorgan cricket – and William Brain as a series of celebratory speeches were made at the club's A.G.M.

Having secured their goal, attention was now given to having the right men, both on and off the field, running the club's affairs. Arthur Gibson – the Yorkshire-born batsman who had played before the First World War for both Cardiff C.C. and Glamorgan – was appointed as secretary, with Billy Bowden – another stalwart figure in the town club – acting as assistant secretary. Dyson Williams was elected as treasurer, while Norman Riches was voted in as captain.

Having been Glamorgan's finest batsman in their minor county days, it was very fitting that in May 1921, Norman Riches should lead out the Welsh county at the Arms Park – the scene of so many of his graceful innings for both the county and the town club – as they played Sussex in their inaugural fixture as a first-class county. It was, in fact, a fairytale start for Riches and his Glamorgan colleagues as they defeated Sussex who were at full strength. The visitors included such notable players as bowler Maurice Tate, batsmen Ted Bowley, England all-rounder Vallance Jupp and the Gilligan brothers, Arthur and Alfred.

Norman Riches and Tom Whittington walk out from the Cardiff pavilion to open the batting against Sussex in Glamorgan's inaugural County Championship match.

County Championship
Glamorgan v. Sussex
Cardiff Arms Park
18, 19, 20 May 1921
Umpires : T. Flowers and A.E.Street
Toss: Glamorgan won and batted
Result: Glamorgan won by 23 runs

Glamorgan	**first innings**			**second innings**		
T.A.L. Whittington	c Street	b A.E. Gilligan	40	c A.E. Gilligan	b Cox	27
*N.V.H. Riches	c A.H. Gilligan	b Jupp	16		b Tate	3
W.E. Bates		b A.E. Gilligan	39	lbw	b Cox	8
W.P. Morris		b Tate	7		b A.H. Gilligan	13
J.R. Tait		b Cox	31		b Tate	96
+G.E. Cording	c Cox	b Roberts	45	c A.H. Gilligan	b Roberts	10
A. O'Bree		b Cox	0		b A.H.Gilligan	8
H.G. Symonds	c Higgs	b Bowley	58		b Cox	20
E. Cooper		b Jupp	12		b Cox	0
H.Creber		not out	7		b Cox	7
A.Nash		b Cox	5		not out	5
Extras	(b5, lb5, w1, nb1)		12	(b13, lb3)		16
TOTAL			272			213
FOW:	1-38, 2-78, 3-99, 4-115, 5-169, 6-169, 7-245, 8-252, 9-262			1-25, 2-41, 3-52, 4-107, 5-120, 6-137, 7-171, 8-171, 9-197		

Bowling	O	M	R	W	Bowling	O	M	R	W
Roberts	15	2	31	1	Roberts	9	0	21	1
Tate	26	12	34	1	Tate	13.2	4	29	2
Jupp	21	5	52	2	Jupp	15	4	37	0
Cox	20.5	5	36	3	Cox	23	4	60	5
A.H. Gilligan	5	0	24	0	A.H. Gilligan	7	0	33	2
A.E. Gilligan	21	3	71	2	A.E. Gilligan	6	2	17	0
Bowley	5	1	12	1					

Sussex		**first innings**				**second innings**	
V.W.C. Jupp	c Cording	b Cooper	34		c O'Bree	b Cooper	5
E.H. Bowley	lbw	b Nash	21			b Nash	146
K.A. Higgs		b Nash	0		lbw	b Creber	5
M.W. Tate		b Cooper	11		c Nash	b Creber	10
F.D. Jenner		b Nash	6		c Symonds	b Cooper	55
+G. Street	c Bates	b Cooper	5	(9)		b Nash	11
*A.E.R. Gilligan		b Cooper	3	(6)	c and	b Cooper	15
G. Stannard	c Tait	b Nash	41	(7)	c Riches	b Cooper	4
G.R. Cox		not out	7	(10)		not out	11
A.H.H. Gilligan		run out	2	(8)	c Tait	b Creber	33
H.E. Roberts	c Cording	b Creber	13		c Morris	b Creber	0
Extras	(lb7, w1, nb1)		9		(b8, lb6, w1)		15
TOTAL			152				310

FOW: 1-44, 2-48, 3-65, 4-78, 5-80, 6-83, 7-103, 8-131, 9-134 | 1-11, 2-45, 3-59, 4-225, 5-249, 6-251, 7-258, 8-289, 9-303

Bowling	O	M	R	W	Bowling	O	M	R	W
Creber	17.5	6	25	1	Creber	19.2	1	78	4
Morris	4	1	12	0	Morris	3	0	20	0
Nash	29	11	45	4	Nash	25	1	86	2
Cooper	16	2	61	4	Cooper	24	3	81	4
Bates	6	0	29	0					
Symonds	1	0	1	0					

Riches struck the first blow by winning the toss and, in front of a crowd in excess of 5,000, basking in glorious sunshine, he opened the batting with Tom Whittington. All of the Glamorgan batsmen proceeded to make useful contributions against the accurate Sussex attack, but it was their number-eight batsman, Henry Symonds, who ended up as top scorer. The thirty-one year old left-hander from Cardiff C.C. made an assured half-century and together with club colleague George Cording, a Cardiff schoolmaster, they shared an attractive seventh-wicket partnership of 76.

Glamorgan were eventually dismissed for 272 and buoyed by the success of their batsmen, the Welsh bowlers soon made early inroads into the Sussex batting. Veteran Jack Nash's off-cutters picked up four cheap wickets, while fast-medium bowler Edgar Cooper, a thirty year old from Briton Ferry, also claimed four victims as Sussex were dismissed for 152.

It was then the turn of Glamorgan's batsmen to struggle against the Sussex bowlers, all that is except Jock Tait, the thirty-four year old amateur from Cardiff C.C. Tait had been born in the Shetland Islands and had already enjoyed quite a distinguished sporting career, winning a Welsh amateur football cap in 1913, as well as playing rugby for Swansea. Despite the loss of partners at regular intervals, Tait unleashed some expansive strokes and, by the close of play on the second day, he was unbeaten on 96 and set to become Glamorgan's first-ever centurion in Championship cricket.

When play resumed on the final morning, Maurice Tate sportingly bowled his namesake a gentle full toss down the legside, hoping that Tait would reach three figures and reach this unique milestone in Welsh sport. But nerves had taken over, Tait swung and missed, and he was duly clean

The crowd engulf the Glamorgan players after their victory in the club's inaugural Championship fixture.

REMARKABLE CRICKET ENTHUSIASM AT CARDIFF.

The montage from the *Western Mail* in 1921 following the historic victory over Sussex.

Billy Spiller, the man who struck Glamorgan's first Championship century.

bowled by Tate's next delivery and dejectedly trudged off the Arms Park, knowing that he had come within a whisker of making history.

By the time the last Glamorgan wicket fell, Sussex were left with a rather stiff target of 334. Their position soon became even worse, as they slumped to 59-3 as Cooper and Creber once again made early inroads. Ted Bowley and Felix Jenner then halted the decline with a spirited stand of 166 for the fourth wicket and their steady efforts increasingly gave the visitors a realistic chance of pulling off a fine victory as, for once, Nash proved ineffective on the Arms Park wicket.

With the Sussex total mounting, Riches was forced to recall Cooper in a desperate bid to break the troublesome stand. It proved a wise decision, as first Jenner was caught by Symonds, before Cooper picked up two further wickets to tip the balance slightly back in Glamorgan's favour. A revitalised Nash then returned to take the wicket of Bowley and the crowd started to sense that a Glamorgan victory might occur.

Alfred Gilligan offered some stubborn resistance, but Creber came on and mopped up the tail. When last man Henry Roberts was caught by Percy Morris, Sussex were two-dozen runs short of their target, and many of the crowd surged onto the field to congratulate Riches and his team.

The two teams then gathered on the balcony of the Cardiff pavilion, with both captains making impromptu speeches. Riches began by paying tribute to Tom Whittington, before Arthur Gilligan graciously congratulated the Welsh side, saying how they 'had given us a magnificent game, and we do not mind being beaten in the slightest. We have been down until today, but today we might have won. We did not – Glamorgan did, and I congratulate them very much.'

Billy Spiller, Glamorgan's first centurion

The inaugural match with Sussex saw 'Jock' Tait narrowly miss out on becoming Glamorgan's first-ever centurion in Championship cricket. This honour eventually fell to Billy Spiller, a stalwart member of the Cardiff club, and a member of the Glamorgan Constabulary.

His feat came in July 1921 against Northamptonshire at the County Ground, Northampton, during an extended break from his duties 'on the beat'. The thirty-five year old had been a prolific batsman with Cardiff for many years, and on 26 July he reached the landmark with an all-run four on the legside after batting for a shade under three hours.

Spiller had first played for Glamorgan in 1905, but his police duties restricted his subsequent appearances, and in the years leading up to the First World War, Spiller mixed regular games of club cricket with occasional matches for Glamorgan. During the winter months, Spiller also found time to play rugby for Cardiff R.F.C. and his strong running in the centre and deft handling skills also won him ten caps for the Welsh side.

FOURTEEN

The Roaring Twenties?

The 1920s were far from being a roaring success for Glamorgan, although at club level Cardiff C.C. enjoyed a series of successful summers on the Arms Park ground. For example, they went through 1920 without a single defeat, while across the river at Sophia Gardens, the Gala Field continued to host a myriad of junior clubs, some of whose members harboured lofty ambitions of one day playing on the Arms Park for both the premier town club and the county side.

Despite Glamorgan's regular failures at county level, their Championship matches at Cardiff were reasonably well attended. To an extent, there was an amount of novelty value about these fixtures, as for the first time Cardiff residents could watch many of the top county teams in action without having to travel across the Severn Estuary to Bristol, or by Great Western express to London.

After their victory over Sussex, Glamorgan only recorded one further win in 1921 – against Worcestershire at Swansea – and lost fourteen out of their nineteen matches, ending the summer in seventeenth and last place in the Championship table. *Wisden*'s correspondent was not very complimentary in his end-of-season review, summing up the situation by writing that, 'It is clear that to hold their own in first-class company, Glamorgan must find young talent and not depend so much on middle-aged men.'

Such a course of action had been inevitable, given the loss of promising young players in the First World War, and the limited capital reserves now available to the club. In fact, only four professionals – the bowlers Hacker, Nash and Creber, plus William Bates, the former Yorkshire batsman – had appeared on a regular basis in 1921, and then on the quite modest terms of £14 for each away match and £10 for each home game. The rest of the line-up chopped and changed on a regular basis, with over thirty players appearing in 1921, followed by forty-three in 1922 as the amateurs juggled their appearances with their business or scholastic duties.

Without a settled XI, there were no regular close catchers and three Cardiff men – Pat Brain, George Cording and Riches – all did duty as wicketkeeper in these early years. In an attempt to address this situation, the Glamorgan officials agreed to hire a couple of professional wicketkeepers, both of whom were in the twilights of their careers: Dennis Sullivan, the thirty-eight year old from Surrey, who had been Herbert Strudwick's understudy for many years, plus Jimmy Stone, the forty-five year old who had spent fifteen years on Hampshire's staff.

Neither were going to have an extended career with the Welsh county, but as far as Stone was concerned, he did play a key role in the defeat of the 1923 West Indians by scoring a superb century as the tourists were defeated by 43 runs at the Arms Park. This game in early August was a major milestone for his new employers, as it was Glamorgan's first victory over a touring team and their only one against a Test team, until Glamorgan defeated India in 1936 and New Zealand twice the following year. It also came at a difficult time for the club, having endured a series of heavy defeats in the County Championship, with forty-five out of their sixty-one fixtures having been lost, including eighteen by an innings.

With several people questioning the recruitment policy and their presence in first-class cricket, few gave the Glamorgan side much of a chance against the West Indian tourists. Their pessimism appeared well founded as Glamorgan mustered just 115 in their first innings, before the visitors from the Caribbean secured a first innings lead of 86. It might have been much more had it not been for the efforts of Trevor Arnott, the cheerful amateur from Cardiff C.C., who opened the county attack. He refused to be downhearted and took 7-40 as the West Indians were bowled out for 201.

Pat Brain with his team which played Glamorgan in a pre-season friendly in 1939. *Back row, left to right*: Bill Hitch, G.N. O'Daly, Trevil Morgan, Tip Williams, Bill Chattin, Bryan Stevens-Davis, Dr Tresawna. *Front row, left to right*: Trevor Arnott, Norman Riches, Pat Brain, Phil Clift and Wilf Wooller.

The Arms Park in the early 1920s.

Batting for a second time, Glamorgan lost Norman Riches for 26, but William Bates then drew on his vast experience to carefully see off the new ball, before Jimmy Stone shared an attractive partnership of 136 in just an hour and a half for the fifth wicket with Frank Pinch, the Cornish-born schoolmaster. After the loss of Pinch for 55, Stone continued to counter-attack the West Indian bowlers and, with useful support from Arnott, the veteran became Glamorgan's first centurion against a touring team.

His brave efforts meant that the West Indians needed to score 239 to win the game and they were set on their way by the clean strokeplay of opening batsman George Challenor. Despite the loss of a few partners, Challenor played almost without fault, and with the score on 185-5, it looked as if he was going to play a match-winning innings for the tourists. But soon after reaching a fine century, Jack Mercer – the former Sussex seam bowler – was brought back into the attack by captain Riches in a late bid to wrest the initiative away from the tourists. It did the trick, as Mercer trapped Challenor lbw, before claiming the last two wickets, as great celebrations began in the Cardiff pavilion.

August 1923 also saw the Welsh cricket team play for the first, and only, time at the Arms Park. It followed the creation of the Welsh Cricket Union by representatives from Glamorgan, Monmouthshire and the North Wales Cricket Association. The union duly organised a series of three-day games, on days when Glamorgan were not involved in Championship fixtures, against the likes of the M.C.C., Scotland, Ireland and various touring teams. These Welsh teams were largely amateur, supplemented by a couple of professionals attached to Glamorgan, who quite enjoyed the opportunity of playing – and subsequently socialising – at places such as Llandudno, Colwyn Bay and Rydal School, as well as in Ireland or Scotland.

The contest in August 1923 saw Ireland visit the Arms Park and after Wales had been dismissed for 153, the Irish batsmen made hay, rattling up 418 with three of their men scoring fluent half-centuries. Facing a sizeable deficit, none of the Welsh top order made any impression once again, and it was left to Jack Mercer, with a vibrant 71, and captain Norman Riches, who was carrying a leg injury, to spare Welsh blushes as the pair added 108 for the eighth wicket before the Irish gentlemen celebrated a comprehensive innings victory.

By the time this match took place at the Arms Park, several improvements had started to take place to the facilities at the ground. These had begun as a change in ownership, following the creation in 1922 of Cardiff Athletic Club and through the amalgamation of the city's rugby and cricket clubs. Each had been granted the use of the park at a peppercorn rate by the Marquess of Bute, but in 1922, as the Marquess began disposing of his property in South Wales, the two clubs had to consider if their future was guaranteed at the Arms Park.

Gone to the Dogs

In the late 1920s, the Cardiff Greyhound Co. transferred their operations from the GKN Sports Ground in Sloper Road – known as the Welsh White City – to a track laid out around the circumference of the rugby stadium at the Arms Park.

For over fifty years, there were regular races on Monday and Saturday evenings, with the fixture list including the Welsh Greyhound Derby and the Welsh Greyhound Grand National, with the final races being run at the Arms Park on 30 July 1977.

Several people and organisations had already cast admiring glances at the Arms Park, close to the bustling business centre in the heart of the city. Eager to preserve their hallowed turf, a series of meetings took place between officials from the town's cricket and rugby clubs, with the outcome being their merger to create the Cardiff Athletic Club. Through the help of Hugh Ingledew, the club were able to purchase the Arms Park, except for a strip of land adjoining Westgate Street, for the sum of £30,000 on the understanding that, in keeping with the Marquess' wishes, it should be preserved for recreational purposes. Shortly afterwards, a limited company was formed after further discussions with the Arms Park (Cardiff) Greyhound Racing Co. and also the W.R.U.

There was a downside to this new arrangement as far as Glamorgan were concerned, as the Cardiff Athletic Club significantly raised the sum that the county had been charged for the use of the Arms Park for their first-class fixtures. This irked many of the county's officials, especially those in the west, but after some gentle persuasion by Norman Riches, the rent was reduced.

Even so, it was still a major financial commitment for Glamorgan, who were operating on a shoestring budget. To show that Cardiff did not have a monopoly on the Championship matches allocated to the east, arrangements were made in 1926 to play Derbyshire at Pontypridd, using the new wicket which had been laid out in Ynysangharad Park, opened three years before as a tribute to the young men of the valley town and surrounding area who had lost their lives in the First World War. The fixture proved a success, and further games were staged at Pontypridd, including the lucrative fixture in 1929 against the South Africans.

By that time, the Athletic Club had overseen a series of other improvements to the Arms Park cricket ground as the facilities started to justify the higher rent. The first phase of improvements saw the installation of improved drainage, completed in 1924, for both the cricket and rugby ground, while a generous grant of £100 from the *Western Mail* newspaper allowed the provision of modern covers for the start of the 1926 season.

That summer also saw Cardiff C.C. participate in the newly-formed South Wales and Monmouthshire League, which had been created in a partnership between the Glamorgan officials and the leading clubs in South Wales. For several years, the county officials had cast envious eyes on the highly competitive Yorkshire and Lancashire leagues, which had provided a welter of talent for these northern counties. After several years of negotiation and discussion, the Glamorgan officials contacted many of the leading clubs, suggesting that it would be better for all concerned if an element of rivalry and competition was introduced, with league matches replacing the traditional friendly matches. Successful replies were obtained from Barry, Briton Ferry Town, Briton Ferry Steel, Cardiff, Gowerton, Llanelli, Neath, Newport and Swansea, while Cardiff businessman Daniel Radcliffe put up a handsome sum for a large silver trophy.

The introduction of the South Wales and Monmouthshire League may have seen changes to the Cardiff fixture list during the late 1920s, but some things were still the same as Norman Riches continued to be a prolific run scorer for both Cardiff C.C. and Glamorgan. On several occasions he showed that despite a receding hairline, he was by no means past his best as a batsman at county level. An example of this enduring ability came at Old Trafford in 1928 as he recorded a superb century against Lancashire, who at the time possessed one of the most potent bowling attacks in the country. They held no terrors though for Norman Riches, as Glamorgan faced a first-innings deficit of 266. Many in the home crowd thought that the Glamorgan batting would meekly subside, but Riches had other thoughts as he crisply struck a series of boundaries in a magnificent 140, and with support from Dai Davies and captain Trevor Arnott, he saw Glamorgan to 370, forcing Lancashire to bat again.

Riches continued to play for Glamorgan until 1935 and even into his fifties, he was still a consistent run scorer for the Cardiff club. Alongside him in the Cardiff side of the late 1920s was Eric Dolman, a prominent figure in the legal world of the city, as well as a couple of younger batsmen who had made a few headlines themselves, winning cricket Blues at Cambridge in the late 1920s. Each were Cardiff-born, with both Trevil Morgan and Maurice Turnbull coming from leading families in the shipping and business world of the city. Trevil came from the family who ran the famous department store in The Hayes, and Maurice from a family of shipowners who were prominent in the comings and goings at the Bute Docks.

Their emergence also signalled the start of a new era in the history of cricket as J.T. Morgan and M.J.L. Turnbull, in their diverse ways, carried forward both the Glamorgan club and cricket in the city during the 1930s and beyond.

Johnnie Clay Remembers the Batting of Norman Riches

In a magazine interview in the 1960s, Johnnie Clay recalled the batting prowess of Norman Riches back in the 1920s, 'He was the only Glamorgan batsman with the technique and application to get runs regularly during the 1920s, and his bald pate moved quicker by yards than many of the supposedly agile younger men! In fact, my chief memory of those days was Norman Riches steadfastly batting it out, while we rabbits came and went.'

FIFTEEN

Testing Times

If Norman Riches was the dominant name in cricketing circles in Cardiff in the 1920s, the leading personality in the 1930s was undoubtedly Maurice Turnbull – a man who many regard to have been the most complete all-round sportsman Wales has ever produced, winning international honours in cricket, rugby, hockey and squash.

Maurice Turnbull

Born in Cardiff in March 1906, the cricketing CV of Maurice Turnbull was most impressive – county cricket for Glamorgan between 1924 and 1939; captain of Cambridge University in 1929; captain and secretary of Glamorgan from 1930 until 1939; nine Test caps for England and a Test selector in 1938 and 1939.

However, on top of all this, he also played rugby for Cardiff, London Welsh and Cambridge University, won two caps at scrum-half for Wales in 1932/33 in addition to playing hockey for Cardiff, Cambridge University and Wales, founding Cardiff Squash Club and winning the Welsh Squash Championships.

Without the dynamic presence of Maurice Turnbull, it is also doubtful whether Glamorgan would have survived a period of extreme financial hardship during the 1930s. When he returned from his first M.C.C. winter tour – to Australia and New Zealand – in the spring of 1930, he assumed the leadership of a county club who were facing some extremely difficult times with a balance sheet rarely out of the red.

The club's officials had already tried to rein in their expenditure by cutting back on the number of professionals they hired, but this was a vicious spiral, as it adversely affected performances on the field and attendances at home matches. With an increased number of amateurs in their ranks, the Glamorgan team of the late 1920s were often defeated inside two days in front of dwindling attendances at the Arms Park.

Glamorgan were not alone in facing financial hardship, as the trade depression had affected many businesses across South Wales, as well as other sporting organisations. Aberdare Athletic and Merthyr Town were forced to withdraw from the Football League, and for a while it looked like Glamorgan might also have reached the end of the road as a first-class county.

But they survived largely through the efforts of Maurice Turnbull, a man who never shied away from a challenge, no matter how daunting, and it was typical of the man that he masterminded a series of fund-raising functions across the length and breadth of South Wales. Together with his great pal Johnnie Clay, he transformed Glamorgan's finances from a parlous state of near bankruptcy into one with a healthy balance in excess of £1,000 pounds.

Maurice put his heart and soul into the affairs of the county club and always put the club first, so much so, that he refused an invitation in 1933 to tour India with the M.C.C., and the chance of winning further Test caps, believing instead that it would be better for him to remain in South Wales during the winter months, combining his work as an insurance broker and sports journalist with securing valuable capital for the county club.

If his efforts off the field were vast, then his presence as a top-class batsman and wise captain were even greater. He inherited a Glamorgan side in 1930 that languished at, or close to, the

Maurice Turnbull, as seen in a studio photograph in 1933.

bottom of the Championship table, winning just twenty-six out of their 216 fixtures, and losing no less than 125. Turnbull proved to be an inspirational leader and a real talisman for the Welsh county. As with the club's finances, Maurice transformed things during the 1930s through astute and dynamic captaincy. Under his leadership in the 1930s, Glamorgan played 264 Championship games, winning forty-five, and losing just eighty-six. Winning, or not losing games, became more of a habit and Glamorgan rarely threw in the towel and meekly surrendered in the way they had in the 1920s.

Many players flourished under Turnbull's leadership, not least Frank Ryan, a talented left-arm spinner with a volatile character and a great thirst. He had arrived in South Wales back in 1921 after having a brief career with Hampshire, during which time he had several run-ins with their aristocratic captain, the Hon. Lionel Tennyson. Following one dispute, and a heavy night's drinking, Ryan literally walked out on the club. At the time, Ryan had barely two pennies to rub together, so he walked and hitch-hiked his way to Bristol hoping that his friend Charlie Tayler would arrange an introduction to the Gloucestershire committee. But Ryan already had a reputation for heavy drinking and a tendency for flying off the handle if he did not get his way, so Tayler advised him instead to approach another old friend, Jack Nash, the groundsman-professional at the Arms Park.

Aware that the Welsh county were looking to bolster their attack, Ryan duly headed for Cardiff and during the August Bank Holiday weekend he arrived at the Arms Park, where Nash and his son were marking out a pitch for Cardiff's afternoon fixture. By this time, Ryan was in a quite disheveled state; at first Nash was unsure who the down and out actually was. After hearing his story about looking for employment, Nash took pity on him, offered him a bath in the Cardiff pavilion plus a decent meal and even placed a few notes in his back pocket, before chatting to Ryan about his prospects with the Welsh county. At the time, the Cardiff club were looking to bolster their side with another professional, and for good measure, by playing for the Arms Park club, Ryan could qualify for Glamorgan.

Frank Ryan demonstrates his bowling action.

It seemed too good an opportunity to turn down, so Ryan duly made his way to Swansea where Glamorgan were playing. Once again, Ryan made his journey by foot, through torrential rain, before arriving at the St Helen's ground, absolutely soaked and quite exhausted. But his efforts were well worth it, as after a brief chat with the county's officials, terms were agreed and Ryan headed back to Cardiff to seek suitable accommodation and to meet the Cardiff officials. He subsequently won a regular place in the Glamorgan side and returned to form under Turnbull's captaincy and gentle encouragement. However, the Glamorgan captain had to use very subtle tactics to get the best out of the maverick spinner.

These were the days when Ryan, like the other professionals, was paid a match fee for each game. On the away trips, Ryan would often have frittered away his fee, well before making the long journey home by train with his thirst quenched and a virtually empty wallet. By that time, the spinner had also got married, so if his wife was meeting him at Cardiff General Station, Ryan would often sneak out of the back door of the station, then find a friend who could lend him some cash, so that he could return home pretending that he still had his fee.

Turnbull knew of Ryan's financial circumstances and his peccadillos, which had prevented him from fully realising his true abilities. Even so, the captain was more than happy to lend Ryan a few pounds if he seemed down on his luck, and he would even slip Ryan a few notes after a fine bowling performance. In this way, he managed to get the best out of the spinner, with Ryan taking 127 wickets in 1930.

During the 1930s Glamorgan steadily relied on fewer players from other English counties as, under the skipper's encouragement, the county developed a stronger Welsh identity. Having more homegrown players in their ranks was, according to Turnbull, the key to preventing further cash problems, as more people would support Glamorgan if players from local clubs were in the county side.

CRICKET TEST TRIAL.

CONTROL BOARD OFFER TO CARDIFF.

MATCH IN JULY, 1932.

GESTURE THAT SHOULD GIVE FILLIP TO GAME.

Cricket in South Wales, and Glamorgan in particular, should receive a fillip as the result of the decision of the Cricket Board of Control to offer a Test trial match to Cardiff on July 27, 28, and 29 of season 1932.

This decision was come to at a meeting of the Board, held at Lord's on Tuesday, when the English Test Match Selection Committee was chosen, with Mr. P. F. ("Plum") Warner as chairman.

Two trial matches will be played in the season 1932, the other game being allocated to Manchester. Should India send a team to this country, a Test match will be played at Lord's in June.

The trial matches next year will be very important in view of the fact that during the following winter the M.C.C. team will tour Australia, and the form of the players in the trial games will be closely watched.

If the offer is accepted it will be the first occasion on which a Test trial match has been staged in Wales.

ATHLETIC CLUB'S GREAT CHANCE.

By "NOMAD."

Followers of cricket in South Wales will be both gratified and surprised by the

Over and over again cricketers have told me it is one of the best pitches in the country—for batsmen. And that, after all,

An extract from the *Western Mail* in 1931 containing news of the proposed Test Trial at Cardiff the following year.

The Fastest Thing Ever Seen at the Arms Park?

The Arms Park cricket ground saw many fast bowlers from several generations strut their stuff on the Cardiff wicket. In 1908 the Philadelphians included Bart King, who was renowned as the fastest bowler in world cricket before the First World War.

During the 1920s and 1930s the likes of Harold Larwood and other pace bowlers from abroad displayed their talents, before Frank Tyson of Northants and the legendary Fred Trueman from Yorkshire picked up the mantle in the post-war era. Glamorgan also had their own fast bowlers who exploited the Cardiff wicket, including Jeff Jones, the left-arm quickie whose sheer pace and hostility frightened many visiting batsmen.

You can also add to this cavalcade of pace a remarkable event on the cricket ground on 6 October 1928 when the members of Cardiff Motorcycle Club held races around the perimeter of the field. The races had the full blessing of the Cardiff Athletic Club, who shortly afterwards replaced the damaged turf as part of the end-of-season work by Trevor Preece and his hard-working groundstaff.

In their early years in the County Championship, one writer had described Glamorgan as a 'ragbag eleven', containing rejects from English counties and only a handful of native cricketers with whom the locals could identify. This all changed under Turnbull's leadership and by the mid-1930s, the club were more clearly representing Wales, playing Championship fixtures at a variety of grounds and staging special friendlies against club sides in almost every part of South Wales.

If the creation of a strong Welsh identity was one legacy that Turnbull left to Glamorgan, another was the resurrection of the quest for Test-match status. As a keen student of history, Turnbull was well aware of the attempts made before the First World War to bring Test cricket to Cardiff and, with Glamorgan now clearly representing Wales, it seemed a most appropriate time to lobby the M.C.C. for a Test match at the Arms Park. Moreover, there were financial benefits that Glamorgan would gain from staging a Test and this greater cash input would only benefit the county.

Turnbull was highly regarded by the mandarins at Lord's and, through his initiative, the M.C.C. agreed to allocate the three-day Test Trial to the Arms Park in July 1932. At the time, it was the finest collection of cricketing talent ever assembled in the city and the chance of seeing the cream of English talent was a mouth-watering one. It certainly left the Glamorgan treasurer rubbing his hands at the thought of such a lucrative fixture that would help to ease the county's financial worries. However, the weather ruined the contest with just three-and-a-quarter hours play on the first day, and nothing at all on the other two. In what little play there was, the crowd saw K.S. Duleepsinhji of Sussex and Douglas Jardine, the England captain, share an unbroken fourth-wicket partnership of 105 in a fraction over an hour and three-quarters.

England v. Rest of England (Test Trial 1932)

At Cardiff Arms Park on 27, 28, 29 July 1932
England won the toss and decided to bat
Result - Match drawn
Umpires: D. Hendren, E.J. Smith

England		**first innings**	
H. Sutcliffe	st Ames	b Mitchell	23
Nawab of Pataudi	c Woolley	b Larwood	3
K.S. Duleepsinhji		not out	92
W.R. Hammond	c Larwood	b Mitchell	8
*D.R. Jardine		not out	40
G.O.B. Allen			
F.R. Brown			
+G. Duckworth			
W. Voce			
E. Paynter			
H. Verity			
Extras	(b5, lb6, nb1, w2)		14
Total	(3 wickets, 79 overs)		180
FOW:	12, 63, 75		

Bowling	O	M	R	W
Larwood	15	4	34	1
Farnes	18	5	37	0
Scott	11	1	31	0
Mitchell	22	7	47	2
Staples	7	2	13	0
Wyatt	6	3	4	0

Rest of England: *R.E.S. Wyatt, K. Farnes, R.S.G. Scott, G.E. Tyldesley, F.E. Woolley, W.W. Keeton, +L.E.G. Ames, T.B. Mitchell, H. Larwood, M. Leyland, A. Staples

The bad weather and loss of gate receipts were further blows to the county whose finances had further worsened by the middle of the year. Upon the final day of the washed-out Test Trial, the club chairman wrote an open letter to the Press in which he outlined the severity of the club's plight:

> At the present moment, the club's indebtedness is just over £4,000. In addition, it is estimated that £1,500 is required to enable it to carry on until the beginning of the 1933 season. If this response is not forthcoming, the committee will have no option but to declare that it is impossible to maintain first-class cricket in Wales. We should welcome assistance in any form. It is essential that this should be given immediately.

Shortly afterwards, the county committee also set up a special appeal called the 'Save Glamorgan Cricket Campaign', which aimed to raise or secure promises for £5,500 by 1 October so that all the debts and liabilities could be wiped out, and a small working balance created for 1933. But the committee realised the gravity of the situation by adding a rider that,'all donations will be returned if it is found impossible to continue first-class cricket in 1933.'

During August, public meetings were held in Cardiff as well as in Swansea and Pontypridd to launch the appeal. A series of sub-committees were also formed across South Wales and the London area to raise funds for the ailing county. Trevil Morgan, who was now helping to run his family's department store in Central Cardiff, acted as secretary of the Eastern Area sub-committee, while Johnnie Clay served as chairman of this group. Together with the Glamorgan captain, they all persuaded influential members of the Cardiff society and business world to take part in the fund-raising events.

Local newspapers soon carried details of the campaign's plans, and the fund-raising began in earnest in late August and early September, with the *Western Mail* running a daily update with news of donations and forthcoming functions. In the first week of the campaign, the column began with the following words,'This is an S.O.S. to tradesmen, businessmen generally, philanthropists and sportsmen, everybody who must feel a wrench at the thought that next season we shall go back to the backwaters of cricket, unless...' The newspaper also pledged 100 guineas themselves, while other leading companies from Cardiff Docks made handsome donations.

A host of events were held in the Welsh capital, including dinners at the Mayfair Café, boxing tournaments, bridge and whist drives, and special collections during the greyhound races at the Arms Park. Sportsmen's evenings were also held at various clubs, where leading personalities from the cricket world and leading local figures pledged their support for Glamorgan.

More often than not it was Turnbull himself who spoke at these functions, as in the case of a gathering at Whitchurch, where he took the stage alongside Sir Herbert Cory, the shipping and colliery magnate, who began by pledging £50. Turnbull then spoke to the assembled mass about the important national role played by the county club:

> The fact that Glamorgan hosted a Test Trial in 1932 at Cardiff showed that the club's status as a first-class county had been recognised and we do not want to lose it. Throughout the country, Glamorgan are regarded as one of the best sporting teams on the road. This accolade means a lot to the team. Our professionals are the finest lot of lads I know – they are very young, but they showed great promise last season.

The buckets were soon jangling after his rallying cry and stirring words; by the end of September over £2,000 had been pledged, together with promises of other handsome sums. However, the fund-raising did not stop there and, during the winter of 1932/33, further activity took place with Turnbull organising carol singing around the city and outside St Peter's Cathedral, together with a concert by the Covent Garden Opera Co. at the Park Hotel. Fund-raising rugby matches were also staged at the Arms Park, including a game between a XV led by Turnbull himself, containing fourteen other internationals against an Anglo-Welsh XV, raised by Frank Instone of London Welsh.

A football match was also arranged at Ninian Park with the county cricketers taking on the Cardiff City F.C. team, while another venture included the production of a county yearbook for 1933 in which all the members of the club were listed, together with a roll call of all of the people who had pledged their financial support. In short, the yearbook was a means of saying thank you to the many organisations who had supported the fund-raising activities; its appearance on the shelves of bookstores and newsagents throughout South Wales was a tangible sign that the club had survived its worst period.

The only blot had been the abandonment of the Test Trial at the Arms Park and a chance to showcase the facilities and the wicket as a potential international venue. At the very least, it had shown to the M.C.C. authorities the way that the hard-working Glamorgan officials could organise and promote a major match. They took their lead from Turnbull himself – a man from whom energy and drive oozed, and someone who, in the middle of a Championship match at Cardiff, once travelled over to Ireland on the Saturday night by ferry to a Papal Mass in Dublin, along with a delegation of Catholics from South Wales, before returning overnight on Sunday and being back on the field at the Arms Park on the Monday morning.

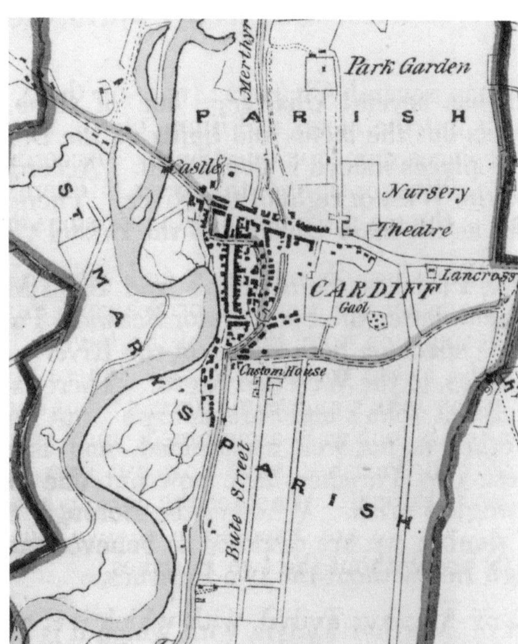

1 A sketch map of Cardiff in 1832, showing the large meanders flowing adjacent to St Mary Street. The area where Sophia Gardens was created is in the top left-hand corner of the map.

2 A sketch of Canton Bridge and Cowbridge Road, *c.*1820. Sophia Gardens were laid out in the left-hand foreground.

3 An image of Sophia Gardens on an Edwardian postcard.

4 The pavilion at Sophia Gardens, as seen in the late 1980s, during a televised Sunday League contest. The building was erected in 1967 when Glamorgan moved away from the Arms Park to the new ground.

5 Len Smith (right) and his staff prepare the Cardiff wicket in the late 1980s. A lot of remedial work took place from the mid-1980s onwards to improve the quality of the surface.

6 Other improvements took place at Sophia Gardens in the 1980s, including the construction of the Vice-President Members' Enclosure, adjacent to the pavilion.

7 Despite the switch to Sophia Gardens, the Cardiff Arms Park was not forgotten as a cricket venue – in 1989 it staged a floodlit match in aid of Rodney Ontong's Benefit Fund.

8 An aerial view of Sophia Gardens in 1999 showing the recently completed National Cricket Centre in the north-west corner of the ground. This was the first phase of the ground-development scheme.

9 Hugh Morris and Matthew Maynard at the opening of the National Cricket Centre in 1999.

10 The National Cricket Centre was created as a centre of excellence, and the photograph above shows Malcolm Price undertaking a coaching clinic in 2000 with several young players who have gone on to play for Glamorgan – to his left is Ben Wright, crouching with the bat is Tom Maynard and on the extreme right is Mike O'Shea.

11 It may have been all change at the Cardiff ground, but the past was not forgotten as the Wooller Gates were formally opened in 2001. The family of the Glamorgan legend stand proudly in front of the gates named in memory of the man who led the Welsh county to their first ever Championship title in 1948.

12 & 13 Viv Richards (above) made a significant impact on Glamorgan Cricket, bringing a wealth of experience and new steel to the club. The West Indian maestro also shared a record stand of 425 with Adrian Dale (left) against Middlesex at Sophia Gardens in 1993.

14 Hugh Morris, the Cardiff-born batsman, who led Glamorgan to their Sunday League title in 1993. His weight of runs and prolific form also saw him appear in three Test matches for England.

15 Behind every team lies fine bowlers; the Glamorgan side of the 1990s was able to call upon the express pace of the Pakistani international Waqar Younis, who in 1997 was the Welsh county's overseas star as they clinched the county title.

16 They also relied on the stalwart services of Steve Watkin, now a highly respected coach in the National Cricket Centre at the SWALEC Stadium.

17 Steve James made his Glamorgan debut in 1985 at Cardiff, but he never took to the field as rain washed out his chance of batting. Twelve years later, Steve hit the winning runs when they won the Championship at Taunton in 1997. He also holds the record for the highest individual first-class score for Glamorgan – 309*.

18 On the bowling front, Robert Croft has given yeoman service during a career that has seen the proud Welshman score over 10,000 first-class runs and take over 1,000 wickets. The Cardiff ground has also seen some fine performances from him in one-day cricket, including 6-20 against Worcestershire in a National League contest in 1994.

19 Another integral member of the Glamorgan side in the 1990s was Tony Cottey – he played a series of gritty innings in the county's Championship-winning year in 1997. Here Cottey receives the Player of the Year Award for 1994 from Byron Denning on the balcony of the Sophia Gardens pavilion.

20 Homegrown stalwarts formed the nucleus of the Glamorgan side that won the County Championship in 1997. Here the team are celebrating at Taunton after clinching the title. *Back row, left to right:* Owen Parkin, Alun Evans, Duncan Fletcher, Dean Conway, Adrian Dale, Robert Croft, Matthew Maynard, Dean Cosker, Steve James. *Front row:* Tony Cottey, Hugh Morris, Waqar Younis, Darren Thomas and Adrian Shaw.

21 The early 2000s saw further success for Glamorgan in one-day cricket, with an appearance at Lord's in the Benson & Hedges Cup final in 2000 followed by title-winning campaigns in the National League in 2002 and 2004. Glamorgan's success was accompanied by formal presentations and celebrations at the Cardiff ground. The team celebrate the 2002 success above. *Back row, left to right:* Matthew Maynard, Jonathan Hughes, Mark Wallace, Robert Croft, Steve James, David Harrison, Keith Newell, Alex Wharf, Adrian Dale, Michael Kasprowicz, Dean Cosker. *Front row:* Darren Thomas, Andrew Davies, Owen Parkin, Michael Powell, Ian Thomas and David Hemp.

22 The Glamorgan team celebrate at Cardiff after winning the 2004 totesport League. *Back row, left to right:* Darren Thomas, Mark Wallace, David Harrison, Adrian Dale, Alex Wharf, Mick Lewis, Matthew Elliott and John Derrick. *Front row:* Andrew Davies, Dean Cosker, Robert Croft, Matthew Maynard, Michael Powell, Ian Thomas and David Hemp.

23 Another of the significant changes at the Cardiff ground has been the staging of regular international cricket from 1999 onwards. Australia were based at Sophia Gardens for the 1999 World Cup and they visited the Welsh capital again two years later. Spectators take in the action between Australia and Pakistan in a One-Day International on 9 June 2001. Australia were victorious by 7 wickets.

24 The match programme from the Australia *v*. Pakistan One-Day International, 9 June 2001.

25 The Australians gather at the fall of another Pakistani wicket.

26 Mohammad Ashraful *(right)* celebrates reaching his century at Cardiff in the 2005 One-Day International against Ricky Ponting *(left)* and his Australian team.

27 In 2006 England visited Cardiff for the first time to play a full One-Day International at Sophia Gardens. Both the hosts and the Pakistani opposition were eventually beaten by the rain.

28 James Harris, Glamorgan's young all-rounder, represents the next generation of homegrown talent to benefit from the world-class facilities at the SWALEC Stadium and the other centres of excellence in Wales. In 2007 James performed a unique feat by taking a wicket with his first delivery for Glamorgan at both Swansea and Cardiff.

29 The changing of the guard: Matthew Maynard, along with Robert Croft, is synonymous with Glamorgan's success over the last fifteen or so years. Now ensconced as Director of Cricket at Glamorgan's headquarters, the photograph above shows Matthew pulling a ball to the boundary of the Cardiff ground during their Championship match with Northamptonshire in 2002.

30 Out with the old and in with the new: Matthew Maynard leaves Sophia Gardens for the final time during his Testimonial Match in 2005, and is replaced at the wicket by his son Tom.

31 Paul Russell, the chairman of Glamorgan Cricket, shows a display of the proposed ground developments to visiting politicians from the Welsh Assembly, who helped to finance the construction of the magnificent new stadium.

32 & 33 A view of Sophia Gardens in August 2007, with construction work well under way (above) and a shot of the completed stadium from the grandstand, taken in June 2008 (below).

The Devout Faith of Maurice Turnbull

The Turnbulls were perhaps the most prominent Catholics in South Wales, and fervent supporters of all the good things that St Peter's R.C. church attempted to do. Indeed, it was for this reason that Maurice and his brothers were educated at Downside, the famous boarding school south of Bath, run by Benedictine Monks attached to the adjoining abbey. Despite his many sporting and business commitments, Turnbull found time each year to take part in the Easter Retreat at his old school and wrote in his diary how, 'to spend Holy Week at Downside is always a source of grace and inspiration. I only wish everyone could be as fortunate as I am.'

Maurice Turnbull.

SIXTEEN

Bodyline at Cardiff

The Bodyline controversy, which erupted in Australia during England's tour Down Under in 1932/33, was one of the most infamous moments in cricket history. 'There are two teams out there, but only one of them is playing cricket,' was the claim of the Australian faction as Larwood and Voce adopted leg-theory tactics, bowling a succession of short-pitched deliveries with a ring of close catchers on the legside, in an attempt to quell the prolific run-scoring feats of Don Bradman, perhaps the greatest-ever batsman to wear the 'baggy green' cap.

Despite being over 10,000 miles away from the Test grounds in Australia, there is a close association with the Arms Park ground because Larwood and Voce experimented with what subsequently became known as 'Bodyline' tactics during their county's closing games of the 1932 season, including the contest with Glamorgan at Cardiff. In fact, in the days leading up to the match with the Welsh county, the Nottinghamshire bowlers had been openly speaking about how they were going to experiment with leg theory in what was a run-of-the-mill encounter at the end of the summer. The experiment turned out to be a failure and as one writer subsequently claimed, 'If fast leg theory had been judged on what Maurice Turnbull and Dai Davies did to it, there would have been no storm later in Australia!'

With the prospect of a most intriguing contest at the Arms Park in August 1932, a massive crowd turned up at the Cardiff ground expecting fireworks from the visiting bowlers. They had to wait, as Nottinghamshire batted first and rattled up 386 before their bowlers were set loose with a ring of leg-side catchers. With Larwood and Voce racing in and pitching short time and again, many expected the regular clatter of wickets, but instead Maurice Turnbull and Dai Davies proceeded to share a record partnership of 220 for the third wicket during a truly memorable three-and-a-quarter hour's play.

The surfeit of short-pitched bowling held no terrors in particular for Turnbull who, in a typically courageous display, constantly pulled and hooked the high rising balls to the leg-side boundary, so much so, that some of the spectators sitting in the seats square of the wicket were more at risk of being hit than the Glamorgan batsmen, as the ball sped to, or bounced over, the boundary rope.

Sitting in the crowd at the Arms Park was a young man called John Arlott, who had travelled by train and bike with a friend from London to watch the fiery Nottinghamshire bowlers prior to their voyage to Australia. Arlott subsequently became the doyen of English cricket writers, and wrote in his memoirs:

> (Turnbull) was wonderful to watch that day. As the ball rose along the line of his body, he hooked it so fiercely that it went with a single, fierce, skiding bounce for four to the square-leg or long-leg boundary. He punished those two England bowlers as I believe no other batsman ever did.

Although he was hit several times on the body, Turnbull never flinched; each time he courageously went back into position during a five-hour innings, which saw him almost single-handedly master the bowlers and saw Larwood revert back to bowling a fuller length, switching his line away from leg stump. It was a truly majestic display of batting from the Glamorgan captain, who finished unbeaten on 160, as his side ended the pulsating day on 354-4, just 32 runs behind, with six wickets in hand. As the Glamorgan captain left the field to a standing ovation from the enraptured crowd, the Nottinghamshire bowlers departed somewhat shamefaced, with some muttering about the feather-bed wicket.

County Championship

Glamorgan v. Nottinghamshire
Cardiff Arms Park
24, 25, 26 August 1932

Umpires: D. Hendren and F. Field
Nottinghamshire won the toss and elected to bat
Result: Match Drawn

Nottinghamshire		**first innings**				**second innings**	
W.W. Keeton	c Duckfield	b Mercer	22			b Lavis	13
C.B. Harris		b D.E. Davies	12		c D.E.Davies	b Glover	20
W. Walker		run out	68			not out	67
*A.W. Carr	c D.E. Davies	b Glover	92	(7)		not out	17
A. Staples	c and	b Mercer	31		c Howard	b Glover	0
F.W. Shipston		not out	102		c D. Davies	b Glover	25
+B. Lilley		b D.Davies	15				
J. Hardstaff		b Mercer	7	(4)	c Howard	b Glover	1
H. Larwood		b D.E.Davies	16				
W. Voce		b D.E.Davies	14				
S.J. Staples		b Lavis	0				
Extras	(lb3, nb4)		7		(b12, lb3, w1, nb2)		18
TOTAL	(all out)		386		(for 5 wickets)		161
FOW:	1-26, 2-42, 3-158, 4-216, 5-238 6-276, 7-291, 8-327, 9-371				1-17, 2-57, 3-61, 4-62, 5-123,		

Bowling	O	M	R	W		O	M	R	W
Mercer	40	12	110	3	Mercer	10	0	24	0
Glover	20	2	97	1	Glover	18	1	52	4
Lavis	25.3	9	65	1	Lavis	9	3	12	1
D.E. Davies	29	2	75	3	D.E.Davies	22	6	40	0
D. Davies	9	2	32	1	Boon	2	0	12	0
Turnbull	1	0	3	0					

Glamorgan		**first innings**	
A.H. Dyson		b Larwood	36
D.E. Davies		b Voce	30
D. Davies	st Lilley	b S.Staples	106
*M.J.L. Turnbull	c Voce	b Larwood	205
R.G. Duckfield		b Larwood	5
+T. Every		not out	58
A.H. Howard	c and	b Larwood	0
R.W. Boon		b Larwood	0
G.Lavis	st Lilley	b Harris	22
J. Mercer	st Lilley	b S.Staples	9
E.R.K. Glover	c A.Staples	b S.Staples	2
Extras	(B 24, LB 4, W 0, NB 1)		29
TOTAL	(all out)		502
FOW:	1-53, 2-96, 3-316, 4-354, 5-436 6-438, 7-438, 8-477, 9-492		

Bowling	O	M	R	W
Larwood	30	2	78	5
Voce	27	4	96	1
S.Staples	48	10	117	3
A.Staples	34	7	89	0
Harris	14	1	64	1
Hardstaff	9	0	29	0

Their complaints about the docile nature of the Cardiff wicket, along with the merits of leg theory itself, raged on long into the night; the hotel bars and pubs adjoining the Cardiff ground were full of talk about the remarkable happenings that afternoon, with the Glamorgan batsmen en route to a record score. The visiting bowlers were soundly of the opinion that the wicket was to blame for the failure of their experiment, and after airing their views about the docile nature of the surface, they returned from the city centre pubs to the Grand Hotel in Westgate Street, where they were staying. But their journey was not a direct one as upon leaving one of the town's pubs frequented by cricketers and a few press men, a group of Nottinghamshire players decided to go back into the Arms Park ground and express their contempt about the lethargic surface by pouring some beer on the wicket.

After climbing over the wall into the ground, they soon encountered Trevor Preece – the Cardiff groundsman – who presumably had been tipped off that the Notts players wanted to revisit the ground. An altercation took place in which Preece was roughed up by the visiting bowlers, who were hell bent on their nocturnal watering of the offending surface. Upset at his manhandling

Harold Larwood of Nottinghamshire and England.

Bill Voce, the other notorious Bodyline bowler from 1932.

Trevor Preece tends the Arms Park wicket with his trusty scythe, watched by Trevor Every, Tom Brierley and Dick Duckfield.

and the watering of the wicket, Preece rang Maurice Turnbull to alert him to the situation. The Glamorgan captain had been dining, as usual, in the Grand Hotel with the Nottinghamshire captain and, after settling the bill, Turnbull hastily made his way across to the Arms Park.

By this time, news of the prank had spread like wildfire around the city centre watering holes, and a couple of local pressmen had wandered into the Arms Park to view the damp and rust-coloured patches on the wicket. One of the journalists who had witnessed the night-time shenanigans was Harry Ditton who wrote under the nom de plume of 'Nomad' and 'Citizen' for *The Western Mail*. Aware that he had a fantastic scoop, Ditton quickly filed his copy, but it never saw the light of day as Turnbull, after re-assuring Preece following his rough treatment, headed across from the Arms Park into the adjoining street where the *The Western Mail* offices were situated.

By now it was almost past midnight and the presses were ready to roll with the early morning edition, but Turnbull successfully persuaded the editor not to run the story. 'Think of the embarrassment it will cause to English cricket and to Glamorgan Cricket in particular,' was Turnbull's heartfelt argument which, much to his relief, won the day as the story about the watering was removed from the copy being assembled on the presses.

Nevertheless, a number of pressmen had been tipped off about the antics of the Nottinghamshire team and, sensing a good story as a follow-up to the Bodyline experiment, a posse of reporters were present at the Arms Park soon after breakfast time as Preece and his colleagues began their preparatory work with the wicket still under cover. Unbeknown to the dozen or so journalists who were hovering near the covers, Preece and his staff had spent much of the early hours removing the damaged turf so that when the covers were rolled away shortly before the start of the day's

Douglas Jardine, England's captain on the infamous Ashes tour of 1932/33.

play, there was nothing to see. The journalists were mightily disappointed at not seeing the telltale signs, and several rounded on Preece hoping that he would spill the beans about what had really happened. But despite having been furious at the damage to his wicket and his rough manhandling by the visiting players, Preece steadfastly refused the offers from the Press to reveal the truth; play started on time with Turnbull resuming his innings.

He showed no sign of tiredness after his nocturnal diplomacy as the Glamorgan captain duly took his score on to 205 during the first hour's play, before he was caught at fine-leg attempting another boundary. He departed with a couple of sixes and two-dozen fours to his name, and received a standing ovation from the enraptured crowd – and many of the Nottinghamshire players as well – before the lower-order batsmen further consolidated on their team's position, as they reached a record total of 502, their highest in the club's history.

When Nottinghamshire batted again, the Welsh county continued to hold the upper hand and after losing several wickets during the afternoon session, the visitors had to stoutly defend in order to stave off an unlikely defeat. Their plight brought a wry smile to Turnbull's face, and with an impish grin, he asked Ted Glover to bowl a brief spell of leg theory to give the Nottinghamshire side a taste of their own medicine. 'It did my heart good to see the Nottinghamshire fellows for once hoisted with their own petard,' he later wrote in a newspaper article, arguing against the legitimacy of Bodyline, which he believed 'was dangerous, over-destructive and unnecessary. It robs cricket of everything that is best, and presents the bowler with a scheme by which he can do no more than stalemate the batsman. The result – slower cricket.'

Turnbull was also upset the following season when Yorkshire's Bill Bowes tried 'Bodyline' against Glamorgan, and proceeded to break one of Johnnie Clay's ribs. It put the spinner out of cricket for a month and when Turnbull was asked to speak at a dinner given by the London Welsh Society in honour of the Glamorgan side, he took the opportunity to once again strongly voice his disapproval of leg theory:

> Poor old Johnnie Clay woke up in severe pain the morning after the Yorkshire match and then read in the morning paper that Douglas Jardine had been cheered at a match at Lord's because he had brought the Ashes back. But the way he brought them back was to introduce Bodyline, and that more than rankled a bit!

His outspoken views against Bodyline brought Maurice a standing ovation at the dinner and had others also spoken out about Bodyline bowling, relations between England and Australia might not have become so soured as they did in the winter of 1932/33.

SEVENTEEN

Steamers, Big Hits and the War

Not many county teams can claim to have sailed to an away match, but in the 1930s this is precisely what Glamorgan were able to do on a regular basis when they played Somerset at Weston-super-Mare, with Maurice Turnbull and his team travelling over to the Somerset resort on a Campbell's steamer from Pier Head in Cardiff Docks. Supporters were also able to travel over on either the early morning or evening sailings, and the annual matches between Glamorgan and Somerset – either at the Arms Park or at Weston – became quite jolly affairs.

Many of the Welsh amateurs had close friendships with their Somerset counterparts in any case, and the games between the two teams saw several light-hearted moments. In one year, Johnnie Clay bowled a rubber ball to C.C. Case, while the following year, the Glamorgan bowler accepted a wager from Case and proceeded to bat left-handed with some effect against the Somerset man, with players on both sides roaring with laughter at the jolly japes.

Details of the fun and games eventually reached the corridors of power at Lord's, where some of the more po-faced and straight-laced M.C.C. officials felt that Clay and Turnbull should have been cautioned for encouraging behaviour on the field of play that bordered on slapstick comedy. But most of the officials viewed it as typifying the happy atmosphere that the Glamorgan captain had gone out of his way to nurture.

There was further evidence of the excellent team spirit in Glamorgan's ranks during 1935 as Cyril Smart produced some record-breaking hitting at the Arms Park with some remarkable, and quite violent, blows against both the touring South Africans and then Hampshire, as he ended the summer with a club record of 30 sixes to his name.

Smart's big-hitting feats began against the touring Springboks, although it was Wilf Hughes, an all-rounder on his county debut, who stole the headlines during a record tenth-wicket partnership. At the time, the twenty-five year old was teaching in Northamptonshire and playing with some effect in the local leagues. When Glamorgan had been playing at Kettering, Ben Bellamy, the Northants wicketkeeper, happened to tell Turnbull, who was ever on the lookout for promising new talent, about the success of the Welsh-born science teacher in local cricket.

On further investigation, it transpired that Hughes had previously played for Monmouthshire when at school in Ebbw Vale, but had left the area, seeking the security of a career in teaching rather than a more precarious one as a professional cricketer. After checking on his credentials, Turnbull invited Hughes to the Arms Park nets during the Whitsun school holidays, and after impressing Bill Hitch, the county coach, and the watching Turnbull and Clay, Hughes was chosen in Glamorgan's side for their game against the Springboks at Cardiff.

Both Turnbull and Clay liked a flutter on the horses, but this was a case of a raw novice being thrown in against some top-class thoroughbreds. However, they had nothing to lose in the friendly against the tourists and, to their great delight, Hughes had a memorable debut, sharing in a rollicking partnership with the big-hitting Smart in Glamorgan's first innings, with their rousing stand helping to save the game after Glamorgan had been forced to follow-on by the South Africans in overcast conditions on the second day.

After the clatter of wickets in their first innings, the wickets continued to tumble when Glamorgan batted for a second time and by the close, Arnold Dyson, Tom Brierley and the two Davies – Dai and Emrys – were already back in the pavilion, with just 10 runs on the board. A Glamorgan defeat looked inevitable on the final morning, as Turnbull was dismissed early on and despite some stubborn resistance from Cyril Smart, further wickets fell to the accurate Springbok bowlers.

A Campbell steamer bound for Weston-super-Mare leaves Pier Head in Cardiff around the time of the First World War.

Cyril Smart, normally a big hitting batsman shows off his defensive strokes.

Glamorgan's eighth and ninth wicket fell with the score on 114, to leave the tourists on the verge of an innings victory. Hughes was the last Glamorgan batsman to come in and as he took guard, surrounded by a cluster of South African catchers, some of the crowd started to leave the Arms Park and headed off for lunch in the city-centre taverns and cafes. They must have wished they had stayed as the raw all-rounder then launched an amazing counter-attack on the Springbok bowling. Hughes shared a quite remarkable last-wicket partnership with Smart, which added a record 131 runs in a dramatic ninety-minute passage of play.

Realising that he had nothing to lose, Hughes counter-attacked with a combination of gusto and glee, completely belying his inexperience as he thrashed the bowling to all parts of the Cardiff ground. His rousing and uninhibited blows brought loud cheers from the supporters, several of whom had left their lunch and hastily returned to the ground after hearing the applause which had rung out to greet Hughes' fierce blows.

In fact, the youngster was the dominant partner, racing to his half-century in just three-quarters of an hour, with four huge sixes and several other crisply timed fours, causing 'Nomad' of the

Western Mail to write that, 'Hughes dominated the game to such a degree that even the eager and enterprising Smart was overshadowed as the South African attack was cut to ribbons.'

As the bowlers became demoralised, Smart started to join in with the big hitting and repeated his feat against Hampshire by striking a series of massive sixes, one of which sailed high out of the ground and straight through the plate-glass window in the foyer of the Grand Hotel in Westgate Street. This shattering blow also saw Smart to a well-deserved century and when the players left the field for lunch, Smart was unbeaten on 114, while Hughes was on 70, with the two men departing to a standing ovation after their rousing display.

As the applause died down, a few wags in the crowd suggested to people leaving the ground that they shouldn't linger for a late lunch because Hughes might make a debut century if he continued with his whirlwind hitting during the afternoon. But light rain started to fall during the interval, causing the resumption to be delayed and, as the afternoon progressed, the rain steadily got heavier. By the tea interval, several pools lay on the outfield with the ground now saturated, the umpires had the formality of calling off play and declaring the match a draw, leaving the South Africans frustrated at the outcome and the Glamorgan supporters gleefully toasting their new heroes.

Smart cut loose again a few weeks later at the Arms Park during the closing stages of the opening day of Glamorgan's match with Hampshire. Prior to his salvo, it had been quite a drab sort of day but in the final hour, Smart was joined by Dick Duckfield, the free-scoring batsman from Maesteg. In the space of sixty minutes, the pair added 130, with Smart savaging Gerry Hill, the visitor's off-spinner. In the process of this assault, Smart created a new world record, as he struck 32 runs in an over.

All were from authentic strokes, cleanly hit in an arc from straight to deep-square leg, as Smart hit Hill for two sixes and a four, followed by two more mighty sixes, and then, from the final delivery, a massive blow on the legside which was inches away from dropping over the ropes again and becoming the fifth six of the over. As Hill later recalled:

> Smart was going along initially like a normal batsman, pushing the singles around, plus the odd boundary. But then he suddenly let loose on me. They were all clean hits, and he wasn't dropped once. In fact, no fielders got anywhere near any of his strokes!

Perhaps inspired by his efforts, the Glamorgan bowlers then forced Hampshire to follow-on before wrapping up a ten-wicket victory. For the second time during a remarkable summer, the Glamorgan players were sitting in the Cardiff pavilion and toasting the explosive batting feats of Cyril Smart.

The Arms Park in the 1930s, following the clearance of Temperance Town to the south of the rugby stadium.

Maurice Turnbull leads out the Glamorgan team against Kent at Cardiff in 1936. His colleagues are, *from left to right*: Jack Mercer, Dick Duckfield, Tom Brierley, (Turnbull), Haydn Davies, Johnnie Clay and Ted Glover.

To the relief of the manager of the Grand Hotel, the autumn of 1935 saw building work on the tennis courts that lined the western edge of Westgate Street as the Marquess of Bute decided to build a block of luxury flats overlooking the Arms Park, thereby putting pay to the risk of more balls flying through the plush hotel's windows.

However, many believe that the real reason for the Marquess' decision was the fact that in 1934 the W.R.U. had built a massive double-decker stand on the northern side of the rugby ground – and between the rugby and cricket pitches – with the new structure offending the Marquess who would often admire the view south from the castle towards Penarth.

Hat-Tricks at the Arms Park

Trevor Arnott was the only Glamorgan bowler to record a first-class hat-trick at the Arms Park. His unique feat came in July 1926 during the Welsh county's Championship encounter with Somerset, as he claimed 5-29, while Jack Mercer pouched 5-27 to dismiss the West Country side for a mere 59.

In 1933 two visiting bowlers each took hat-tricks against Glamorgan. In the match against Yorkshire in May, George Macauley dismissed Trevor Every, Dick Duckfield and George Lavis in consecutive deliveries. Every and Lavis were involved again in July as George Paine claimed a hat-trick for Warwickshire during their drawn match with the Welsh county.

Building the South Stand at the Arms Park.

The North Stand also became used by the cricketers as the decorative old pavilion was dismantled and new changing rooms were incorporated into the new stand, together with a members' lounge on the mezzanine floor. The scoreboard, which had also been adjacent to the old pavilion, was moved to the north-east corner of the ground and in 1937 a new cricket pavilion and tea room, solely for the use of the cricket section of Cardiff Athletic Club was built in the south-east corner of the cricket ground.

It may have been no coincidence but 1937 was Glamorgan's most successful season in first-class cricket, with their eleven victories helping Maurice Turnbull's team clinch seventh place in the table. His side also inflicted a six-wicket defeat on the New Zealand tourists at the Arms Park in May, before doing the 'double' over the Kiwi's in August at Swansea.

Sadly, the Welsh county slipped back to sixteenth place in 1938, before rising back up to thirteenth place in the Championship the following year. Their last game at the Arms Park in 1939 took place in the third week of August – a time when dark clouds had firmly gathered over Europe, and just a fortnight before Neville Chamberlain's historic announcement that Britain and Germany were at war. Understandably, the players on both the Glamorgan and Northamptonshire sides, as well as the spectators at the Arms Park in late August could therefore be excused for having other things on their minds as the game ended in a draw.

Within a few weeks, the military authorities had taken over both the Arms Park and Sophia Gardens, where the junior clubs of Cardiff had continued to play cricket, hockey and rugby in the balmy summer sunshine. The Glamorgan hierarchy, as well as the Athletic Club, each set up emergency committees to oversee the running of the clubs as their member's swapped sports kit for military uniform.

During the course of the next two years, very little sporting activity took place on the Arms Park and Sophia Gardens, as both became military training camps. Bombing raids brought home the reality of war and in January 1941 a German landmine landed on the North Stand, causing a fair amount of damage to the massive grandstand. Other devices left craters on the rugby and cricket grounds, while similar damage was caused a mile or so away at Sophia Gardens.

However, as far as Glamorgan were concerned, more devastating blows occurred in 1944 shortly after the Normandy invasion. Both Jim Pleass and Maurice Turnbull – now a major in the Welsh Guards – were on the frontline during the summer of 1944, with the Glamorgan captain landing at Arromanches a week or so after D-Day. As always, Major Turnbull led from the front and, during

A cartoon from *The South Wales Echo* in January 1941 after wartime damage at the Arms Park.

Maurice Turnbull and his wife Elizabeth in 1941.

their advance into Northern France, he led several raids on Nazi troops as the Allied Forces moved forward.

However, in one of these raids during August, near the small town of Montchamp, Turnbull was to pay the highest price for his bravery, as he was shot and killed instantly by gunfire from a German tank as he and his colleagues launched a counter-attack against an advancing column of Panzer tanks. Even in these final, grim hours, Turnbull's faith and his family remained foremost in his mind. The final entry in his diary dutifully records taking Mass and Holy Communion on the morning of the raid on Montchamp, and prior to leading the fateful raid on the German tanks, Turnbull took out his wallet from his pocket and looked at the photograph of his wife and three small children.

News of Turnbull's tragic death filtered through to South Wales during the course of mid-August. At the time, Glamorgan were engaged in a series of fund-raising matches at the Arms Park and, shortly after the sad news of his death was posted on the noticeboard in the Cardiff pavilion, the crowd spontaneously rose and stood in a minute's silence in tribute of a man whose life had been devoted to sport in the Welsh capital and raising the fortunes of Glamorgan.

As his great friend Johnnie Clay later wrote:

> It was somehow quite fitting that the news of Maurice's death should have arrived in Cardiff at a time when Glamorgan were playing a wartime fixture. As the crowd stood in respectful silence to mark his passing, perhaps the more imaginative or sentimental among them may have pictured for a fleeting instant the well-known figure out there on the field, and derived some small measure of comfort. For Glamorgan were carrying on and above all else, Maurice would have wished that.

WELSH SPORTS LTD.

THE SPORTS AND ATHLETIC OUTFITTERS

CASTLE ARCADE
CARDIFF

Telephone: Cardiff 1708

Score Card Price 3d

In aid of
MAURICE TURNBULL MEMORIAL FUND

WEST OF ENGLAND XI
v.
GLAMORGAN

CARDIFF ARMS PARK

Saturday, 18th August, 1945
Commencing 11.30 a.m.

Western Mail & Echo Ltd., Cardiff.—6805N.

The scorecard for the Maurice Turnbull memorial match held at the Arms Park in 1945 – the scene of some of his finest innings.

EIGHTEEN

Wooller Takes Over

The Second World War may have robbed Glamorgan of their influential leader, but when the county's players regrouped at the end of hostilities, they were determined to continue his good work and to build on the developments that had taken place in the 1930s. It was Turnbull's close friend, Johnnie Clay, who oversaw events in 1946 as Glamorgan C.C.C. swung back into action, with the veteran taking over the captaincy on an interim basis.

Several of the seating areas at the Arms Park had disappeared for other uses during the war effort, but, fortunately, there had been little damage to the major buildings at the ground and its immediate surroundings.

The damage to the North Stand was soon repaired and as the Arms Park, like Sophia Gardens, had been used as glorified camp-sites, there was not too much to be done in getting the Cardiff wicket back into shape for Championship action. In fact, several one-day friendlies were held at the Arms Park from 1942; Glamorgan's emergency committee had organised a series of fund-raising matches in 1944 and 1945, including a memorial match for Maurice Turnbull.

Soon after accepting the captaincy, Johnnie Clay made contact with several members of Cardiff C.C. and the city's sporting community to see if they would lend him a hand in getting the county going again. G.V. Wynne-Jones, the well-known broadcaster and rugby writer, agreed to lend a hand as honorary treasurer, while Austin Matthews and Wilf Wooller – who had each played for the county before the war – agreed to help out as assistant secretaries, together with Les Spence, another prominent figure with both the rugby and cricket sections of Cardiff Athletic Club.

Matthews had been a close friend of Turnbull's, having played alongside him for Cardiff C.C. back in the mid-1920s. After attending St David's College, Lampeter, the talented all-round sportsman turned down an offer to play for Glamorgan and instead accepted an alternative offer to move to the East Midlands to play for, and captain, Northampton R.F.C. While in Northamptonshire, he decided to give county cricket a go and, from 1927, he acted as their opening bowler. At the end of 1936 he failed to reach new terms with the county and accepted instead a coaching post at Stowe School. The following summer he returned to his family home in Penarth. Rather fortuitously, it was at a time when Glamorgan were struggling with injuries. After hearing of his friend's return, Turnbull approached his chum about turning out for the Welsh county. He agreed to help out and duly made his Glamorgan debut against the New Zealand tourists at Swansea at the end of July.

Matthews proceeded to worry the Kiwi batsmen with his brisk away swingers and then, in the following match against Sussex at Hastings, he returned match figures of 14-132 on a perfect batting wicket. Aware of how the experienced bowler had caused problems for the Kiwi batsmen, the England selectors called up Matthews for the Third Test at The Oval – remarkably, his only appearance at international level. He continued playing for the county in 1938 and 1939, and with his experience of coaching and organising games at both Stowe and Cambridge, Clay knew how Matthews' skills off the field, as well as on, would be invaluable to Glamorgan as they groomed the next generation of county players in the nets at the Arms Park.

Wilf Wooller was another talented all-round sportsman who played rugby for Wales and cricket for Glamorgan. He had spent much of the Second World War in a Japanese P.O.W. camp, and upon returning to the UK in 1945, he valiantly tried to resume his sporting career. However, his loss of weight meant that he had to retire from club rugby, and aware of eagerness to forge a new career, Johnnie Clay invited Wooller, and his good friend Les Spence – with whom he had played rugby for Cardiff before the war – to act as Glamorgan's assistant secretaries. The two pals quickly agreed and together with the rest of the county's officials, they got on with the task of re-equipping the Arms Park.

Wilf Wooller

Born and raised in North Wales, Wilf Wooller was a member of the Welsh rugby team that became the first Welsh side to defeat England at Twickenham in February 1933. Not a bad achievement for Wooller, who at the time was still a sixth-former at Rydal School.

In the autumn of 1933, Wooller went up to Cambridge, where he won Blues for both cricket and rugby, and continued to live life to the full, before moving to Cardiff to work for Herbert Merrett, a wealthy businessman and sports enthusiast who ran a coal-exporting business based at the Bute Docks.

Wooller continued his international rugby career while playing for the Cardiff club but, initially, he had little time for county cricket, playing just at the weekends for the St Fagans club. Turnbull, however, knew of Wooller's prowess at cricket and he persuaded the burly all-rounder to turn out for Glamorgan in 1938 when the side was badly affected by injury.

Wooller had an immediate impact, taking 5-90 on his debut against Yorkshire at the Arms Park – a performance which refuelled his enthusiasm for the county game. The following year, Wooller hit 111 in two hours against the West Indies at the Arms Park and helped to steer Glamorgan to another well-deserved victory over the tourists from the Caribbean.

With the wicket in good condition, the main concern was providing new enclosures for the public, as austerity calls had resulted in the loss of several seating areas. There was also the need for outdoor-practice facilities, so a Seating and Nursery Fund was created, with Wooller persuading his former employer Sir Herbert Merrett to act as president of the fund, which would, according to the flyer they produced, '... attempt to raise money so that proper coaching facilities could be provided for all young cricketers and thereby build up a team composed mainly of our own players, which will be able to entertain us, accommodated in decent facilities, with cricket of the highest possible class.'

Like many other aspects of life in post-war Britain, there was great optimism about the scheme and reflecting this enthusiasm, the initial target for the Seating and Nursery Fund was £10,000. Within a few weeks, over £1,000 had been raised and the money continued to roll in during 1946. Gate receipts also reached record levels, as people flocked in their droves to watch Glamorgan's home games, glad to see the team playing again and doing quite well. The August Bank Holiday encounter at Swansea with the Indians drew a crowd in excess of 50,000, and to the delight of the Glamorgan officials the gates had to be closed shortly after lunch on the second day, leaving long queues of disappointed people outside the St Helen's ground.

Earlier in the season, the match against India at the Arms Park had also drawn a healthy crowd. With rain having interrupted proceedings on the first two days, when play duly commenced at 2.30 p.m. on the third afternoon, a dull draw seemed inevitable as Glamorgan resumed their first innings in reply to the tourist's total of 376-6 declared. But, the Indian bowlers exploited the damp conditions and forced the home county to follow-on.

With under two hours play left, and with a decent crowd in the ground, Johnnie Clay – who was the non-striking batsman when the tenth wicket fell – decided to reverse the batting order and treat the crowd to some big hitting. He also waived the interval between innings and stayed out in the middle with his partner Peter Judge, who had just been bowled by the spin of Chandra Sarwate. Remarkably, Judge was then bowled by the Indian with the second delivery of

Austin Matthews, as seen in a photograph from 1946.

Wilf Wooller demonstrates aggressive strokes at the Arms Park.

the second innings, and departed for the changing rooms in the North Stand with the dubious distinction of being dismissed twice within a minute!

1946 was a turning point in the club's finances for, at the end of the season, Glamorgan had its healthiest-ever bank balance. Through the hard work and persuasion of Wilf Wooller and his team, the Seating and Nursery Fund raised £8,000 by June, resulting in the target being increased to £15,000. The cash continued to flood in and by the end of the year, the fund stood at £12,000, allowing the Glamorgan committee to agree that if the fund continued to swell, then county officials would contact the Cardiff Athletic Club to discuss the purchase of the cricket ground, thus allowing the creation of a headquarters for Glamorgan Cricket.

These were lofty ambitions and a few informal approaches were made by Glamorgan officials to the Athletic Club in the afterglow of 1946. But it soon became clear that the Athletic Club wanted to maintain the status quo, with the county still paying a fee for the use of the Arms Park for their fixtures in both the County Championship, as well as the Minor County Championship in which the Glamorgan Second XI, under the captaincy of Trevil Morgan, participated.

Even though creating their own headquarters at the Arms Park was out of the question, the Glamorgan officials were able to sit down at the end of 1946 and plan how they would spend the money which the fund had raised. Freed from the anxiety of financial loss and having to release professionals, over the course of the next few years they authorised the creation of improved seating areas at the Arms Park, with new terraces at the Castle End, while in 1953 the members enclosure in front of the North Stand was enlarged to a covered structure with four-tiers of wooden seating.

New enclosures were also installed at the Westgate Street end, together with new facilities for the scorers and the Press, as the capacity of the Arms Park rose to around 12,000. In February 1949 indoor nets were also laid along the corridors of the top floor of the North Stand, creating an area where Wooller and George Lavis enthusiastically oversaw a winter coaching programme, eager to identify and nurture any promising youngsters.

Memories of the Indoor School in the North Stand

In Volume One of the *Pelham Cricket Year* (1979), Peter Walker, the great Glamorgan all-rounder, recalled the days of the indoor school in the North Stand at the Arms Park:

'It provided nets of the most primitive kind. Added to the often sub-zero temperatures was the fact that this narrow space was some hundred feet in the air, so besides nearly dying of exposure, a coach often suffered from severe vertigo!

'One cheerless January evening, Jim Pleass, the former Glamorgan batsman, was doing some indoor coaching and attempting to instil some of the game's rarer subtleties into a frozen and largely bored group of teenagers, press-ganged by their parents into compulsory nets to keep them out of the city's coffee bars.

'In an effort to grab their attention, Jim stopped the session and grabbing a bat, walked to the receiving end *sans* pads, gloves and box in order to give them a mind-arresting example of how the thing should be done.

'But the whole exercise was brought to a sudden halt when the first ball from a left-arm seamer struck Jim in what is euphemistically called mid-ships. Falling to the ground in a jack-knife position, Jim was duly carried down the six flights of stairs and laid to rest in the rugby physiotherapy room!'

Plans were also made in 1946 for the future on the field, with Johnnie Clay grooming Wilf Wooller as the next captain of the club, as the forty-eight year old veteran slipped into semi-retirement. Wooller was the ideal man for the job, given his amateur status and playing experience with the club, plus his times at Cambridge and on the rugby fields of Wales and England. After surviving the horrors of Changhi, he was also eager to channel his enthusiasm and efforts into Glamorgan Cricket, and during the 1946 season he spent many long hours with Clay, discussing tactics and playing resources before accepting the offer from the committee to lead the club in 1947.

With the financial reserves in a healthy state, Wooller was also able to acquire a group of new professional talent. The partial retirement of Clay and the complete retirement of Closs Jones left the spin-bowling department quite bare, so terms were agreed with Len Muncer of Middlesex, who could bowl both leg and off-spin. The following year, another former Middlesex man was hired. Norman Hever, a twenty-three year old fast-medium bowler joined the Welsh county, and when Arnold Dyson indicated that 1948 would be his last season, a third Middlesex man joined the staff as Jim Eaglestone, a left-handed batsman, was signed.

They joined a crop of young homegrown talent which had helped Wooller lift Glamorgan to ninth place in the county table in 1947. These included all-rounder Allan Watkins and batsman Phil Clift – each from Usk – plus batsmen Willie Jones from Carmarthen, Gilbert Parkhouse from Swansea and Cardiff's Jim Pleass, who had shown rich promise with the town club in the late 1930s before swapping his cricket whites for military uniform and taking part in the Normandy Landings in 1944.

Willie Jones and Gilbert Parkhouse walk out from the dressing rooms in the North Stand for Glamorgan's celebratory match against an All-England XI in 1948.

Len Muncer plays a stroke during a special publicity photograph at the Arms Park in 1954.

Wilf Wooller greets Norman Hever *(right)* and Jimmy Eaglestone as they arrive at the Arms Park in the spring of 1948.

Wilf Wooller and the Glamorgan squad that won the County Championship in 1948. *Back row, left to right*: Willie Jones, Phil Clift, Jim Pleass, Allan Watkins, Hugh Griffiths, Len Muncer, Norman Hever, Gilbert Parkhouse and Jimmy Eaglestone. *Front row, from left to right*: Haydn Davies, Emrys Davies, Wilf Wooller, Arnold Dyson and George Lavis.

There was plenty of experience as well in the shape of the two Davies' - all-rounder Emrys and wicketkeeper Haydn – plus the Monmouthshire veteran George Lavis, who also accepted an offer to take over as the county's coach. It was a feather in the cap of Glamorgan's new captain that he was able to blend this mix of youth and experience into a side that won the County Championship for the first ever time in 1948.

Wooller's side launched their campaign with a five wicket victory over Essex at the Arms Park in early May, and by the time they returned to Cardiff in the first week of June, his team had added innings victories over Worcestershire and Kent – against whom Willie Jones scored 207 at Gravesend – plus a 137-run win at Swansea over Somerset, their 100th victory in the Championship, which put Glamorgan into a lofty position at the top of the table, ahead of Middlesex and Yorkshire.

The winning run was maintained as Hampshire were defeated at Cardiff by 70 runs, with the visitors struggling against Willie Jones' left-arm spin on the final afternoon as they attempted to chase 220. Spin was to the fore again in the next match at Swansea, as Stan Trick of Neath joined forces with Muncer to share eighteen wickets as Kent were beaten again by 278 runs. With morale in the Welsh camp sky high, Glamorgan then travelled to Brentwood where Essex were beaten by an innings after Willie Jones and Emrys Davies had shared a record-breaking third-wicket partnership of 313, both men confounding the Essex fielders by calling to each other in Welsh!

After a draw at Trent Bridge and another victory at Swansea over Nottinghamshire, the winning run came to an end when Wooller and his team returned to the Arms Park during the last week of June to play Middlesex. The visitors were without both Bill Edrich and Denis Compton, who were on England duty, and after their purple patch earlier in the month, the Welshmen fancied their chances of recording their first-ever win over the London side. But after being left a target of 275 on the final day, a watchful 150 from Syd Brown guided Middlesex to a thrilling victory by two wickets.

Wilf Wooller leads out the Glamorgan team for their match against Surrey at the Arms Park in 1948. *From left to right*: Wilf Wooller, Arnold Dyson, Norman Hever, Johnnie Clay, Len Muncer, Jimmy Eaglestone, Haydn Davies, Gilbert Parkhouse, Jim Pleass and Emrys Davies.

Glamorgan's position at the top of the table was then whittled away during July. Despite victories over Warwickshire at Neath and Sussex at Swansea, two games ended in draws, while two others were lost, including the match at the end of the month against Leicestershire at the Arms Park as Glamorgan dramatically collapsed chasing 195 to win. They had appeared well set on 120-3, but they then lost seven wickets for 31 runs to the cunning spin of Australians Jack Walsh and Vic Jackson.

Many thought that Glamorgan's bubble had burst, with Surrey and Yorkshire closing the gap. Wooller and his team knew they had to return to winning ways in August if they were going to sustain their title challenge. After a draw at Ebbw Vale, they recorded a nail-biting win over Somerset at Weston-super-Mare, before drawing against Middlesex at Lord's. With four games to play, Glamorgan returned to the Arms Park in mid-August for back-to-back matches with Northamptonshire and Surrey, who themselves were mounting a late challenge for the title, first visiting Cheltenham to play Gloucestershire before returning to Cardiff to play the Welsh county. Glamorgan's game with Northants was interrupted by the weather on the third day, and as rain ended the game in mid-afternoon at the Arms Park, Wooller and his team faced an agonising few hours as they waited to hear whether the band of rain had moved east up the Severn Estuary and descended upon Cheltenham, where Surrey were in a strong position after setting the home team an unlikely target of 291 on a crumbling wicket. To the delight of the Welsh team, news eventually reached Cardiff that Gloucestershire had hung on at 124-9 to deprive Surrey a vital win.

Everyone's attention then turned to the home encounter with Surrey, which over the next three days was likely to decide the outcome of the county title. With Allan Watkins having been called up to play for England in the Ashes series and Phil Clift carrying an injury, Wooller decided to recall Johnnie Clay for the vital match, a decision which initially raised a few eyebrows but proved to be one which was to reap rewards beyond even the wildest hopes of the Glamorgan captain.

The Arms Park was still quite damp after the heavy overnight rain as the two teams gathered at the Cardiff ground. Nevertheless, play got underway on time, with Wooller winning a vital toss and deciding to bat first in the belief that the wicket would not get any better. His decision was vindicated as Arnold Dyson and Emrys Davies launched the innings with an opening stand of 91, before the skipper came in and counter-attacked with glee during the course of scoring 89 with some powerful drives and square-cuts.

When Glamorgan were eventually dismissed for 239, Surrey had just over an hour's batting on the opening day, so when Hever and Wooller took the new ball, most people anticipated a quiet few overs as the visitors built a platform upon which they could consolidate the following day. To everyone's amazement, and the delight of the home crowd, Surrey dramatically collapsed in the most eventful sixty minutes of cricket ever seen at the Cardiff ground.

The new-ball bowlers made immediate inroads as Surrey slipped to 22-3, and when Wooller turned to spin by introducing Clay and Muncer into the attack, further wickets tumbled. Clay removed Arthur McIntyre, Eric Bedser and Jim Laker in the space of one very dramatic over, prompting the visiting horde of journalists to quickly rewrite their copy as wickets fell, in the words of 'Nomad' of the *Western Mail*, 'like a mower moving through ripe corn.'

Surrey ended the dramatic day on 47-9, with Wooller and his joyful team leaving the field as cheers echoed around the Arms Park, in scenes reminiscent of a Welsh rugby victory over England. In excess of 5,000 people were inside the ground before the start of play the next morning as Clay polished off the Surrey resistance in the fourth over, before Wooller – wreathed in smiles – invited the visitors to follow-on.

Their openers duly added 38 runs without loss, before Wooller turned to spin and, once again, induced a clatter of wickets. Micky Barton was bowled by Muncer, before Clay trapped Stan Squires leg before. Laurie Fishlock was then smartly stumped by Haydn Davies as he tried to drive Muncer, and as two more Surrey batsmen departed, news quickly spread around the adjoining streets that Glamorgan were on the verge of a historic victory. Shops and offices emptied and there were around 10,000 people in the ground after lunch as Surrey resumed on 88-6.

Clay soon bowled Jim Laker and then had Tom Clark snaffled at short leg, before Stuart Surridge and Bernie Constable opted to go down fighting, producing a few lusty blows against the Glamorgan spinners. But it was only a matter of time before they swung once too often, and with the score on 144-8, a slower ball from Clay deceived Constable, before John McMahon spooned a drive against Jones into Clay's safe hands at mid-off as Glamorgan won the game by an innings and 24 runs.

With tumultuous applause and loud cheers echoing around the ground again, Clay left the field with the remarkable match figures of 10-65 as hundreds of office clerks and shop workers quickly scurried back across Westgate Street, in the hope that their bosses did not mind about their extra-long lunch hour!

The delighted Glamorgan players assemble on the balcony of the Dean Park pavilion at Bournemouth in August 1948.

County Championship

Glamorgan v. Surrey
Cardiff Arms Park
18, 19 (20) August 1948

Glamorgan won the toss and batted
Result: Glamorgan won by an innings and 24 runs
Umpires: T.J. Bartley, B. Flint

Glamorgan		**first innings**	
D.E. Davies	c Parker	b Laker	47
A.H. Dyson	lbw	b Laker	51
W.G.A. Parkhouse		b Laker	0
W.E. Jones	st McIntyre	b Laker	1
*W. Wooller	lbw	b Squires	89
J.T. Eaglestone	c Squires	b Bedser	6
J.E. Pleass	lbw	b Bedser	0
B.L. Muncer	c Laker	b Bedser	4
+H.G. Davies	c Bedser	b Squires	17
N.G. Hever		not out	1
J.C. Clay	st McIntyre	b Laker	4
Extras	(16b, 1lb, 1nb, 1w)		19
Total	(all out)		239
FOW:	1-91, 2-91, 3-97, 4-138, 5-167, 6-167, 7-179, 8-223, 9-234, 10-239		

Bowling	O	M	R	W
Surridge	6	1	11	0
Parker	9	1	24	0
Laker	44.2	10	86	5
McMahon	14	8	33	0
Squires	10	5	11	2
Bedser	30	13	55	3

Surrey		**first innings**			**second innings**	
L.B. Fishlock		b Hever	7	st Davies	b Muncer	38
*M.R. Barton		b Wooller	2		b Muncer	12
H.S. Squires		b Hever	5	lbw	b Clay	9
+A.J.W. McIntyre	st H.G. Davies	b Clay	17	c Clay	b Jones	19
J.F. Parker		b Muncer	6		b Muncer	0
E.A. Bedser	lbw	b Clay	3		b Clay	1
B. Constable	c Dyson	b Muncer	1		b Clay	30
J.C. Laker	lbw	b Clay	0		b Clay	11
T.H. Clark	lbw	b Clay	0	c Wooller	b Clay	0
W.S. Surridge		b Clay	9		not out	33
J.W.J. McMahon		not out	0	c Clay	b Jones	6
Extras			0	(5b, 1lb)		6
Total	(all out)		50	(all out)		165
FOW:	1-9, 2-9, 3-22, 4-32, 5-40, 6-40, 7-40, 8-40, 9-42, 10-50			1-38, 2-61, 3-61, 4-61, 5-62, 6-87, 7-115, 8-117, 9-144, 10-165		

Bowling	O	M	R	W	Bowling	O	M	R	W
Wooller	6	1	14	1	Wooller	5	1	11	0
Hever	10	2	14	2	Hever	6	1	13	0
Clay	8.2	3	15	5	Clay	27	9	51	5
Muncer	4	1	7	2	Muncer	25	5	61	3
					Jones	5	1	23	2

A few days later, their attention turned to cricket again as they desperately sought news of Glamorgan's fixture with Hampshire at Bournemouth with the Welsh county needing just one more victory to clinch the county title. At first, it was gloomy news as after just ten minutes play, rain swept in from the English Channel and prevented any further action on the Saturday.

The following day, many prayers were uttered on behalf of Glamorgan and fine weather on the South Coast in the churches and chapels throughout South Wales. Their requests were answered as the sun shone down on the Monday morning, allowing the Glamorgan batsmen to resume their innings and by 5.30 p.m. they had amassed a decent total of 315. As in the match with Surrey, the Glamorgan bowlers then struck decisively in the final hour, as Hampshire lost six wickets to a combination of fine deliveries and deft fielding.

After half-an-hour's play on the final morning, Wooller was able to enforce the follow-on again, and his bowlers were soon among the wickets as Hampshire batted again, with Clay taking 6-48 as the Welsh county quickly swept to an innings victory to secure the county title.

Wooller and his delighted team then gathered on the balcony of the pavilion to Dean Park to celebrate their magnificent achievement in winning the county title. With Wooller having to travel on to Lord's to play for the M.C.C. against the Australians, it was rather fitting that Clay should lead the delighted Glamorgan party back by train to Cardiff General. With news of their success having spread by evening newspaper and radio across the city, there were thousands of people at the railway station as Clay and the team arrived home. A mighty cheer went up as they got off the

Johnnie Clay arrives back at Cardiff General railway station with the victorious Glamorgan team after clinching the 1948 Championship title with victory against Hampshire. The interviewer holding the microphone is Alun Williams of the BBC.

train and, after some impromptu speeches at the entrance to the booking hall, the players, officials and the delirious supporters headed off to Cardiff Athletic Club for a champagne celebration that went on long into the night.

The following week, arrangements were made for a couple of celebratory matches at the end of the season, starting with a three-day game in mid-September against a South of England XI at Swansea, followed by another three-day contest against an All-England XI at the Arms Park. Initially, there had been thoughts that the fixture at Cardiff could be against a Commonwealth XI, with Wooller making contact with the Australian tourists to enquire if Don Bradman and a few others in the touring party would agree to play at the Arms Park as Glamorgan celebrated their Championship success.

The thought of the great batsman playing at the Cardiff ground was a mouth-watering one, but the approach came to nothing and it was another figure from the Bodyline series who took centre stage, as Douglas Jardine agreed to come out of retirement and play alongside Len Hutton, Bill Edrich, Maurice Leyland, Johnny Wardle, Norman Yardley and Alf Gover in the England XI who ended up drawing the game with the newly crowned champions. Added to this galaxy of star names was Jack Hobbs, who agreed to stand as one of the umpires in the three-day contest together with Norman Riches who was only too delighted to take time off from his dental practice to join in with the celebrations to round off the greatest year in the history of Cardiff and Glamorgan cricket thus far.

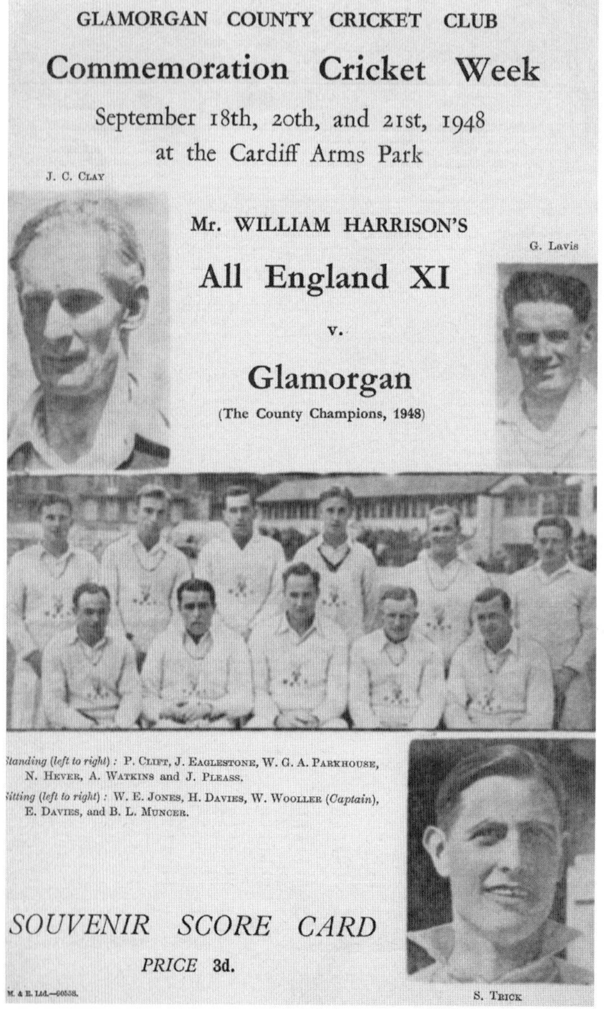

GLAMORGAN COUNTY CRICKET CLUB

Commemoration Cricket Week

September 18th, 20th, and 21st, 1948
at the Cardiff Arms Park

J. C. Clay

Mr. WILLIAM HARRISON'S

G. Lavis

All England XI

v.

Glamorgan

(The County Champions, 1948)

Standing (left to right): P. Clift, J. Eaglestone, W. G. A. Parkhouse, N. Hever, A. Watkins and J. Pleass.
Sitting (left to right): W. E. Jones, H. Davies, W. Wooller (Captain), E. Davies, and B. L. Muncer.

SOUVENIR SCORE CARD

PRICE 3d.

S. Trick

The scorecard from the All England XI *vs.* Glamorgan match in 1948.

NINETEEN

Developing Sophia Gardens?

If 1948 was a great year for Glamorgan cricket, the previous year was a key year in the history of Sophia Gardens, as all of the extensive parkland and open space owned by the Bute Estate, were given to the City Corporation in September 1947 on the understanding that the land was not used for building and reserved instead by the city fathers for healthy recreation.

During the inter-war era, the number of teams and organisations using the Sophia Gardens Recreation Field had steadly fallen. Fewer civic events were also staged at the gardens and the whole area became frequented by fewer teams playing rugby, football, cricket or hockey. The reasons for this were twofold - the geographical growth of the 'coal metropolis' and the availability of open space elsewhere in the sprawling city and its suburbs.

By the mid-twentieth century, Cardiff was no longer a compact town. Instead, it had extensive suburbs to the north, west and east of the city centre, and with ever-improving transport provision, the affluent owners of the substantial villas in Cathedral Road had also moved to new and spacious homes in the outer suburbs.

Either side of the First World War, other recreational areas in Cardiff increased in popularity. Some had been developed by the Bute Estate, such as the Roath Recreation Ground to the south of the impressive lake and its leafy walks, which had been presented to the inhabitants of the city by the Marquess in 1887. The Recreation Ground only staged a small amount of cricket, and became a centre for rugby, football, baseball and hockey instead, as the suburbs of Penylan, Cyncoed and Lakeside rapidly developed during the inter-war period.

To the north of the city, Llandaff Fields became a popular recreation area following their purchase in 1897 at a cost of £69,000 by the City Corporation and, aided by a generous gift from the Thompson family, the seventy-one acres of parkland became used for football, cricket and rugby, while a bowling green, miniature golf course, tennis courts and open-air swimming pool were also provided.

To the west of the city, Victoria Park – opened in 1897 – became a popular destination for bowls and tennis, while to the south-east of the central areas, Splott Park – presented to the Corporation in 1901 by Lord Tredegar – became used for tennis and football, while an open-air swimming pool and bowls green were also laid out. All of this meant that, by the end of the Second World War, there were a plethora of places within the city boundaries where the city's residents could take part in healthy reaction. Shortly after the end of hostilities, another group of recreational areas became available as Blackweir and Pontcanna Fields – which during the war had been used as market gardens producing food and fresh fare for the city's inhabitants – reverted back to recreational usage and, within a few months, became the base for matches in the Cardiff and District Cricket League, which by the early 1950s boasted four divisions.

With fewer people using the Sophia Gardens Recreation Field, a few people also suggested that the area could be used for housing, as the Bute planners had originally intended. Others suggested it be used as the site for a new city hospital, but the Fifth Marquess and his advisors were keen that the city kept its magnificent green heart and, in September 1947, he handed over the gardens and the rest of his family's estate to the City Corporation on the understanding that they could not build any houses or factories on the gardens or the Recreation Field.

The next few years therefore saw the city fathers develop the area as a centre for entertainment and recreation. Firstly, the castle grounds were turned into a city-centre parkland, while in the southern part of Sophia Gardens, a large pavilion was developed, adjacent to the bowling club, as a centre for indoor recreation, as well as music, drama, exhibitions and conferences.

An aerial view of the Sophia Gardens pavilion in the 1960s, with Cardiff Bowls Club to the north.

The Sophia Gardens pavilion was, in fact, a converted RAF hangar that had originally been at Stormy Down near Bridgend during the Second World War. In the early 1950s, the hangar was moved to Cardiff and after being converted, it was formally opened by the Lord Mayor, Alderman George Williams, as a centre for indoor recreation on 27 April 1951. In a glowing and at times quite flowery speech to the assembled party of 2,500, the Lord Mayor described the new structure as 'a beautiful pavilion, set in a beautiful park and within a beautiful city.'

But he also made reference to the pavilion being a temporary facility which could do service for ten or fifteen years until something else, purposely built, was erected in the city centre. At the time, the city planners were looking ahead to the next couple of decades, and their future schemes included a city centre conference hall.

As it turned out, the Sophia Gardens Pavilion did yeoman service until the 1980s. Within a year or so of its opening, the pavilion had become a popular venue for boxing and wrestling, as well as exhibitions such as Ideal Homes and the annual Welsh Trade Fair. Other high-profile concerts and stageshows were also held in the pavilion from the mid-1950s, with a number of well-known celebrities from the world of entertainment appearing, including Sir Cliff Richard, Danny Kaye and Gracie Fields.

An advertisement feature from the *South Wales Echo*, following the completion of building work on the Sophia Gardens pavilion in 1951.

Centuries against Touring Teams at the Arms Park

In the post-war era, several Glamorgan batsmen recorded centuries against touring teams in matches at the Arms Park. In 1961 Jim Pressdee became the first Glamorgan batsman to hit a hundred against Australia as he struck 118*. Two years before, he had registered 113 to set up a thrilling victory over the 1959 Indians, while in 1962 Alwyn Harris, the young opening batsman, made 101 against Pakistan.

In 1965 Tony Lewis struck a magnificent 169 against the New Zealanders, but perhaps the finest achievement at the Arms Park against touring teams came in the early 1930s when Arnold Dyson struck 100 against India in 1932, followed by 147 against the West Indies the following year.

The early 1950s also saw the Sophia Gardens Recreation Field stage other recreational events including grass-track cycle racing, motor-cycle racing and international baseball. In June 1950, and again in 1951, the Welsh Grass-Track Championships were staged around the perimeter of the Recreation Field, with a crowd estimated at around 5,000 watching the riders with geared bikes in a series of keenly contested races.

1950 also saw the Sophia Gardens Recreation Field stage the annual baseball international between Wales and England. The contest had previously been staged at the Arms Park, with the contests in 1924, 1926 and 1930 all taking place on the cricket ground, before moving to the rugby ground for the matches in 1934, 1936 and 1938. A crowd in excess of 8,000 turned up in 1950 to see Wales defeat England and the success of the venture at the Recreation Field saw the contests in 1952 and 1954 – both of which Wales won – also allocated to Sophia Gardens.

Another exhibition international between Wales and England took place at Sophia Gardens in August 1957 as part of a lavish sporting gala held by the City Corporation to raise funds for the 1958 Commonwealth Games. Among the other activities on the Recreation Field was a special penalty

Jim Pressdee and Alwyn Harris return to the Arms Park pavilion after their match-winning stand against the 1962 Pakistanis.

shoot-out competition involving the staff of Cardiff City F.C., plus a series of schoolboy boxing bouts, a show-jumping demonstration including a guest appearance by Col. Harry Llewellyn and his horse, Foxhunter, plus a 'Cardiff Queen of Sport' beauty pageant.

With the city of Cardiff continuing to grow in size and stature, the city fathers continued to think about how their parkland could be developed further for recreational purposes. Their successful bid to host the 1958 Commonwealth Games helped to focus their thoughts and, in the mid-1950s, various plans were set in motion to provide the facilities for the Empire Games, which would further enhance the city's facilities.

A variety of ideas were considered, starting in 1953 with a plan to develop a racecourse running north from Sophia Gardens into Pontcanna Fields. Since 1855 the city had staged horse racing, initially at The Heath, before the creation of Ely Racecourse on the western outskirts. The latter played host to the Welsh Grand National from 1895 until the outbreak of war, but the races on 27 April 1939 at the Ely course proved to be the final meeting. After the war, the defunct racecourse was developed for housing, with a few areas of open space allocated for rugby, football, hockey, cricket and baseball.

The racecourse scheme at Sophia Gardens was first discussed by the city planners in the summer of 1953. The plan had the full support of Alderman Jack Morgan who, as a journalist with the *Western Mail* and *South Wales Echo*, had covered many of Glamorgan's matches since the mid-1920s and, when covering events as a war correspondent in Normandy in 1944, had been the last person closely associated with the Welsh county to have seen, and spoken to, Maurice Turnbull prior to the Welsh Guards' fateful assault on Montchamp.

Jack Morgan had been a city councillor since 1934, and now as chairman of the City Parks committee, he was tasked with overseeing the further development of Cardiff's recreational facilities, as well as the use of the former Bute Estate property. Like other members of the Parks committee, he was frustrated by the fact that the City Corporation were having to spend upwards of £3,000 per annum on the upkeep of Pontcanna and only allowing livestock to graze on the fields, simply so that it could be used for agricultural shows, horse trials and other events.

Overall, the Corporation had seen little return from the acquisition of Pontcanna Farm in 1949 and many felt that it could be put to a better and more lucrative purpose. With the support of the local horse-racing community, Jack Morgan set in motion a scheme to convert Pontcanna Fields into a racecourse, with the area inside the circular track also being used for other recreation, including rugby, hockey, football and cricket. As far as the racing was concerned, the draft plans were for an outer flat course, with a National Hunt course inside, plus a seven-furlong shute – similar to the one at Chepstow – running north towards Llandaff Cathedral, together with a parade ring, stable block and grandstand in the southern part of Pontcanna and on the Sophia Gardens Recreation Field, adjacent to the main access point via Sophia Close.

In early December 1953, the City Council gave outline approval to the draft plans and instructed the Parks committee to progress the plans further and to obtain detailed costings. In the week before Christmas, Maj. John Netherside, the Jockey Club's Inspector of Courses, met with the City Parks committee and also spent time visiting the 200 acres of Pontcanna Fields and the Recreation Field earmarked for the racecourse. Maj. Netherside was very impressed with the site, telling local journalists that the land 'was one of the finest natural sites for a racecourse in the country.'

But the cost of converting the farmland into a racecourse, and the money needed to construct the stands, stables and other buildings were considerable. With the city planners drawing up the blueprint for Cardiff into the 1960s and beyond, there were many other considerations on the financial wish-list, including a new west–east road bypassing the city centre, more housing and schools, as well as a modern hospital. The city fathers had already agreed to setting aside finance for enhancements to Cardiff's sporting facilities ahead of the 1958 Empire Games, so after due consideration of the plans for the racecourse on Sophia Gardens and Pontcanna, they decided in 1955 against allocating further funds towards the scheme.

But this was not the end of the issue as other schemes for the Sophia Gardens area and Pontcanna Fields were submitted, including one which would convert the playing fields at Sophia Gardens into a multi-purpose recreation complex, including a skating rink, bowling alley and a ballroom. During 1957, Glamorgan also became involved, as the county officials realised the potential for developing their own headquarters at Sophia Gardens. Most of the other English counties had developed impressive headquarters and were generating revenue from their facilities. It was completely different as far as Glamorgan were concerned, who by the 1950s were still paying quite high sums to the likes of Cardiff Athletic Club, Swansea Cricket & Football Club and Newport Athletic Club for the use of their facilities in staging County Championship fixtures.

Despite the improvements, the facilities at the Arms Park were still very cramped and the stands were frequently crammed full. In the Championship-winning year of 1948, around 3,000 people were left outside the ground, as the gates were closed for the first day of the vital match against Surrey, while in the game against Middlesex, 15,000 people were allowed in, but only after the visitors had agreed for the ropes to be brought in, so that the overflow of people could sit on the grass.

There were other issues to be considered, especially their modest indoor-coaching facilities at Cardiff, with the coaches utilising one of the corridors in the North Stand. Proper indoor schools had been created, thanks to the Seating and Nursery Fund, at the cricket clubs in Neath and Ebbw Vale, but as far as the Arms Park ground was concerned, the facilities indoors were still quite limited. Aware of the criticisms about the limited facilities, the management committee of the Athletic Club took action in December 1954 to rectify matters by giving their approval to the construction of a clubhouse, costing the club around £25,000, in the south-east corner of the cricket pitch.

Pontcanna 'Ideal For Racecourse'

PONTCANNA lands and Sophia Gardens field, Cardiff, provide "one of the finest natural sites for a racecourse in the country."

Major John Nethersole, Inspector of Courses of the Jockey Club, said this yesterday after he inspected the 200 acres at the invitation of the city parks committee.

The committee have recommended the establishment of a racecourse there.

Last week, when the City Council approved the proposal in principle, it was pointed out that Pontcanna was bought by the corporation in 1949 and since then the cost to the city had been about £126,000 against an income of only £1,900.

Major Nethersole visited the site with members of the Pontcanna lands development sub-committee including the chairman (Alderman J. H. Morgan)

Impressed

Major Nethersole told the *South Wales Echo*: "I was tremendously impressed with the physical properties of the site which has a very good seven-furlong straight and a very fine round course with the possibilities, if required, of an independent National Hunt and hurdles course inside the flat course."

There was ample room for stable yards, a parade ring and other course requirements. There were also three straight avenues of trees, about seven furlongs in length, which would make excellent gallops for exercising horses.

Major Nethersole will now report to the Jockey Club who, in the event of an application being made, would have to license a racecourse.

Plans for the racecourse on Pontcanna and Sophia Gardens are aired within the pages of the *The South Wales Echo.*

SOUTH WALES ECHO

MONDAY JUNE 10 1957 — FOUNDED 1884 — A KEMSLEY NEWSPAPER

LATE CITY

IT'S BRAINS STRONG ALE YOU WANT

3d.

Tourists' lowest score—then Glamorgan wickets tumble

IT'S ALL SHOCKS AT ARMS PARK

HOLIDAY CROWD PACK GROUND

GATES were locked at Cardiff Arms Park this afternoon when a capacity crowd saw Glamorgan end the West Indies innings at 119—their lowest total so far.

McConnon, whose bruised finger caused anxiety on Saturday, took the field and ended the innings. His figures were six for 50.

Then the West Indies struck back and Glamorgan were dismissed for 77.

Fans began to queue outside the Arms Park at 8 a.m. And when they began streaming into the ground nearly three hours later the queues were lengthening instead of getting shorter.

Six to eight deep, they stretched along Westgate-street for some hundreds of yards and in the other direction over Canton Bridge.

It was a colourful crowd sat in their shirt sleeves and the women with gay summer dresses. The West Indians were not without their supporters.

People were sat on the grass all around the boundary, and still the officials were finding spaces for more spectators.

"We do not want to close the gates unless we can help it," said former secretary Les Spence who with assistant secretary Phil Thomas, was engaged in packing the crowds to make more room.

'NO DEATH SENTENCES ON BRITONS'

From Reuter and British United Press Correspondents

CAIRO, Monday.

VERDICTS in the Cairo "spy" trial were today postponed until June 22, except for one of the Egyptian accused, Amin Mahmoud, who was sentenced to death.

Judge Abdel Latif said the ...

KILLED GOING TO SEE FATHER

PLANS for a holiday reunion between an Abertillery father and his daughter were shattered on a road near Oxford over the week-end.

Boat capsized, crew saved

The front page of the *South Wales Echo* for 10 June 1957, showing the crowded enclosures.

Despite the construction of the clubhouse with new bars, lounge areas and a spacious dining room, there were still issues over the lack of space for additional seating, especially to the south and west of the cricket ground, because of the tennis courts and bowls green belonging to Cardiff Athletic Club. It seemed to be a case of too many large eggs being forced into a small basket. Just to add spice to the arguments, a growing number of people started to pass adverse comments about the drainage at the ground and the qualities of the wickets, with five out of the six matches held at Cardiff in 1957 ending inside two days, resulting in the loss of an estimated £500 in gate receipts.

At the end of the Championship match with Yorkshire in August 1957, a formal complaint was also lodged with the M.C.C. by Billy Sutcliffe, the visiting captain. 'The Cardiff wicket is not fit for first-class cricket. It is the worst dry wicket I have ever played on,' he told the local journalists after his team's match with Glamorgan had also ended inside two days. It wasn't a case of sour grapes either, as the White Rose county had won a close encounter by just four runs, but the match had only seen an aggregate of 486 runs, while all forty wickets tumbled with just one batsman – Glamorgan's Bernard Hedges - passing fifty.

Glamorgan had already put down a marker to indicate that the Athletic Club did not hold a monopoly over cricket in Cardiff by staging several matches at the Barracks Field ground in Maindy, a couple of miles to the north of the city centre. The Barracks had been opened in 1876, with the military authorities laying out a sports field to the west of the camp so that the military personnel could partake in healthy recreation.

By the 1930s, a decent wicket was in place and in August 1945, with the Arms Park and the St Helen's ground in Swansea both being unavailable, the ground was used by Glamorgan for their one-day friendly between a Glamorgan Past XI and a Glamorgan Future XI. The Barracks ground was also the venue for Glamorgan's two-day friendly against the RAF in August 1949, and in the early 1950s various Second XI and club and ground fixtures were staged at Barracks Field.

Conversations also took place with officials from Swansea Cricket & Football Club, with several people on the Glamorgan committee hoping that talk of moving the county's base to the St Helen's ground would prompt the officials in Cardiff Athletic Club into doing something to improve the situation at the Arms Park. The availability of land at Sophia Gardens, however, was an entirely different proposition and during 1957 a sub-committee was formed by the county club to discuss, and plan, how the Sophia Gardens Recreation Ground could be acquired.

A group of young players in the mid-1950s training at the Arms Park ground. *From left to right*: Tudor Hargest, Billy Davies and Peter Walker.

The nets at Cardiff Arms Park in the mid-1950s.

Allan Watkins *(left)* puts his pads on prior to a batting session in the Arms Park nets with Norman Hever, Jimmy Eaglestone and Phil Clift in 1948.

The Cardiff Athletic Club tearoom, as seen during an interval in a Championship match in 1958.

An aerial view of the Barracks cricket ground in the top left-hand corner, adjacent to Maindy Stadium.

The discussions took place at a time when concerned voices were being raised about the state of club wickets in the city. Many officials from clubs using the park wickets in the Cardiff and District Mid-week League were getting increasingly frustrated that the general poor standard of playing surfaces in the city would stifle the development of young batting talent. These worries reached the letters page of the *South Wales Echo*, where a correspondent, fittingly called Blackeye, wrote on 25 May 1957 that:

> Apart from Blackweir, I do not know of any park in Cardiff which has anything resembling a decent cricket pitch. I have lived in several towns and Cardiff possesses the worst cricket facilities of them all. It would appear that the popularity of baseball in Cardiff is due to the fact that the City Corporation finds it easier and cheaper to mark a baseball pitch. No wonder Glamorgan are the Cinderellas of county cricket when the premier city of Wales cannot give the youngsters good wickets to develop on. Playing correct strokes is out the question when one is wondering if every ball received may knock one's head off!

Developing their own ground at Sophia Gardens would allow Glamorgan to create a nursery and spacious practice facilities where youngsters from the city's junior clubs could practice and develop their skills. Having a purpose-built stadium would also act as a catalyst for cricket in the area, thereby encouraging the Corporation to improve the standards of groundsmanship and wicket preparation in the surrounding parks.

After lengthy consultation within the sub-committee, a formal approach was made to the City Corporation for developing approximately a third of the Sophia Gardens Recreation Field, leaving the remaining two-thirds for civic events, horse shows and other sports. Their approach initially met with a favourable response and at the council meeting in December 1957, the scheme was broadly approved. A few opponents suggested that the land should remain as public open space, with Alderman A.J. Williams saying, 'To allow this private concern seven acres of our Sophia Gardens would be robbing the people of Cardiff.' But Jack Morgan, who by now was Lord Mayor, argued instead that the area was not being fully used, with only the Cardiff youth rugby team, as well as junior hockey and teams using the field. He concluded, 'The Corporation was not making the full use of this wonderful asset at present.'

Buoyed by this support from on high, the Glamorgan committee held further discussions during January with council officials, including W.M. Brook, the city estates manager. The upshot was that the Council suggested to the Glamorgan officials that the club could have a fifty-year lease at £300 per annum, with work starting in 1958/59 on a practice ground. Indoor facilities could also be built, followed at a later date by the creation of a proper stadium, once a suitable wicket had been developed.

It seemed a fantastic opportunity, especially when the club were paying around £500 each year for the use of the Arms Park, but the provisional agreement between Glamorgan C.C.C. and Cardiff Corporation stirred up something of a hornets' nest, starting with opposition from the West Area committee who felt that agreeing to the creation of a nursery ground in Cardiff would ultimately lead to fewer matches in Swansea, Llanelli and Neath or even none whatsoever. Wooller and others tried to allay their fears and a special committee meeting was held at Bridgend in January 1958 in a attempt to resolve the issue. Johnnie Clay summed up the feelings of many members by telling the meeting that, 'All we want is a good cricket side, and the object in going to Sophia Gardens would be for that purpose.' Even so, feelings were running high among the West Area, and Col. J.M. Bevan, the chairman of the county club – himself a former player with both Neath and Glamorgan – quelled their fears by adding that 'they could be absolutely certain that there would be no change in the allocation of fixtures.'

His comments proved persuasive and the committee duly authorised the sub-committee to proceed with their negotiations with Cardiff Corporation over the fifty-year lease at Sophia Gardens. But this prompted dark mutterings from a few senior members of Cardiff Athletic Club with whom Wilf Wooller had not exactly seen eye to eye, especially concerning the quality of the wicket and the drainage at the Arms Park.

For their part, the Athletic Club liked the fact that county cricket was staged at the Arms Park, in the heart of the Welsh capital, and as far as the cricket section was concerned, having Glamorgan as one of their tenants was a useful weapon in fighting off the growing calls from the rugby and tennis sections to expand their areas of the park. The thought of county cricket moving away from the Arms Park upset several of the Athletic Club's senior members, who were only too mindful of the strong historic link between the county and the Arms Park. Therefore, a delegation from the Athletic Club met with Jack Morgan, the Lord Mayor of Cardiff, prior to the Corporation meeting up to discuss the proposal that Glamorgan should be offered a lease for Sophia Gardens Recreation Field.

Subsequently, the Lord Mayor's stance changed towards the scheme, with Morgan suggesting to the Parks Committee that the financial terms of £300 were far too low. Knowing that Glamorgan were unable to afford a much higher figure, the Corporation suggested that the annual rent should be in excess of £475 or £500. Some council officials supported the view that Glamorgan were getting something at the ratepayer's expense, but others felt that the terms, as suggested by Wooller, were quite reasonable and would preserve the ambience of the gardens. With the Corporation equally divided over the issue, the mayor used his casting vote to terminate the discussions and the scheme, much to the disgust of the Glamorgan lobby, was thrown out.

The following day, Wilf Wooller spoke out in a typically vehement way, 'As a rate-payer, I am extremely surprised that the Council, which has spent vast sums on minor sports, should not keep the opportunity of having the Sophia Gardens Field developed as a first-class cricket ground which could prove to be great value to Glamorgan and South Wales cricket.' The secretary's comments about minority sports were based on figures from the Council's balance sheet, which showed that providing bowls and tennis in the city's parks cost £17,000 yet only brought in a revenue of £4,000. Other Glamorgan officials agreed that it seemed perverse that the Council should be raising the proposed rent for Sophia Gardens when other sports were given quite favourable terms.

In another fierce broadside at the Council, Wooller announced to journalists that Glamorgan's future may loom elsewhere, even outside the capital city, in order to develop their headquarters:

> We have great need of a ground to develop our young talent, but we cannot afford to pay exhorbitant rents as the Council suggest. Here we are with twenty-six players on our books, and coaching up to 100 schoolboys every year, and we have not a ground to accommodate them.

With Glamorgan's officials still deeply unhappy about the Council's apparent u-turn, it was not long before the 1958 season began and attention switched to events on the field. It was a historic summer for the city of Cardiff, hosting the Commonwealth Games yet, ironically in the aftermath of the games, the Glamorgan cricket officials gained a new and politically powerful ally in their bid to secure their headquarters at Sophia Gardens.

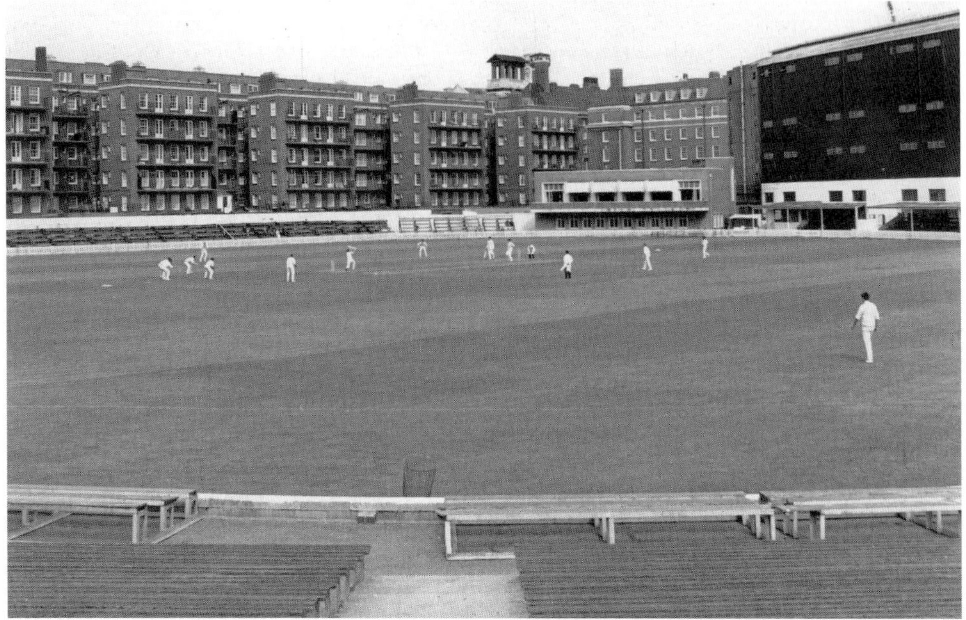

Cardiff Arms Park, 1960.

Wilf Wooller.

Cardiff may lose county cricket

By MALCOLM LEWIS

DISAPPOINTED over the initial failure to reach terms with Cardiff Corporation for the lease of seven acres of Sophia Gardens Field, Glamorgan County Cricket Club may have to look elsewhere for the site of their proposed first-class cricket ground.

Glamorgan captain Wilfred Wooller said today that the club were not bound in any way to carry out their developments in Cardiff. If necessary, they would search for a suitable site outside the capital of Wales.

"We have great need of a ground to develop our young talent," Wooller said, "but we cannot afford to pay an exhorbitant rental. Here we are with 26 players on our books and coaching up to 100 schoolboys every year and we have not a ground to accommodate them!"

No profit made

The Glamorgan club feel strongly over the action of the city council in turning down the £300 a year ground rental, which had been agreed between the club and the city estates manager.

Glamorgan, in fact, have not made county cricket pay in gate receipts for the past six years. Last season, county games at Cardiff brought in only £1,771, and it is only through outside revenues, such as the share of Test match profits, TV fees and supporters' clubs, that they are able to pay their way.

Severe blow

Their idea of a "cricket factory" at Sophia Gardens has received a severe blow as a result of the city council's decision. They feel it should be up to the council to give them every encouragement in providing this amenity, instead of putting obstacles in the way.

Many believe that Glamorgan were getting their site in Sophia Gardens at "fantastically low" terms, but in actual fact they would have to spend thousands of pounds on developing it.

In no way can the corporation be considered the losing partner. They intend to keep the car parking fees and would have additional revenue from the club buildings, which would all be rateable.

LATE NEWS

NEW TYNE TUNNEL

Government has agreed to a new Tyne tunnel to be started next financial year, 1958-59.

RHIGOS MAN JAILED

Edwin Richard John Preece, aged 28, colliery worker, of Rhigos, near Aberdare, was at Glamorgan Assizes today jailed for 21 months for shop-breaking, larceny, forgery and obtaining money by forgery.

4.25—Tommy Long, Clanyon and Chatelet do not run.

THE QUEEN MOTHER

Entebbe, Uganda, Wednesday.—Queen Elizabeth, the Queen Mother, left here today by air for London.—Reuter.

DAVIES WINS

M. Davies (Wales) defeated A. R. Mills (Lancs) 9-11, 6-4, 7-5, 2-6, 6-4, in quarter finals covered courts tennis championships.

F—Swansea U 3pts Bristol U 0

4.25—1 CAESAR'S HELM, 2 Irish Coffee, 3 Fine Point

Betting—9-2, 8-1, 9-1 [illegible]

[illegible] Non-rnrs: Wild Knave, Solarient, Woodfield Melody.

An article from the *South Wales Echo* in 1958, as Wilf Wooller shows his displeasure about the Council's decision to reject Glamorgan's application to develop a nursery ground at Sophia Gardens.

TWENTY

Creating a National Rugby Stadium

The 1958 Commonwealth Games were the biggest event that the city of Cardiff had hosted, with the local councillors and the leading members of the sporting community hoping that the fortnight of competition in July would be a fitting celebration of sport in the Welsh capital. The opening and closing ceremonies at the Arms Park were the showcase events as the games went off with few hitches. But in their aftermath, they drew attention to many of the problems with the Arms Park as a modern sporting venue and confirmed what many people within the Glamorgan committee had thought about the antiquated drainage system.

The Commonwealth Games comprised nine sports – athletics, boxing, cycling, fencing, lawn bowls, rowing, swimming (and diving), weightlifting and wrestling – with a variety of locations in Cardiff being used. The newly built Empire Pool, to the south-west of the Arms Park, hosted the swimming and diving events, while the cycling races were held at Maindy Stadium, adjacent to the Barracks Ground north of the city. The boxing and wrestling bouts took place in the Sophia Gardens Pavilion, while Cae'r Castell School in Llanrumney was used for the fencing. The Mackintosh and Penylan clubs each hosted the lawn bowls competition, along with the Cardiff Bowls Club whose green in Sophia Gardens – created in 1879 – staged the final rounds of the competition. Some events were also held outside the city, with the weightlifting staged at the Barry Memorial Hall and the rowing at Lake Padarn in Snowdonia, North Wales.

The showpiece opening and closing ceremonies, plus the athletics events, were allocated to the Arms Park rugby ground. The races had initially been allocated to Maindy Stadium, but concerns over the latter's size and suitability meant that they were transferred, at a late hour, to the Arms Park with a running track being hastily laid on top of the greyhound track running around the perimeter of the rugby pitch.

After the games ended, the arena had to be quickly restored to its normal state, with the greyhound track being reinstated and the rugby pitch being available for the pre-season practices and trial games. But in their haste, the workmen forgot to fork and break up the sub-soil which had been intensively packed and rolled before the games so that the athletes could run on a level and firm surface. Other areas, closer to the central part of the rugby pitch where hundreds of people had gathered had also become compacted, and the net result was that the turf never recovered from the pounding it received.

To make matters worse, the following winter was a wet one, with the River Taff overtopping and spilling in excess of two feet of floodwater over the cricket and rugby ground. With the First and Second XVs of Cardiff R.F.C., plus Cardiff Schools, the Barbarians and Wales all staging a plethora of games and training sessions at the Arms Park, it meant that the rugby ground frequently resembled a muddy quagmire, with many adverse comments being made about the quality of the matches in the boggy conditions.

This caused considerable embarrassment to the W.R.U., who had long treasured the thought of a stadium of their own to match those at Twickenham and Murrayfield. In March 1959, the W.R.U. created a development sub-committee which was tasked to find solutions to:

i) The poor state of the Arms Park pitch,
ii) The inadequate and unsatisfactory seating accommodation,
iii) The lack of the kind of facilities offered at other national grounds.

The opening ceremony of the Empire Games at the Arms Park in July 1958.

Staff remove the cinder-track laid at the Arms Park for the Empire Games in 1958.

The answer was clearly a Welsh National Stadium, preferably in Cardiff, and the W.R.U. soon began negotiations with Cardiff City Council and Cardiff Athletic Club over a couple of possible sites at Ely Moors and the Arms Park. The former quickly became a non-starter when surveys found that the land was liable to flooding. Talks then focussed on the Arms Park, but a sticking point developed when the W.R.U. said that it wanted to restrict the number of games played by Cardiff on the Arms Park, so that the pitch could be in pristine condition for international matches.

Officials from Cardiff Athletic Club did not like the prospect of having to move from what they viewed as their natural home. Having reached an impasse over their preferred location in Cardiff, the W.R.U. instructed the development sub-committee to find an alternative site in South Wales, somewhere between Newport and Swansea, and adjacent to the main railway line.

After several weeks of deliberation, attention focussed on a ninety-acre site at Island Farm, near Bridgend. The latter was equidistant between Cardiff and Swansea, and with fewer international

The runners in the marathon in the 1958 Empire Games leave the Arms Park and head up Westgate Street.

Rain stops play at Cardiff in the late 1950s as the Glamorgan players sit in the changing rooms in the North Stand. *Left to right*: Wilf Wooller, Peter Walker, Frank Clarke, Louis Devereux, David Evans and Gilbert Parkhouse.

matches having been staged at St Helen's after the Second World War, playing at a 'halfway house' in Bridgend would appease grumbles from the West.

Dunraven Estates, the owners of Island Farm, were most amenable to approaches from the W.R.U. and after several productive meetings they offered their land to the W.R.U. for £19,250. News that the sale was progressing came as a bombshell to the city councillors in Cardiff – not to mention the officials of Cardiff Athletic Club – all of whom did not like the thought of the Arms Park ground losing its kudos and the city losing international rugby.

Having previously opposed the move of the cricket section to Sophia Gardens, the officials of Cardiff Athletic Club now considered this area as an overflow site for other sections of the club in order to keep top-class rugby at the Arms Park. Moreover, it would allow both of the existing tenants at the Arms Park – Glamorgan C.C.C. and the W.R.U. – a chance to develop their own grounds.

Officials from Cardiff Athletic Club held a meeting with the Lord Mayor, Alderman Clifford Bence, and the outcome was that in the winter of 1962/63, prospective plans were drawn up

David Evans (wicketkeeper) and Peter Walker (batting) practice in the nets at the Arms Park in 1957.

by Ken Harris and Hubert Johnson, later to be chairman and president of the Athletic Club. Their scheme was duly presented to the Council on 29 January 1963, with their masterplan involving the enlargement of the existing Arms Park into a 60,000-seat complex National Stadium, which would be used for major games by Cardiff and Wales, with a smaller rugby ground alongside the National Stadium on the site of the cricket ground for club and junior matches.

In addition, the cricket, tennis and hockey sections of the Athletic Club would move to a ten-acre site on the Sophia Gardens Recreation Ground, with Glamorgan being able to pursue several of their dreams in the abortive scheme proposed a few years earlier. Glamorgan were now in a better position than in 1958 because in order to gain their support, the Cardiff Athletic Club agreed to subsidise the removal costs of the seating areas and stands, as well as paying for the costs of the erection of a new pavilion and scoreboard.

In presenting the plans to the Council, Wyndham Richards, the chairman of the Cardiff Athletic Club, said that the plan would mean that certain sacrifices would have to be made – especially by the cricket section – but, 'It is in the best interests of the club, the citizens of Cardiff and, in the long run, the W.R.U. We feel that we are the custodians of the past, and the architects of the future. This is no dream. It is something we feel must happen.' There were a few dissenting voices, with some suggesting that the W.R.U. were blackmailing Cardiff, arguing that if the Corporation did not agree to Cardiff Athletic Club leasing land in Sophia Gardens, they would take international rugby to Bridgend instead.

Shortly after plans for the redevelopment of the Arms Park were published, a few difficulties started to arise over the Island Farm plan. The planners at Glamorgan County Council were concerned about the impact the matches would have on the road network around Island Farm, while the Ministry of Transport also lodged a protest. Members of the W.R.U. duly met with officials from the Ministry to discuss their fears about traffic jams on the main A48 running from Cardiff to Swansea. In contrast, there was general support within Cardiff for the redevelopment of the Arms Park. All of the sections within the Athletic Club, plus Glamorgan C.C.C., were in favour, and with the City Corporation heartily supportive, Cardiff Athletic Club formally offered the Arms Park to the Welsh Rugby Union as a site for the National Stadium.

With more and more doubts being raised about the Island Farm site, including the viability of creating a suitable and freely drained rugby pitch on the farmland, the Union dropped their plans for the Bridgend site, and in 1964, to the delight of the officials of the Athletic Club and the county cricket club, plans were set in motion for the redevelopment of both the Arms Park and the Sophia Gardens Recreation Field.

Initially, the plan for Sophia Gardens involved laying out a greyhound track, plus two rugby pitches, a row of tennis courts and a new cricket pitch whose outfield during the winter months would also be used for hockey. However, there were concerns raised about transferring the greyhound track from its cosy home at the Arms Park, so it was dropped from the final draft which was submitted to the City Corporation for their approval. A few months later the city fathers rubber stamped the scheme, giving Cardiff Athletic Club a ninety-nine-year lease on the Sophia Gardens Recreation Field. At long last, work could begin on the creation of a permanent headquarters for Glamorgan C.C.C.

SOUTH WALES ECHO

No. 21,992 EST. 69 YEARS Tel. Cardiff 33022 & EVENING EXPRESS SATURDAY, JULY 17, 1954 A KEMSLEY NEWSPAPER 2d.

DISLEY AND JONES THIRD AT WHITE CITY

There *WAS* Play At Cardiff After All

POOLS CHECK

Australian Soccer Results

Bannister's Relay Team Fail In Record Bid

WELSH Empire Games captain John Disley and his team mate for Vancouver Ken Jones both finished third in their respective races in the international athletics meeting at White City to-day.

Great Britain despite a gallant solo last leg by Roger Bannister, failed to break the world record for the 4 x 1,500 metres relay. The team finished 1.8 seconds outside the official record which is British held.

British women's team broke world record for 3 x 880yds. relay held by Britain by three seconds.

• Turn to Back Page

At Carmarthen Park

Richards Wins Six-Mile Race

Blank Day Cost Glamorgan £500

By JIM HILL

"NO play to-day" signs went up outside Cardiff Arms Park shortly after 2 p.m. to-day as rain ruined the start of Glamorgan's match with Gloucestershire and cost the Welsh county another £500 or so.

Already in this monsoon summer which cricketers are calling the worst for years, Glamorgan, in common with most other counties, have sustained serious financial losses.

The *South Wales Echo* laments another blank day at the Arms Park in July 1954 thanks to the poor drainage.

Standard Metal Windows – Standard Industrial Sashes

SOUTH WALES ECHO

FOUNDED 1884 TUESDAY JANUARY 29 1963 3d.

WELSH TWICKENHAM PLAN

Arms Park offer to WRU

By MALCOLM LEWIS

CARDIFF ARMS PARK AS THE WELSH NATIONAL RUGBY STADIUM.

A NEW GROUND FOR CLUB RUGBY ON THE PRESENT ARMS PARK CRICKET SITE.

THE COUNTY CRICKET GROUND, PLUS HOCKEY AND RUGBY PITCHES, IN SOPHIA GARDENS.

These are the main proposals in a bold plan revealed today by Cardiff Athletic Club—a plan which would give Wales its "Twickenham," uniquely placed in the heart of the capital city.

Committee say 'yes' to scheme

By PETER O'CONNELL

FOR this afternoon's meeting of Cardiff City Council General Purposes Committee—at which the whole scheme was being explained by members of Cardiff Athletic Club—the council chamber ...

The whole concept was put before Cardiff City Council, sitting as a general purposes committee, this afternoon.

They must give approval to leasing part of Sophia Gardens to the Athletic Club before the project receives the consideration of the Welsh Rugby Union.

If the WRU approve, it is, of course, for them to decide how the Arms Park main stadium would be developed. The plans put before the city council today by the Cardiff Athletic Club are a suggestion of what might happen.

The Cardiff club are willing to give up their birthright at Cardiff Arms Park in a bid to retain the world-famous arena as the national rugby stadium of Wales.

They see their plan as the only way of keeping international rugby in the capital in the face of WRU investigations to build a national ground in ...

BUTLINS IN BARRY BY 1964

A BUTLINS holiday camp should be established at Barry Island by 1964, Mr. Billy Butlin told a South Wales Echo reporter in Cardiff today.

"We are negotiating with Blackpool, Weymouth and Barry, but I am satisfied that Barry ...

Market talks fail—and Britain is out

BRUSSELS, Tuesday.

COMMON Market negotiations on British entry collapsed today when the "Six" announced "the impossibility of coming to an agreement."

France refused to yield and a conference spokesman said, "The conference is over."

Government circles in London were suggesting that in terms of "bread and butter" the consequences of the breakdown in Brussels need not really be con...

MISSING GIRL FOUND DEAD IN

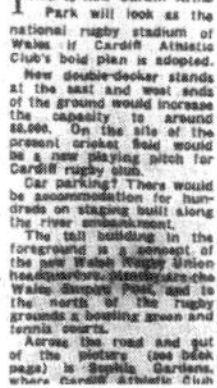

THIS is how Cardiff Arms Park will look as the national rugby stadium of Wales if Cardiff Athletic Club's bold plan is adopted.

New double-decker stands at the east and west ends of the ground would increase the capacity to around 60,000. On the site of the present cricket field would be a new playing pitch for Cardiff rugby club.

Car parking? There would be accommodation for hundreds on staging built along the river embankment.

The tall building in the foreground is a concept of the new Welsh Rugby Union headquarters ... the Wales Empire Pool, and to the north of the rugby grounds a bowling green and tennis courts.

Across the road and out of the picture (see back page) is Sophia Gardens, where Cardiff Athletic Club ...

The *South Wales Echo* in January 1963 announces the redevelopment of the Arms Park and the creation of a National Stadium.

Left: The Arms Park and Sophia Gardens in the early 1960s, with the Empire Pool also seen in the bottom left-hand corner.

Below: Tony Cordle bowls to a Leicestershire batsman during their Championship match at Sophia Gardens in 1971.

The Greatest Spell at the Arms Park?

May 1963 saw one of the finest bowling performances ever seen at the Arms Park, as Cardiff dismissed Pontypridd for just 15, with the damage done by two bowlers, each with county connections – Peter Gatehouse, a university student from Caerphilly, and Tony Cordle, a fast bowler from Barbados. Gatehouse returned figures of 9-2-11-6, while Cordle produced the amazing return of 8.1-8-0-4.

It was the Bajan's second season with Cardiff, having emigrated to the UK and spending a few weeks in London before moving to the Welsh capital to live with a brother. There were few things about Cardiff in the winter of 1961/62 that reminded Cordle of the West Indies, but to his delight, in the spring, he saw early season practices taking place on the outfield at the Arms Park. He gleefully joined the club, and after performances such as the one in May 1963, he made his debut for Glamorgan Second XI before making his first-class debut and subsequently becoming a stalwart of the county side.

TWENTY-ONE

Bumps, Bruises and Cheers

August 1966 saw the final county cricket match at the Arms Park, almost 100 years to the date when the Marquess of Bute had first agreed to allow Cardiff C.C. to have sole use of the Park's cricket ground. During that summer, a series of commemorative matches were staged by Cardiff C.C., while on 13 August the last Championship fixture began at the ground as Glamorgan played Somerset. The Welsh county failed to mark the occasion with an historic victory. The West Country team set Ossie Wheatley's side a target of 223 in three hours, but after Alan Jones had given them a flying start with a half-century in the first hour, their middle order collapsed for the umpteenth time that season and Glamorgan ended up losing by 71 runs as Brian Langford and Peter Robinson shared eight wickets between them.

County Championship
Glamorgan v. Somerset

Cardiff Arms Park on 13, 15, 16 August 1966
Somerset won the toss and decided to bat
Result: Somerset won by 71 runs
Umpires: J.F. Crapp, F. Jakeman

Somerset		**first innings**				**second innings**	
G. Atkinson	c Walker	b Wheatley	16		c Shepherd	b Slade	15
R.T. Virgin	c Walker	b Shepherd	8		c Evans	b Cordle	10
M.J. Kitchen	c Evans	b Shepherd	1		c Jones	b Shepherd	48
G.I. Burgess		b Shepherd	6		c AR Lewis	b Slade	13
W.E. Alley	c Wheatley	b Shepherd	55		c Slade	b Cordle	28
*C.R.M. Atkinson	c Evans	b Cordle	20		c Slade	b Shepherd	0
K.E. Palmer	lbw	b Wheatley	6	(9)		not out	21
+G. Clayton	c Rees	b Shepherd	16	(8)	c Walker	b Wheatley	9
P.J. Robinson	c Evans	b E.J. Lewis	25	(7)	c Walker	b Cordle	28
B.A. Langford	c Walker	b Shepherd	25			run out	2
F.E. Rumsey		not out	0			not out	1
Extras	(2lb, 4nb)		6		(8b, 4lb, 2nb, 5w)		19
Total	(all out)		184		(9 wickets declared)		194
FOW:	1-18, 2-20, 3-28, 4-46, 5-96, 6-116, 7-122, 8-146, 9-178, 10-184				1-17, 2-56, 3-82, 4-126, 5-126, 6-130, 7-140, 8-187, 9-189.		

Bowling	O	M	R	W		O	M	R	W
Cordle	23	5	56	1	Cordle	24	7	48	3
Wheatley	25	8	42	2	Wheatley	15	5	28	1
Shepherd	38.3	17	64	6	Shepherd	34	17	51	2
E.J. Lewis	9	4	16	1	Slade	18	4	46	2
Walker	4	3	2	0					

Ossie Wheatley.

Glamorgan		**first innings**				**second innings**	
A. Jones		b Robinson	48		c Alley	b Langford	51
B. Hedges	c Robinson	b Palmer	2			run out	11
P.M. Walker	c Clayton	b Rumsey	9		c G. Atkinson	b Robinson	20
A.R. Lewis	c Robinson	b Langford	0	(8)	c and	b Robinson	5
A.H.M. Rees		not out	35	(4)	c Kitchen	b Robinson	6
W.D. Slade	c Alley	b Langford	0	(5)		b Langford	4
+D.G.L. Evans	c Burgess	b Robinson	15	(6)		b Langford	1
E.A. Cordle		b Langford	25	(7)	c Alley	b Robinson	28
D.J. Shepherd	c Alley	b Robinson	7			not out	13
*O.S. Wheatley		b Robinson	5			b Langford	0
E.J. Lewis		absent ill				absent ill	
Extras	(2b, 4lb, 3nb, 1w)		10		(6lb, 1nb, 5w)		12
Total	(all out)		156		(all out)		151
FOW:	1-4, 2-21, 3-72, 4-72, 5-100, 6-109, 7-137, 8-147, 9-156				1-48, 2-91, 3-91, 4-97, 5-106, 6-106, 7-115, 8-127, 9-151		

Bowling	O	M	R	W		O	M	R	W
Rumsey	12	5	18	1	Rumsey	6	1	23	0
Palmer	13	6	27	1	Palmer	12	5	24	0
Langford	35	24	45	3	Langford	16	5	41	4
Alley	16	8	20	0	Robinson	9.3	2	51	4
Robinson	18.5	6	36	4					

Cardiff C.C. continued to play at the ground until mid-September when their last First XI fixture was staged against Lydney C.C. On 17 September, the final cricket match was staged at the Arms Park as Cardiff Athletic Club entertained the Glamorgan Nomads. Fittingly, Norman Riches – now the venerable president of the club – was called out to the middle to stand as umpire on the ground where over sixty-five years before he had first played for Glamorgan.

After the match, which ended in a draw, a ceremonial burning of the wicket took place as 'Auld Lang Syne' and 'Now is the Hour' were sung by the players and officials who had gathered around the large brazier where the stumps and turf were being burnt. The following day, the bulldozers moved in and work began on the construction work for the new, smaller rugby ground.

Meanwhile, frenetic work took place at Sophia Gardens, laying the new wicket which would be suitable for county cricket and during the second half of the 1966 season, a number of practice games were successfully held on the new surface, followed on 21 August by the first-ever match between Cardiff Athletic Reserves and Newport Athletic Reserves.

Soon afterwards, some of the seating areas were transferred from the Arms Park to Sophia Gardens, with the low covered stand that had been in front of the North Stand being erected at the River End, while the seats that had previously lined the Westgate Street side of the ground were installed at the Cathedral Road End. Work building the new pavilion and changing room block by Taylor and Co. of Treforest also began at the southern end of the new ground, while in the north-western corner a scoreboard was created at a cost of £3,500, donated by Sir Edward Lewis, the well-known London Welsh sportsman and chairman of Decca.

However, a few delays occurred in completing the new pavilion and when the inaugural match took place at Sophia Gardens – against India at the end of May 1967 – the players had to eat in a series of marquees alongside the newly finished building. Other areas of the ground still looked like a building site when the tourists arrived for the first day's play at Sophia Gardens. The weather, however, had the last laugh as rain washed out play and persistent drizzle on the following day meant that a start could not be made until 3.35 p.m., with India winning the toss and electing to bowl first.

Sadanand Mohol duly bowled the first ball to Alan Jones, who opened the batting with Alan Rees. The pair added a watchful 47 until the tourists' three spinners, Bhagwat Chandrasekhar, Erapalli Prasanna and Bishen Bedi, were each introduced into the attack. They soon exploited the conditions as Glamorgan subsided to 117-8 before rain interrupted play again on the final day. It eased off to allow the tourists some brief batting practice and to allow the legendary Don Shepherd a chance to display his skills with a superb spell of 10.3-6-10-4 as the inaugural match at the new ground ended in a soggy draw.

The Arms Park cricket ground, as the bulldozers move in, September 1966.

Gordon Eccles plays a model forward-defensive stroke as Cardiff Second XI play a trial match at Sophia Gardens in 1966

Alan Jones and Alan Rees walk out from the Sophia Gardens pavilion for Glamorgan's inaugural match at their new ground in Cardiff in 1967.

Glamorgan v. Indians

Sophia Gardens, Cardiff on 24, 25, 26 May 1967
The Indians won the toss and decided to field
Result: Match drawn
Umpires: J. Arnold, W.F.F. Price

Glamorgan		**first innings**	
A. Jones	c Surti	b Prasanna	36
A.H.M. Rees	c Surti	b Chandrasekhar	12
P.M. Walker	c and	b Chandrasekhar	2
*A.R. Lewis		not out	19
K.S. Jarrett	lbw	b Prasanna	0
M.A. Nash	c Pataudi	b Prasanna	17
E.A. Cordle		b Prasanna	0
B. Lewis	c Engineer	b Bedi	0
+D.G.L. Evans	st Engineer	b Prasanna	1
D.J. Shepherd		not out	15
I.J. Jones			
Extras	(11b, 4lb)		15
Total	(8 wickets declared)		117
FOW:	1-47, 2-59, 3-67, 4-68, 5-76, 6-96, 7-97, 8-100		

Bowling	O	M	R	W
Mohol	9	5	5	0
Surti	3	0	9	0
Prasanna	10	3	21	5
Chandrasekhar	16	8	40	2
Bedi	13	5	27	1

Indians		**first innings**	
+F.M. Engineer	c B. Lewis	b Shepherd	30
B.K. Kunderan	c A. Jones	b Shepherd	9
R.F. Surti	lbw	b I.J. Jones	0
C.G. Borde		b Shepherd	3
*Nawab of Pataudi	lbw	b Shepherd	0
R.C. Saxena		not out	24
A.L. Wadekar		b Cordle	21
S.N. Mohol		not out	3
E.A.S. Prasanna			
B.S. Bedi			
B.S. Chandrasekhar			
Extras	(4 b)		4
Total	(6 wickets)		94
FOW:	1-36, 2-41, 3-45, 4-45, 5-46, 6-91		

Bowling	O	M	R	W
I.J. Jones	8	1	31	1
Cordle	4	1	10	1
Shepherd	10.3	6	10	4
B. Lewis	9	2	24	0
Nash	4	0	15	0

The poor weather did not, however, dampen the enthusiasm of the Cardiff club, and to celebrate their move, they held a festival in the first week of July with matches against St Fagans C.C., the Glamorgan Nomads, a West Wales XI, a North Wales XI, Newport C.C. and Lydney C.C. There was also a game against the XL club, who included Wilf Wooller and Harold Gimblett, the former Somerset and England batsman who had been coaching at Ebbw Vale C.C. There was also a fixture against the M.C.C., who selected Eric Russell and Alan Moss of Middlesex, plus Stan Trick, the former Glamorgan spinner.

By the time this cricket week took place, the pavilion at the Sophia Gardens ground had been duly completed, and on 3 July it was formally opened in a ceremony involving two stalwarts of the Cardiff club, Norman Riches and Eric Dolman, who by now had risen to the rank of Lord Mayor of Cardiff.

Alan Jones Recalls the Move from the Arms Park

At the time, I was disappointed at moving for the Arms Park was a nice ground. It was close to the city centre, which meant that at lunch times, office workers used to help swell the crowds. This fact accounted for the lunch interval at Cardiff being taken at 2.00 p.m.

The Arms Park also had a nice wicket and I enjoyed playing there. Sophia Gardens is a more picturesque ground, but the wickets were at first lively and inconsistent in bounce.

A lot of rain fell during the week leading up to our first match there against the touring Indians and the outfield was waterlogged. It was not the best conditions to test either the pitch or the Indian XI. I think it was a mistake to have played that match and perhaps the committee were too keen on seeing the new pitch in use.

(from *Hooked on Opening* by Alan Jones with Terry Stevens, Gomer Press, 1984)

Having staged their pre-season games at Barry Island, Glamorgan had agreed to stage a minimum of six matches per annum at their new ground, and their first Championship match at Sophia Gardens took place on 7 June 1967 against Northamptonshire. The game proved to be a low-scoring affair with complaints from several batsmen on both sides about the irregular bounce. With added problems with the drainage, a few people suggested that the new system had been incorrectly installed with the drains running across, rather than at right angles to the pitch, creating a ridge midway down the wicket.

The formal opening of the Sophia Gardens scoreboard in 1967.

Tony Lewis plays and misses in a Championship match with Gloucestershire at Sophia Gardens in 1968.

These claims, however, were unfounded, but with the seating at the River End occupying more land than originally expected, the square was not precisely situated in the location earmarked on the original plans. As more balls rose up sharply off a good length, the M.C.C. Inspector of Pitches visited the Cardiff ground during the second half of the 1967 season, and as a result, the autumn months saw remedial work undertaken by the Athletic Club's groundsman Les Gerry and his team.

The surface steadily became more reliable the following summer as Glamorgan defeated Hampshire at Sophia Gardens by an innings and 16 runs at the end of June, followed later in the season at their new ground by a four-wicket victory over Lancashire. Tony Lewis's team had certainly become a highly effective unit and at Swansea in August 1968 they confirmed this by defeating the Australians – who they had also defeated in 1964 – by 79 runs.

The nucleus of a successful side had been created in the previous few years, with Alan Jones and Roger Davis opening the batting, followed by Majid Khan, the gifted Pakistani stroke-maker, at number three ahead of captain Tony Lewis, Trinidadian Bryan Davis, Peter Walker and wicketkeeper Eifion Jones, before bowlers Tony Cordle, Malcolm Nash, Lawrence Williams and the veteran Don Shepherd, who had over 1,900 victims to his name after many years of excelling as a bowler of off-cutters.

With the wicket gradually settling down at Sophia Gardens, there was great optimism in the Glamorgan camp for 1969; a summer that also saw Prince Charles, now the club's Patron, become invested as Prince of Wales at Caernarvon Castle, as well as the Welsh county being crowned County Champions exactly 100 years after the first attempt to form a county side.

The summer of 1969 began with Glamorgan drawing their Championship matches with Yorkshire, Hampshire and Kent, before overwhelming Somerset by ten wickets inside two days at Sophia Gardens. After winning the toss, Somerset were soon in trouble against the Glamorgan attack, as Malcolm Nash's left-arm swing and the lively seam bowling of Lawrence Williams, in his first full season of county cricket, cut swathes through the visitor's line-up. Majid Khan also picked up three wickets as Somerset limped to 121 in the seventy-second over.

Roger Davis, the young batsman from Cardiff C.C., then anchored Glamorgan's reply with a doughty 74 as his side secured an invaluable first innings lead of 101. Then when Somerset batted again, it was over to the Glamorgan spinners, with seven wickets falling to the off-cutters of Don Shepherd and Peter Walker's left-arm spin, with only Greg Chappell, the young Australian batsman, looking comfortable against the Glamorgan attack as they recorded their first victory of the summer.

After draws with Lancashire and Hampshire, Glamorgan returned to their new Cardiff ground in mid-June to complete their second victory of 1969, beating Sussex by an innings and 23 runs.

A Hampshire batsman plays to leg, watched by wicketkeeper Eifion Jones, Peter Walker and Roger Davis.

Glamorgan's Championship-winning team of 1969, plus club officials, at a special function at Cardiff Castle with the Lord Mayor. *Standing, left to right*: Roger Davis, Malcolm Nash, Eifion Jones, Tony Cordle, Peter Walker, Bryan Davis, Ossie Wheatley, Majid Khan and Wilf Wooller. *Sitting, left to right*: Don Shepherd, Tony Lewis, Sir Lincoln Hallinan, Judge Rowe Harding and Alan Jones.

After being put in to bat, the visitors collapsed dramatically to 32-6 in the face of further high-class bowling by Williams and Nash. Only two of the Sussex batsmen got into double figures as they were dismissed for a paltry 79.

The Glamorgan batsmen then dominated proceedings, with Roger Davis, Majid Khan and Peter Walker all scoring half-centuries before Tony Cordle, the West Indian all-rounder, became the fourth batsman to reach fifty in a vibrant seventh-wicket partnership with Walker as Tony Lewis ended the run-spree by declaring on 325-6. Like their previous win at Cardiff, it was then the spin of Shepherd and the swing of Nash that caused problems for the visiting batsman, as Glamorgan wrapped up a comfortable innings win.

A Gloucestershire batsman plays and misses at Sophia Gardens in 1968. Tony Lewis is fielding in the gully, with Roger Davis at short leg.

Tony Cordle batting in a Championship match against Warwickshire at Sophia Gardens, July 1971.

Majid Khan plays forward against Hampshire at Sophia Gardens in 1969.

The following month Sussex were beaten again by 72 runs at Hastings, and with another victory in the bag at Worcester, Glamorgan moved up into second place in the county table, some 50 points behind Gloucestershire. The runaway leaders were Glamorgan's next opponents at Sophia Gardens in mid-July, with the contest proving to be the turning point in Gloucestershire's fortunes as they crashed to a demoralising 208-run defeat by a rampant Glamorgan team.

Half centuries by Tony Lewis and Majid Khan, followed by swashbuckling fifties from Malcolm Nash and Tony Cordle saw Glamorgan amass 337, before the latter took 6-21 to rip the heart out of the visitors batting as they were dismissed for a paltry 117. With the weather set fair, Lewis then opted to bat again rather than enforce the follow-on, and the astute Glamorgan captain duly added another fifty before he declared on the final morning, leaving the West Country side a target of 364. With his bowlers having rested, they proved to be a handful for the Gloucestershire batsmen, as Lawrence Williams took 5-30 to see the Welsh county to an overwhelming victory.

Victories at Derby and Northampton helped Glamorgan to further close the gap behind Gloucestershire, before the two counties met up again at Cheltenham, where the Welsh side recorded an innings victory, thanks to fine swing bowling from Malcolm Nash, penetrative spin from Don Shepherd and some brilliant batting from Majid Khan and Bryan Davis.

Aware that the Glamorgan team were on the crest of a wave, a massive crowd then turned up at Swansea in the last fortnight of August to witness further victories over Middlesex and Essex, which consolidated Glamorgan's charge for the county title. Their three-wicket win over Middlesex took them to the top of the table, before a pulsating one-run victory off the final ball of the game with Essex put Tony Lewis' team into a virtually unassailable position, needing one more win in their final two matches in September – against Worcestershire at Cardiff and Surrey at The Oval – to guarantee the title.

There were 10,000 people inside the Cardiff ground on 3 September for the first day of the match with Worcestershire, and they were fortunate to witness one of the finest innings of the entire summer, and all on a wicket that still had a capricious nature. The uneven bounce, however, did not worry Majid Khan, as the graceful Pakistani remained unruffled against the waspish pace of Vanburn Holder and Brian Brain, plus the wily spin of Norman Gifford. Even though wickets fell at regular intervals at the other end, Majid used his magical charm to play a series of perfectly timed and elegant strokes, in an innings of 156 which completely mastered the Worcestershire attack.

In reply to Glamorgan's 265, Worcestershire could only muster 183, with all of their batsmen finding run-scoring difficult against the home county's attack. With a useful lead of 82, Tony Lewis gathered his team around him in the Sophia Gardens dressing room and, sensing the Championship was there for the taking, he told his batsmen to go for quick runs. Peter Walker responded with an aggressive 63, while wicketkeeper Eifion Jones made a breezy 39 before being felled by a skiddy bouncer from Holder.

The doughty wicketkeeper – who in the victory over Essex had whipped off the bails with Essex's last man inches from the crease – was helped into the dressing room still in a dazed condition. The

Majid Khan addresses the crowd, watched by Eifion Jones, still bearing a plaster on his forehead after being felled by a bouncer during Glamorgan's victory over Worcestershire at Sophia Gardens in 1969.

St John's Ambulance staff advised him to rest, so still feeling giddy, he handed the gloves to Majid Khan as Lewis challenged the Worcester men to score 255 and stop the title coming to Wales.

Nash and Cordle made early inroads with the new ball, with Ron Headley and Alan Ormrod departing with just 36 runs on the scoreboard. Rodney Cass and Basil D'Oliveira then took the score to 60, before five wickets fell for the addition of just 21 runs as Cordle enjoyed a fine second spell from the River End, while Don Shepherd came on at the Cathedral Road End and immediately caused alarms in Worcestershire's ranks. The veteran off-cutter steadily worked his way through the lower order and in the process claimed his 2,000th first-class wicket. With the crowd standing ten deep around the boundary rope, he duly finished proceedings as Brain was caught at slip off bat and box as Glamorgan recorded a 147-run victory to become County Champions for the second time in their history.

That Magical Moment in the Summer of '69

Don Shepherd may have taken 2,174 wickets for Glamorgan but it was the wicket of Brian Brain that was, as far as his colleagues in 1969 were concerned, the most important as it clinched the county title.

As Tony Lewis recalled, 'It was a moment of sheer delight for Shep and myself as the umpire quickly raised his finger before quickly pulling up the stumps. As the crowds raced onto the field, I immediately looked for Don, and he for me. We hugged each other briefly, and then walked off together. We had hit near perfection – his caution, control and devoted professionalism, and my own musketeering instincts with a team of many skills and adaptability, and without too many egos getting in the way of an overall design which called for unselfishness.'

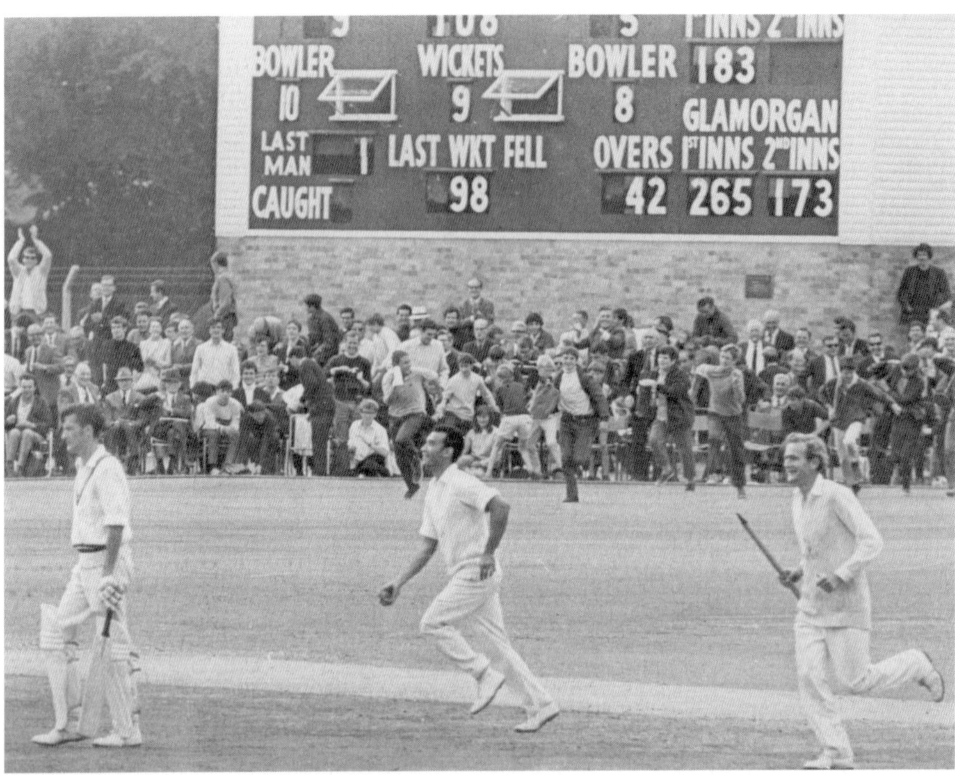

Don Shepherd claims the final wicket in Glamorgan's match with Worcestershire at Sophia Gardens, leaving Bryan Davis and Malcolm Nash to grab stumps and celebrate the Welsh county's title success.

Wilf Wooller commentates on Glamorgan's victory over Worcestershire in 1969 as delighted supporters swarm onto Sophia Gardens to celebrate their Championship success.

The delighted crowd gather in front of the Cardiff pavilion after their victory against Worcestershire in September 1969.

Tony Cordle and Malcolm Nash look on as the crowd celebrate.

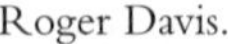

Roger Davis.

Malcolm Nash.

The crowd swarmed onto the field to cheer their heroes off the field, before the jubilant team gathered on the balcony of the Cardiff pavilion to celebrate their success with their elated followers. Songs of every description rang out from the balcony, as the Welsh national anthem was sung, followed by other traditional melodies, plus a few Caribbean calypsos from Bryan Davis and Tony Cordle.

The Championship-winning party went on for many hours in the small bar in the pavilion as the players chatted and reminisced with their friends and supporters. Roger Davis was one of the happy Glamorgan players standing on the pavilion balcony, but as he chatted away, with a champagne glass in his hand, recalling some of the great moments of the summer of 1969, little did he know that he was looking down on the ground where eighteen months later he nearly died in one of the most serious incidents ever seen on a cricket field in Cardiff, or for that matter, in the entire country.

This near tragic accident came during the visit of Warwickshire to Sophia Gardens in May 1971, with Davis, as usual, crouching in his customary position of short leg. The Cardiff-born all-rounder had developed into a quite fearless and brilliant fielder close to the bat, in these days before shin-pads, helmets and other associated body armour were *de riguer*. With just a box for protection, he thrived at short leg through a combination of alert reflexes, good technique and sharp instincts. Even these proficient skills could not prevent a macabre sequence of events, as Neal Abberley – the Warwickshire opening batsman – middled a leg glance off a rare loose delivery from Malcolm Nash. It struck Davis a sickening blow on the temple and the stricken fielder collapsed as an eerie silence descended over Sophia Gardens. As Davis went into violent convulsions, his legs twitching and jerking, fielders on the boundary immediately ran into the pavilion to summon medical help. Fortunately, a doctor called Colin Lewis sprinted out from the members' enclosure at the River End, while Greg Brick, the duty doctor also came out from the pavilion. After quickly assessing the dire situation, with Davis' face turning dark blue, Dr Lewis then gave mouth-to-mouth resuscitation and, with Dr Brick, placed Davis into the recovery position.

Thankfully, Davis started to breathe again and, after twenty minutes, an ambulance crew, who had dashed from St David's Hospital in Cowbridge Road, carried Davis off the field and took him to hospital. The shaken Glamorgan team resumed the match, with Tony Cordle taking over at short leg wearing a motor-cycle helmet. But, like the rest of the Glamorgan team, his thoughts were on the other side of the city as Davis received further emergency treatment. At first the news was not good, as Davis could not speak coherently, and there were fears that he was suffering from brain damage. But after a week or so, he dispelled these concerns by regaining his speech, and after three weeks in hospital he was allowed to go home. There was a happy ending as well, because Roger made a full recovery and was back in the Glamorgan team in 1972, although he was wise enough never to field at short leg again.

Tony Lewis tests the Sophia Gardens wicket in August 1967.

Roger Davis Recalls 'That Moment' in 1971

I was fielding at short leg just behind the batsman Neal Abberley and very close. Neal is the same age as me – we'd gone through junior cricket together and he'd become a big friend of mine.

I must have seen the ball because I turned my head. It must have been going at about eighty or ninety miles per hour. Anyway, it hit me right in front of my ear. There's a vein near it which connects to the brain. If it had hit that, I would have died.

The doctors and surgeons told me at first that I'd never play again. But I decided to get back and play, otherwise I wouldn't. Playing cricket was all I had ever wanted to do, and it was my living.

TWENTY-TWO

One-Day Success

The 1960s and 1970s saw the introduction of various one-day competitions into the county calendar in an attempt to boost attendances which, across the country, had been dwindling. The one-day revolution began in 1963 with the seventeen county teams taking part in a 65-overs contest, sponsored by Gillette. Glamorgan's inaugural match in the new competition took place against Somerset at the Arms Park on 22 May, with the game proving to be the only limited-overs match held by Glamorgan at their Cardiff ground.

It proved to be a closely fought game, with Glamorgan wining by 10 runs, thanks to a fine century from Bernard Hedges and some fiery new-ball bowling by Jeff Jones. However, a Glamorgan defeat had looked on the cards as the Welsh county faltered in the opening overs after electing to bat first. Ken Palmer dismissed opening batsman Alwyn Harris and then Alan Jones was caught and bowled to leave Glamorgan on 11-2. But captain Tony Lewis and Bernard Hedges then added exactly 100 for the third wicket to wrest the initiative back in Glamorgan's favour.

Gillette Cup (65 overs)

Glamorgan v. Somerset
Cardiff Arms Park
22 May 1963

Umpires : A. Jepson and N. Oldfield
Glamorgan won the toss and batted
Result: Glamorgan won by 10 runs
Man of the match : B. Hedges

Glamorgan		**first innings**	
A. Harris	c Virgin	b Palmer	6
A. Jones	c and	b Rumsey	5
*A.R. Lewis	c Alley	b Doughty	40
B. Hedges		not out	103
J.S. Pressdee		b Rumsey	16
A. Rees		b Rumsey	0
+D.G.L. Evans		b Rumsey	0
W.D. Slade		b Palmer	0
E.W. Jones	c Stephenson	b Palmer	16
H.D.S. Miller		not out	13
I.J. Jones			
Extras	(b2, lb4, w1, nb1)		8
TOTAL	(for 8 wickets)		207

FOW: 1-6, 2-11, 3-111, 4-146, 5-152, 6-152, 7-153, 8-187

Bowling	O	M	R	W
Palmer	15	2	39	3
Rumsey	15	6	24	4
Alley	15	1	49	0
Langford	2	0	10	0
Greetham	11	0	46	0
Doughty	7	0	31	1

Somerset **first innings**

C.R.M. Atkinson		b Hedges	31
R.T. Virgin	c Lewis	b I.J. Jones	1
P.B. Wight	c Hedges	b I.J. Jones	11
W.E. Alley	c A. Jones	b Hedges	19
M.J. Kitchen		b I.J .Jones	25
C.H.M. Greetham	c Hedges	b Pressdee	26
K.E. Palmer	c Evans	b Pressdee	1
*+ W.H. Stephenson	c Lewis	b Pressdee	4
B.A. Langford	c Pressdee	b Miller	56
D.G. Doughty	c I.J.Jones	b Evans	20
F.E. Rumsey		not out	0
Extras	(lb1, nb2)		3
TOTAL	(all out)		197

FOW: 1-3, 2-28, 3-64, 4-65, 5-107, 6-116
7-121, 8-121, 9-196, 10-197

Bowling	O	M	R	W
I.J. Jones	15	5	34	3
Evans	8.2	1	37	1
Miller	10	0	31	1
Hedges	8	5	17	2
Slade	7	2	29	0
Pressdee	14	4	46	3

Despite the departure of Lewis for 40, and the loss of three further wickets for just seven runs, Hedges kept the scoreboard ticking over with deft placement, plus the occasional boundary. Hedges received valiant support from wicketkeeper Eifion Jones and all-rounder Hamish Miller, and the Pontypridd-born batsman eventually reached a well-deserved century in the penultimate over as Glamorgan ended on 207-8.

Bernard Hedges returns to the Arms Park changing rooms after his match-winning century in the 1963 Gillette Cup match against Somerset.

With West Indian Peter Wight and Australian Bill Alley in their batting line-up, Somerset looked well placed to chase this target, but their run chase faltered as a result of a fine opening burst from left-arm quickie Jeff Jones. The young pace bowler claimed the valuable wickets of Roy Virgin and Wight in a hostile opening spell. Hedges's gentle medium pace then accounted for Colin Atkinson and Alley, before Jones returned to clean bowl Merv Kitchen for 25.

Then it was the turn of Jim Pressdee's spin to put the visitors under pressure and the all-rounder claimed the wickets of Chris Greetham, Ken Palmer and Harold Stephenson to leave Somerset teetering on 121-8. But thoughts of a comprehensive Glamorgan victory were quickly dispelled as the ninth-wicket pair of Brian Langford and David Doughty then counter-attacked adding 75 runs in rapid time.

When Langford reached a well-made half-century, it even looked as if Somerset might pull off a quite remarkable victory, but he was well caught in the deep by Jim Pressdee and, in the following over, Doughty was dismissed to give Glamorgan a hard-earned victory by 10 runs. It had been a highly entertaining contest, as well as being a good way to launch the new competition. After his all-round contributions with both bat and ball, Bernard Hedges deservedly won the Man of the Match cheque for £50.

Six years later, on 1 June 1969, Somerset were Glamorgan's opponents again in the inaugural Sunday League encounter at Sophia Gardens as a 40-overs league competition was added to the county calendar. It was the Welsh county's seventh match in the new competition, having staged home games earlier in the summer at Neath and Swansea. Once again, Glamorgan won the toss but this time they elected to bowl first against a useful Somerset side who included the highly promising Australian batsman Greg Chappell in their line-up. But the twenty year old was one of three victims for Don Shepherd who produced a masterly spell of controlled spin, taking 3-15 in his eight overs which filleted the visitor's middle-order after Tony Cordle and Malcolm Nash had made inroads with the new ball.

Majid Khan also claimed the wickets of the Palmer brothers, Roy and Ken, as the West Country side desperately tried to rebuild their innings, but when captain Brian Langford was run out off the penultimate delivery, the visitors had only mustered 122. Glamorgan's batsmen, at first, also found run-scoring difficult as Graham Burgess produced a devastating opening spell which reduced Glamorgan to 11-3. But Majid then strolled to the wicket and unfurled some exquisitely timed

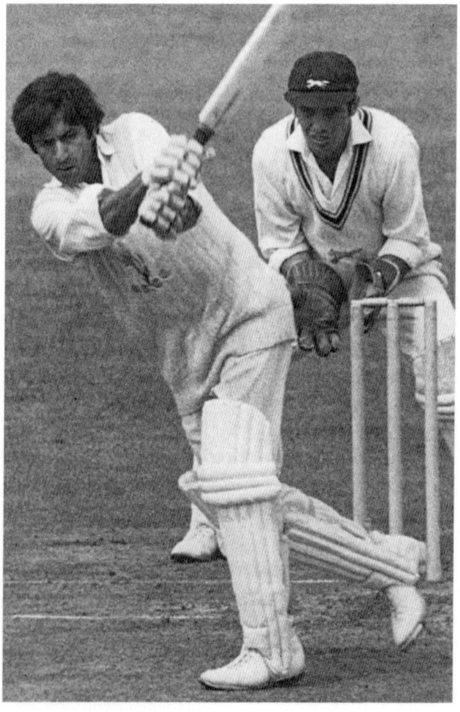

Majid Khan.

The National Sports Centre for Wales

In 1964 the Welsh committee of the Central Council of Physical Recreation called for 'the need for a National Sports Centre for Wales which will provide facilities for the training of coaches and leaders, sports coaching at all levels and international competition.'

In 1969 agreement was reached over funding and negotiations began with Cardiff Corporation over a suitable site in the city. Realising the importance of this amenity, they offered land in Sophia Gardens in between the cricket ground and Cardiff Bowls Club, and work commenced constructing the large indoor sports centre in 1971 – it is now known as the Welsh Institute of Sport.

The capital costs exceeded £500,000, with the three-storey building including a main hall on the ground floor, a gymnasium, weight-training room, lecture theatre and meeting rooms, a series of squash courts, a swimming pool, bar and restaurant, a residential block, and a series of offices for the Sports Council of Wales, plus an upper hall which included a series of cricket nets regularly used until the late-1990s by Glamorgan players and club cricketers from the Cardiff area.

strokes to show that run-scoring was perfectly possible, despite the slow and low bounce. Together with Alan Jones, the Pakistani shared an unbroken stand of 113 which saw Glamorgan to a seven-wicket victory with fourteen balls to spare.

This was just one of many breathtaking innings that Majid played at Sophia Gardens in the early 1970s, with the home crowd in raptures time and again; he produced some scintillating displays of batsmanship, full of wristy and inventive strokes, as well as effortless drives through the covers to leave the visiting bowlers cursing their fortune. He led the county as well from 1973 but sadly, things turned sour as the team struggled to win on a regular basis, and following the retirement of several experienced players, the youngsters who had replaced them failed to make an impact.

There were rumours of a rift between the players and the committee, and things finally came to a head during the long, hot summer of 1976, as Majid quit in mid-season, followed by the departure of several other players amid dark mutterings about dressing-room strife. The club were also languishing at the foot of both the Championship and Sunday League table, and to make matters worse their final league game of the summer – against Somerset on 5 September – saw the West Country side travel to Sophia Gardens needing one more win to clinch their first-ever county title.

Given Glamorgan's very modest form, it looked a formality that Somerset would win the Sunday League, and over twenty coaches and mini-buses full of their supporters descended on the Cardiff ground soon after 11 a.m. with the visiting supporters eager to get their seat and share in what they hoped would be a piece of history for the Somerset club.

As far as Glamorgan were concerned, their arrival en masse caused another embarrassing episode during what had already been a sorry summer for all concerned, both on and off the field. The gates into the ground had already been opened by officials of Cardiff Athletic Club, as a rugby match was taking place on the pitch in the northern part of the ground and, with the Glamorgan stewards not arriving until 11.30 a.m., some two and a half hours before the scheduled start, the visiting supporters were able to wander into the ground without paying.

The stands quickly filled up with Somerset supporters, all of whom had not paid a penny to enter the ground, leaving disgruntled Glamorgan members few spaces to sit in their regular enclosure. In an attempt to recoup the gate receipts, buckets were carried around the ground by the stewards. To their credit, the visiting supporters contributed over £1,000, but even so, there were still several red faces in the Glamorgan office as they counted up the money.

Events on the field, however, soon gave Glamorgan more to smile about as in the early overs, Brian Close, the stalwart Somerset skipper, dropped a chance from Alan Jones. It proved to be a very costly miss as the Glamorgan captain went on to make 70 and with a few hefty blows from Malcolm Nash, who was promoted up to number four, Glamorgan were able to set Somerset a target of 192 in 39 overs.

There were quite a few nerves jangling in the visitor's dressing room as Somerset began their reply, and their cause was not helped by a superb opening burst of left-arm swing from Nash, who dismissed Peter Denning, Brian Close and Ian Botham to leave Somerset reeling at 27-3.

The members stand at the River End, packed out for a match in the late 1980s.

Ian Botham of Somerset practices in front of an excited crowd at Sophia Gardens in 1979. The caravan to the right of the pavilion was the Glamorgan office.

Brian Rose and Merv Kitchen then steadied the ship with a stand of 70 for the fourth wicket, before Graham Burgess and Dennis Breakwell continued their good work as Somerset entered the last six overs needing twenty to win, with five wickets in hand.

The mass of Somerset supporters began to prepare their victory celebrations, but their plans were quickly thrown awry as Nash returned to the attack and bowled Breakwell. With the total on 180, wicketkeeper Derek Taylor was then run out. As the tension mounted in the final over, another mix-up occurred, with Keith Jennings following in similar fashion, and number-ten batsman Colin Dredge made his way to the wicket. But Graham Burgess was still there and the experienced batsman faced the final ball from Nash with Somerset needing three runs to tie the game and secure the Sunday League trophy.

Burgess boldly hit the ball back over Nash's head down to the sightscreen at the Cathedral Road end of the ground. The Somerset supporters started to cheer, believing that Burgess had hit the winning runs, but Alan Jones calmly ran around the boundary, threw the ball back to Nash as Burgess and Colin Dredge completed their second run. The visitors had to get a third run in order to win the trophy, so they set off in desperation as Nash lobbed the ball gently back to Eifion Jones. The wicketkeeper then removed the bails with Dredge well short of his ground, as Glamorgan won by one run.

Sunday League

Glamorgan v. Somerset
Sophia Gardens, Cardiff
5 September 1976

Glamorgan won the toss and elected to bat
Umpires: W.E. Alley and J.F. Crapp
Result: Glamorgan won by 1 run

Glamorgan		**first innings**	
*A. Jones		b Dredge	70
G.P. Ellis	c Taylor	b Botham	12
D.A. Francis		b Jennings	36
M.A. Nash		b Moseley	43
J.A. Hopkins		run out	7
A.E. Cordle	c Rose	b Botham	9
+E.W. Jones		run out	0
G. Richards		not out	0
A.H. Wilkins			
B.J. Lloyd			
D.L. Williams			
Extras	(b12, lb1, nb1)		14
TOTAL	(for 7 wickets)		191

FOW: 1-31, 2-123, 3-134, 4-145, 5-180, 6-189, 7-190

Bowling	O	M	R	W
Moseley	8	0	31	1
Botham	7	0	41	2
Burgess	8	0	32	0
Jennings	8	0	39	1
Dredge	8	0	34	1

Somerset		**first innings**	
B.C. Rose	c E.Jones	b Williams	39
P.W. Denning	lbw	b Nash	6
*D.B. Close	c Wilkins	b Nash	1
I.T. Botham	c and	b Nash	9
M.J. Kitchen		b Wilkins	46
G.I. Burgess		not out	48
D. Breakwell		bNash	21
+D.J.S. Taylor		run out	8
K.V. Jennings		run out	1
C.H. Dredge		run out	0
H.R. Moseley			
Extras	(lb10, nb1)		11
TOTAL	(for 9 wickets)		190

FOW: 1-11, 2-15, 3-27, 4-97, 5-127, 6-171, 7-180, 8-188, 9-190

Bowling	O	M	R	W
Nash	8	1	35	4
Cordle	8	1	38	0
Ellis	8	0	34	0
Lloyd	4	0	17	0
Williams	7	0	32	1
Wilkins	4	0	23	1

This thrilling victory could not mask what had been a very sorry summer of county cricket at Sophia Gardens, with a lot of turmoil and public debate. By the time Christmas came, everyone connected with the club vowed to put their grievances behind them and get down to the task of restoring the team's pride and standing on the county circuit. They did so with almost unbelievable results, and not even the most romantic of Hollywood scriptwriters could have penned the scenario for 1977, which saw Glamorgan play in a one-day final at Lord's for the first time.

It was even more remarkable given their erratic form in limited-overs cricket – their highest-ever position in the Sunday League had been tenth. They had also made little impact in either the Gillette Cup, the 60-overs knockout competition, or the Benson & Hedges Cup, the 55 overs-a-side zonal competition which had been introduced in 1972. But despite this modest run of form, Alan Jones's side enjoyed a purple patch of form in the Gillette Cup where, after a bye in the first round, they defeated Worcestershire at New Road by four wickets, thanks to a spirited innings of 62* from Arthur Francis.

Their prize was a quarter-final contest against Surrey at Cardiff on 3 August and from soon after breakfast time, the Sophia Gardens ground filled up with Glamorgan supporters who, after the misery of the previous summer, were only too glad to voice their support of the team's sterling efforts. Their optimism, though, looked mis-placed as Surrey's opening pair of Alan Butcher and captain John Edrich brought up the half-century with few alarms, but soon after, Edrich damaged a calf muscle and had to call for a runner.

In an attempt to force the pace, Butcher was then bowled by the experienced Tom Cartwright, who had joined the Welsh county for the summer. The new batsmen then found life difficult against the accurate off-spin of Gwyn Richards, with the twenty-five year old from Maesteg claiming the prized wicket of Edrich shortly after the Surrey captain had reached his half-century.

Surrey's middle-order continued to struggle against the lively bowling of Alan Wilkins, the Cardiff-born left-arm seamer, whose father Haydn had been a stalwart figure in the Athletic Club 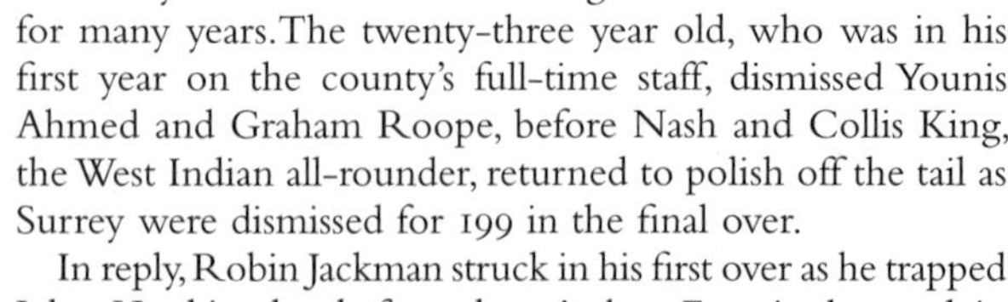
for many years. The twenty-three year old, who was in his first year on the county's full-time staff, dismissed Younis Ahmed and Graham Roope, before Nash and Collis King, the West Indian all-rounder, returned to polish off the tail as Surrey were dismissed for 199 in the final over.

Alan Wilkins.

In reply, Robin Jackman struck in his first over as he trapped John Hopkins leg before, then Arthur Francis departed in similar fashion with the total on 28. Alan Jones found a useful ally in Collis King, as the pair added 101 to wrest the initiative back from the visitors. Both batsmen fell soon after reaching their half-centuries, but any nerves in the Glamorgan dressing room were dispelled as Mike Llewellyn struck a belligerent 37 to see Glamorgan home by four wickets.

To the delight of their supporters, cheers echoed around the Cardiff ground, and a few weeks later, after a thrilling semi-final victory over Leicestershire at Swansea, there was excited chatter around Sophia Gardens, as Middlesex were confirmed as Glamorgan's opponents in the final on 3 September. Queues of people soon formed outside the club's match-day office alongside the Cardiff pavilion, as well as up the stairs leading to their permanent offices in the High Street, as cup-final tickets became like gold dust.

By a wonderful coincidence, Glamorgan's first appearance in a one-day final came on the fiftieth anniversary of

The stands at the River End in the early 1980s, showing the small Radio Wales commentary box, press box, scorer's box and the President's Room.

The Glamorgan squad of 1976. *Standing*: Allan Lewis Jones, Arthur Francis, Tony Allin, John Hopkins, Barry Lloyd, Alan Wilkins, Kevin Lyons, Gwyn Richards. *Seated*: Eifin Jones, Tony Cordle, Alan Jones (captain), Laurence Williams, Malcolm Nash.

Cardiff City's famous victory in the F.A. Cup final at Wembley; in the week leading up to the Gillette Cup final, there was much talk of Glamorgan matching the Bluebirds' feat. Film crews and journalists duly swarmed around Sophia Gardens as Glamorgan entertained Gloucestershire in a Championship encounter on the eve of their big day at Lord's.

Alan Jones' team did not get the send-off they wanted, however, as the pace bowling of Mike Procter and the left-arm spin of John Childs saw Gloucestershire to a 37-run victory. The cup final itself also ended in defeat for Alan Jones' team, despite an aggressive 62 from Mike Llewellyn, as Middlesex were able to canter to a five-wicket victory.

At the end of the match, you could have been excused for thinking that Glamorgan had won, as Welsh supporters jubilantly gathered in front of the historic pavilion and sang their hearts out. Despite the defeat, the match had marked the coming of age for Glamorgan as a club, and now with a one-day final under their belt – plus a rapidly improving new ground in Cardiff – they could look forward to a bright future after several years of turmoil.

TWENTY-THREE

Centenary Celebrations

Glamorgan's appearance in the Gillette Cup final of 1977 was a brief high point during a decade which saw Glamorgan struggle to recapture their successes of the 1960s. The retirement of the old guard, the introduction of new faces and a change of captain did not produce any long-lasting improvements.

But off the field, the club underwent some successful changes as important developments took place during the early 1980s in the administration and marketing of Wales' only first-class county. Wilf Wooller and Phil Clift each retired after many years of loyal service as players, coaches and secretaries. The club's new secretary, Phil Carling, then oversaw several changes which revolutionised the way Glamorgan operated, starting in December 1985 with the erection of an administration block on the Sophia Gardens ground and the sale of the club's old offices at 6 High Street.

Glamorgan's Offices move to Sophia Gardens

April 1986 was a landmark month in the history of Glamorgan cricket as the club finally vacated their small offices at 6 High Street, and moved to the Sophia Gardens ground.

The cricket section of Cardiff Athletic Club had acquired the spacious Portakabins, previously used as the site offices for the Ely Link Road. The county moved into these portakabins during the spring of 1986, which were sited in the south-west corner of the ground, adjacent to the main entrance from Sophia Close.

Secretary Phil Carling and his small team of administrative staff occupied much of the rear of the unit, while the pitch-facing rooms were converted into a committee room, plus a series of hospitality suites named after some of the legends of the county club, with the principal room being the Wilf Wooller Suite, opened by the club's great leader on 2 July 1986.

The club's newly created marketing department also swung into action, tapping into the corporate world of South Wales, with back-to-back Championship matches in mid-summer at the Cardiff ground being re-branded as the Cardiff Festival, with many marquees lining the boundary ropes. Other changes saw the creation of a main electronic scoreboard replacing the old manual board at the Cathedral Road End, as well as a smaller board in front of the Vice-President's Enclosure at the River End, which was used by Cardiff C.C. and built in memory of Dan Herbert, one of the club's leading former players and officials.

Allied Steel and Wire became Glamorgan's new sponsors in 1987 and in the course of the next few years, the Cardiff-based company helped to fund a number of initiatives, including a coaching scheme in south-east Wales, an improved system of covers and a new covered complex at the River End of the Sophia Gardens ground, which included a hospitality box named in memory of Maurice Turnbull. A new media centre and scorer's box, which replaced the old wooden units transferred from the Arms Park, were also added.

During 1987, the club also launched their Centenary Year with a 40-overs friendly between Glamorgan and Gloucestershire on Monday 6 July, a very appropriate date in the club's history, and very fitting opponents given the involvement of the Brain family around the turn of the century.

The Glamorgan offices, as seen in 1986, painted in the colours of Cardiff Athletic Club.

Sue Wood (left) and her colleagues in the Glamorgan office in 1986.

The weather gods also smiled on the Welsh county, as the match for the Severn Trophy was played in temperatures which rocketed into the low eighties.

It was also a right royal occasion as the contest was attended by the patrons of the two counties, HRH The Prince of Wales and his wife Diana, HRH The Princess of Wales. Both teams were formerly introduced to Prince Charles and his charming wife, and the pair also mingled with the hundreds of specially invited guests in the large marquees erected at the Pontcanna end of the ground. At the end of the day, it was Diana who had most to smile about, as Gloucestershire won the match by seven wickets with Tony Wright scoring an unbeaten 99.

A view of the Sophia Gardens cricket ground in 1979.

The pre-season press call at Sophia Gardens in 1999. Note the changes at the River End, compared with the photograph above.

Sophia Gardens during the Cardiff Festival in the early 1990s, with the sponsors' marquees alongside the rugby pitch in the northern end of the ground.

Action from the floodlit match at the Arms Park in 1989.

Floodlit Cricket at the Arms Park

Glamorgan had staged floodlit cricket matches at the St Helen's ground in Swansea since the early 1980s, with exhibition games against a Rest of the World invitation team. On 17 May 1989 a floodlit game took place at the Arms Park, as part of the events held in aid of Rodney Ontong's Benefit year, with Ontong leading the Glamorgan side of 1989 against the Championship-winning team of 1969, led by Tony Lewis.

The 30-overs friendly, on the Cardiff R.F.C. ground, saw Matthew Maynard blast 110 for the 1989 team, before Peter Walker struck an imperious 105 for the 1969 team. Don Shepherd, who was now the county's bowling coach, turned out for the 1989 side against his former colleagues, and delivered the only maiden of the evening as Tony Lewis' team fell four runs short.

1988 also saw the return of Tony Lewis, as chairman of the club, with Gerard Elias acting as Centenary Appeals Director and presiding over a series of functions which celebrated all of those who had flown the flag of Welsh cricket. The first event of the summer was the magnificent London Centenary dinner, held in the Long Room at Lord's, while on the actual anniversary of the club's formation – 6 July 1988 – Glamorgan were engaged in a second round NatWest Trophy match against Lancashire, fittingly enough at Sophia Gardens, and a contest they duly won by 31 runs, thanks to a four-wicket burst from John Derrick, plus a three-wicket haul by Ravi Shastri, the Indian all-rounder who had joined the Welsh county in 1987. The anniversary celebrations drew to a close in the autumn with a Daffodil Ball at St Mellon's Country Club, by which time the wheels had been set in motion for another major development in the club's history – the signing of West Indian legend Viv Richards.

During the Centenary celebrations, Tony Lewis was asked many times to set out the two most important goals for the club to achieve during their second century. The answer, each time, was firstly success on the field, and secondly a permanent home of their own. The signing of Viv Richards was the first element of the blueprint, with the news formally announced on 17 January 1989 that the former Somerset batsman had joined the ambitious Welsh county. However, illness and injury prevented the 'Master Blaster' from appearing until 1990, during which time he rolled back the years in a masterly display of batting, amassing 1,425 runs at an average of 62. His tally contained seven centuries, including 119 on his Championship debut against Leicestershire at Sophia Gardens – a match that saw his new team follow-on, before going down to a nine-wicket defeat.

One of the marquees used for hospitality in the late 1980s.

Sophia Gardens, during Glamorgan's County Championship match against Leicestershire in the early 1990s.

Headway with the second objective – a permanent home for the club – also took place in the Centenary year with the celebrations helping to sharpen people's minds about the need to secure a base, especially when the club were still incurring the costs of playing at, and equipping, up to eight grounds a year; plus the cost of renting equipment and seating, and missing out on the lack of any winter income from bars, restaurants or conference facilities.

During 1989 the committee drew up a list of possible sites where Glamorgan could develop their headquarters. Sophia Gardens was the obvious candidate at the top of the list but, at the time, delegates from Cardiff Athletic Club were not interested in the loss of their premises. Consequently, other sites were considered in and around Cardiff, including sites at Pentwyn, Radyr, Wentloog, Whitchurch and also in Cardiff Bay, as well as at other locations in South Wales, including Swansea, Bridgend, Llandarcy and Hensol.

All of these options, for one reason or another, proved unacceptable and it came as a relief when, in 1993, a chance conversation at Sophia Gardens was to initiate a renewed dialogue between the county club and Cardiff Athletic Club, the outcome of which led to the county commencing discussions over how to acquire the head lease of the ground.

It proved to be a complex deal, with the Athletic Club being paid for thirty years' investment in the ground, specialist machinery and buildings, as well as the costs of relocating their tennis, cricket, hockey and rugby sections, together with a premium which would induce them to vacate Sophia Gardens. Eventually, agreement was reached for the vacation of the ground by October 1997, totalling £2.5 million, while discussions began with the City Council over the terms of the new lease, as well as with the club's financiers, Midland Bank, over the monetary aspects of the scheme. To help generate capital which would assist with the purchase of the ground, a new ten-year category of membership was introduced, with 1,000 members taking out Premier Membership.

The Council and the bank duly reached agreement with the cricket club's officials and the dreams of Turnbull and Wooller became a reality on 24 November 1995 as Glamorgan C.C.C. formally acquired from Cardiff Athletic Club a new 125-year lease of the Sophia Gardens ground, with the documents being signed by the club's Trustees – Tony Lewis, Gwyn Craven and Gordon Jones.

After several months of detailed planning, Glamorgan duly announced in October 1996 their plans to redevelop the Sophia Gardens ground over the course of the next fifteen years, and to create a twenty-first-century headquarters with a capacity in the region of 9,750, with twenty-four new corporate hospitality boxes, a new media centre, an indoor school, new practice facilities, plus new grandstands and seating enclosures.

In announcing the plans, Gerard Elias, the club's deputy chairman, said, 'Our aim is to develop a centre of excellence for cricket in Wales so that players and spectators alike can obtain the maximum benefit and enjoyment from the most popular of summer games.' Similarly, Tony Dilloway, the then director of marketing, said:

> We want to build a ground of which our members, the people of Cardiff and the whole of Wales can be proud. Glamorgan are no longer prepared to be in the shadows of county cricket. We want our light to shine brightly and allow our spectators to enjoy the best.

The signing of the lease for Sophia Gardens by Glamorgan officials and their trustees. Seated at the table are David Morgan (chairman), Tony Lewis, Wilf Wooller, Gwyn Craven and Gordon Jones.

The tennis courts at the rear of the Sophia Gardens scoreboard in the mid-1980s with the Athletic Club's rugby pitches in the rear. This is the land where the National Cricket Centre stands.

The initial plans for Stadium Sophia in 1996

Glamorgan Cricket, in partnership with various organisations including HLN Architects, devised the following for phase two of the ground development:

i) A new pavilion and media centre at the Cathedral Road End, with the complex also housing bars, hospitality suites and new retail outlets.
ii) A new, three-tiered grandstand with up to 3,000 seats, plus twenty-two hospitality suites, and public bars and restaurants.
iii) A leisure complex adjacent to the Wooller Gates with a gymnasium and other facilities.
iv) A crèche on the site of the Vice-President's Enclosure, catering both for families on match days, as well as others throughout the year.

TWENTY-FOUR

A Canterbury Tale

The promotion of Glamorgan as the truly Welsh cricket team, and Sophia Gardens as the centre of Welsh cricket, had been one of the mantras followed by Tony Lewis during his chairmanship. Others agreed that the route to success lay from within, and events on the field during the 1980s highlighted the inadequacies of an import-based strategy, with several signings from other English counties proving to be very disappointing and, in truth, a waste of money.

Nurturing the development of homegrown talent began in the late 1980s, as several Welsh-born players came to the fore through the coaching structures set up by the Welsh Cricket Association. The creation of a Glamorgan Colts team in the South Wales Cricket Association further boosted the emergence of talent, while the promotion of Glamorgan and its Welsh identity came to the fore in 1993 as a membership campaign began, with specialist help from Andersen Consulting.

With the advice of the consultants it was agreed that the vision of the club should be, 'the highly successful, widely supported, universally recognised representative of the Welsh nation at cricket.' Three core objectives were also identified, as follows:

i) To provide the opportunity and means for the Welsh nation to identify with, and express support for, Glamorgan Cricket.

ii) To strengthen and prove legitimacy for the cause of Welsh cricket by promoting Glamorgan to a constituency beyond Wales.

iii) To secure the financial well-being of Glamorgan Cricket into the medium- and long-term.

A meeting took place in the spring of 1993 at a plush London hotel, where at the top of the agenda was a simple question, 'How to achieve these targets?' The meeting, attended by leading Glamorgan officials, a group of players and advertising executives from Andersen Consulting, came up with a reduced membership package, lowered from £45 to just £15, and a membership campaign, highlighting the club's Welsh identity.

Both were promoted during a walk around Wales, as players and office staff took to the road, visiting sixty venues, attending over a dozen sports forums and arranging photo calls with local dignitaries and personalities. There were many smiles as the players, dressed in their dark blue and yellow Sunday League kit, mingled with the general public, signing autographs and handing out thousands of leaflets. But their hard work paid off, as Glamorgan's membership soared from 3,600 to 11,000 – the second highest in the country – and the club's income was boosted by £137,000.

With the promotion of homegrown talent being at the top of the priority list, there were few signings during 1992/93, but one new face proved to be invaluable, as Glamorgan acquired the services of Roland Lefebvre, the thirty year old seam bowler who had spent the previous three years with Somerset. His acquisition proved to be an inspired one as 'Roly' brought an added element of control to the county's one-day attack. He proved to be the ideal foil to Steve Watkin with the new ball throughout 1993, so much so that opposing batsmen were often frustrated by the time the off-spin of Robert Croft or the off-cutters of Steve Barwick were introduced into the attack.

The Sophia Gardens pavilion in the mid-1990s, as seen from the club offices.

Coach Alan Jones leads a fielding practice in 1991. The Cardiff Athletic Club's rugby pitch and floodlights are in the background.

Matthew Maynard on the Strategy for 1993

'Hugh's policy was to bat first if we won the toss, confident that we had the bowlers to constrict the opposition, even if we were defending a small total. Eight of the twelve victories came after we had had first knock.'

'On the four occasions when we batted second, the largest total we had to chase was 208 and with bowlers like Roly Lefebvre, Steve Barwick, Steve Watkin and Robert Croft, no one took liberties with us.'

'Anyway, we always had Viv Richards and Adrian Dale as back-up. Hugh planned the campaign with military precision, operating his bowlers in pairs, and it worked before teams got used to it the following year.'

Glamorgan's playing staff for 1991 stretch their legs in a pre-season training session at Sophia Gardens.

Matthew Maynard demonstrates his batting skills at Sophia Gardens.

Glamorgan were also able to call upon the services of Viv Richards, who had announced that 1993 would be his final summer of county cricket. Viv was eager to go out on a high and thank Glamorgan for the faith they had shown in him. It was evident from the outset that the great West Indian meant business, for in the opening game of the summer – the friendly against Oxford University at The Parks – he raced to a hundred off 94 balls and shared a rollicking partnership of 233 in just 33 overs after tea with Matthew Maynard.

It was then the turn of Sussex to be overwhelmed in the opening Championship match of the season at Sophia Gardens, with the visitors capitulating after lunch on the final day as they chased

Adrian Dale.

385 to win. Steve Watkin and Robert Croft shared seven wickets between them as Sussex were bowled out for 110, leaving Glamorgan cock-a-hoop after their opening four-day encounter. A fortnight later they were celebrating a second win, as Derbyshire were beaten by 191 runs, thanks to impressive centuries from Hugh Morris and Matthew Maynard, plus another immaculate bowling performance from Steve Watkin.

A week or so later, Glamorgan began their campaign in the AXA Equity & Law League, which had been extended to a 50-over-a-side competition for 1993. In keeping with their vision of promoting Glamorgan as a Welsh county and their membership campaign, the county's officials allocated league matches to no less than seven grounds, including Pentyrch, an outer suburb of Cardiff.

The addition of the Parc-yr-Dwrlyn ground followed a few difficulties which Glamorgan had experienced when playing at Pontypridd in the previous few years. The club had a lucrative agreement with Taff-Ely Borough Council to stage matches inside their boundaries and, fortunately, the Pentyrch ground fell inside the Taff-Ely boundaries. But the change of venue did not change Glamorgan's one-day fortunes as Northants successfully chased a target of 170 with two balls to spare.

Away victories over Yorkshire and Surrey kick-started their Sunday campaign and buoyed by their rising fortunes in the one-day game, plus their lofty position in the Championship, Glamorgan then overwhelmed Durham at the Rhos-on-Sea ground in Colwyn Bay. They won by 113 runs, with plenty of Welsh flags flying at the picturesque ground in the North Wales resort.

July 1993 then saw Glamorgan complete an emphatic 121-run victory over Middlesex, as the Welsh batsmen romped to 287-8, their highest-ever total in the competition. Steve James led the way with a career-best 94, but seven days later, against Sussex at Llanelli, he struck his maiden one-day league century. For the second week running, James shared a sizeable partnership with Hugh Morris to steer Glamorgan into a healthy position, before their accurate bowlers strangled the opposing batsmen and set up a win that took the Welsh county to the top of the table.

The Sophia Gardens scoreboard in July 1993 after the record stand by Adrian Dale and Viv Richards against Middlesex in their County Championship match.

The Best-Ever Stand at Cardiff

In early July 1993, Adrian Dale and Viv Richards each scored double-hundreds in the Championship match with Middlesex at Cardiff, with the pair sharing an unbroken stand of 425 for the fourth wicket, the highest-ever partnership in the history of the club.

As Adrian Dale later recalled, their stand helped to rebuild the innings, 'We had lost three early wickets, so at first, we played watchfully but everything soon clicked and the runs started to flow. I remember one shot in particular when Angus Fraser bowled a rare loose delivery that I hit to the boundary. Even though the ball was going for four, instinctively I set off up the wicket, only to see Viv still standing there, leaning on his bat handle. With a broad grin on his face, he said, "Don't run youngster – you spoil the shot!"

'Later on, Viv got a bit fed up with me scampering quick singles so he said to me with a wry smile, "From now on, we're only going to run easy singles down to third man or fine leg, but God willing, we'll just be dealing with fours." His words lifted my confidence and it was a great feeling to reach a double-century, and do it matching him run for run.

'At the end of our stand, Viv made a big point of letting me walk off first, and afterwards he sat in the dressing-room so proud of what we had both accomplished, but also so pleased that he had proved to the critics who had written him off that he could still do the business against a quality attack.'

County Championship

Glamorgan v. Middlesex
Sophia Gardens, Cardiff
1, 2, 3, 5 July 1993

Glamorgan won the toss and batted
Umpires: J.C. Balderstone and V.A. Holder
Result: Middlesex won by 10 wickets

Glamorgan		**first innings**			**second innings**	
S.P .James	c Carr	b Tufnell	42		b Tufnell	11
*H. Morris	c Brown	b Williams	27	c Brown	b Tufnell	14
A. Dale		not out	214	lbw	b Tufnell	14
M.P. Maynard	c Gatting	b Feltham	14	c Carr	b Tufnell	32
I.V.A.Richards		not out	224	c Carr	b Tufnell	0
P.A.Cottey					run out	15
R.D.B.Croft					not out	2
+C.P. Metson				c Gatting	b Tufnell	0
R.P. Lefebvre					b Tufnell	0
S.L. Watkin				c Carr	b Tufnell	0
S.R. Barwick				c Carr	b Emburey	1
Extras	(b4, lb13, w1, nb23)		41	(b6, lb4, nb10)		20
Total	(for 3 wickets declared)		562	(all out)		109

FOW: 1-50, 2-86, 3-137 | 1-25, 2-49, 3-62, 4-62, 5-95, 6-102, 7-102, 8-104, 9-104, 10-109

Bowling	O	M	R	W		O	M	R	W
Williams	26	5	85	1	Williams	3	0	16	0
Fraser	33	3	127	0	Fraser	3	2	2	0
Feltham	27	4	117	1	Emburey	23.2	6	52	1
Emburey	35	5	102	0	Tufnell	23	8	29	8
Tufnell	45	8	114	1					

Middlesex		**first innings**		**second innings**	
D.L. Haynes	lbw	b Watkin	73	not out	50
M.A. Roseberry	c Cottey	b Watkin	58	not out	31
J.E. Emburey		b Dale	123		
*M.W. Gatting		b Lefebvre	173		
M.R. Ramprakash	c Morris	b Dale	4		
J.D. Carr	c Croft	b Watkin	18		
+K.R. Brown	not	out	88		
M.A. Feltham	lbw	b Watkin	0		
N.F. Williams		b Croft	21		
A.R.C. Fraser	c Dale	b Croft	5		
P.C.R. Tufnell	c and	b Croft	5		
Extras	(b9, lb5, nb2)		16	(b 4, lb 3)	7
TOTAL	(all out)		584	(for 0 wickets)	88

FOW: 1-22, 2-135, 3-397, 4-441, 5-441, 6-493, 7-493, 8-561, 9-575, 10-584

Bowling	O	M	R	W		O	M	R	W
Watkin	31	4	87	4	Watkin	2	0	7	0
Lefebvre	30	8	72	1	Barwick	3	0	9	0
Barwick	44	14	131	0	Croft	8.4	2	45	0
Croft	54	9	174	3	Richards	6	0	20	0
Dale	22	6	55	2					
Richards	13	1	51	0					

It had been a good week for the club, a few days before they had also reached the quarter-final of the NatWest Trophy, having recorded a comprehensive second-round win over Durham at Cardiff. Their reward was a quarter-final tie against Worcestershire at Swansea and the resultant capacity crowd, which thronged into the St Helen's ground in mid-July, saw Glamorgan record a 104-run win and a place in the semi-final for the first time since 1977.

The club's fine form in both the one-day and four-day games meant that there was a definite buzz whenever Glamorgan were playing, and wherever the club played there was always a decent and partisan crowd, eager to cheer on Hugh Morris and his men. Morale was, therefore, sky high as the Glamorgan players made their way to Hove for the NatWest Trophy semi-final against Sussex on 11 August.

A veritable army of Welsh supporters also made the journey down to the South Coast with everyone hoping that the contest would end with the Welsh side securing a fairytale cup final at Lord's in Viv Richards' last summer. The game proved to be a turning point in the season, as Sussex won by 3 wickets, leaving the Glamorgan players to rue missed opportunities. The defeat at Hove could have had major implications on previous Glamorgan teams, but not the Glamorgan side of 1993, which had matured into an older and wiser unit. As a result of the Hove match and after acquiring an almost addictive winning habit in the Sunday League, they were eager to return to winning ways.

Captains Hugh Morris and Graham Gooch shelter under an umbrella as rain ruins the Sunday League encounter between Glamorgan and Essex at Sophia Gardens in September 1993.

The Vice-Presidents' Enclosure alongside the pavilion in the early 1990s.

This unified purpose was very evident as they swiftly put the disappointments of the semi-final defeat behind them the following weekend at Leicester, bouncing back with an eight-run victory which returned Glamorgan to the top of the table, ahead of Kent, with whom they competed with to win the league all the way to the final month of the season.

All Washed Out

There have been several occasions in the past when the River Taff has burst its banks during the winter months, spilling water over the Arms Park ground, Sophia Gardens and into Bute Park.

The last great flood came in 1979 when the cricket pitch at Sophia Gardens was inundated, as well as other areas of Riverside, Llandaff and Pontcanna. The aftermath of this flood was to see the implementation of a flood alleviation scheme on both the west and east banks of the river by the City Council, with raised levees, gabions being installed into the river banks and a deeper channel being dredged.

While flooding can be controlled, heavy rain cannot be stopped, and May 1981 saw the abandonment of Glamorgan's Championship match at Cardiff with Gloucestershire. No play was possible on any of the three days. In 2008 torrential rain left the Cardiff ground in a saturated state leading to the abandonment of the four-day contest with Worcestershire.

One match was also lost to the elements at the Arms Park and that was the three-day contest in late August 1924 against Somerset.

It looked like being a nail-biting end to the Sunday season, as Essex travelled to Sophia Gardens on 12 September, as Kent – who Glamorgan were due to meet the following weekend in the final game of the season – had gone clear by two points after beating Northants the previous weekend. Kent, however, were not involved over that weekend and 4,000 extra seats were installed at the Cardiff ground in anticipation of a bumper crowd. The contest was reduced to something of a damp squib, as rain forced the match to be abandoned with Essex on 7-2. But the two points allowed Glamorgan to move level with Kent and all concerned travelled to Canterbury the following weekend for a head-to-head to decide the outcome of the title.

19 September 1993 proved to be a historic day for Hugh Morris's side, as they completed a thrilling victory, but only after some heart-stopping moments at the St Lawrence ground, which had been buzzing with Welsh voices since early in the morning. Kent won the toss on a slow, low pitch and were given a brisk start by a few lusty blows from Matthew Fleming. But the Glamorgan bowlers kept the home batsmen in check, with Steve Watkin and Roland Lefebvre inducing a late-order collapse that saw Kent lose their last five wickets for 14 runs, leaving Glamorgan a target of 201.

Alan Igglesden soon raised Kent's spirits by removing Steve James with just six runs on the board, but Hugh Morris and Adrian Dale skilfully saw off the new ball in a second-wicket stand of 78, before both fell attempting to force the pace. Viv Richards then came in to a spontaneous and emotional standing ovation from the crowd of 12,000 and, after the departure of Matthew Maynard, Tony Cottey came in to keep Glamorgan's hopes alive.

The scriptwriters still had a few tricks up their sleeve, as Richards was firstly hit on the chest by Duncan Spencer – Kent's Anglo-Australian pace bowler – and then the West Indian was caught off a bouncer. It looked as if Spencer had dealt a match-winning blow, but the umpire called no-ball to a massive roar of delight from the Welsh supporters, and Richards remained at the crease.

This was the defining moment of an enthralling contest, as from this point onwards, everything went in Glamorgan's favour and Kentish spirits started to wilt. The pair duly added 60 in ten overs, as Cottey struck the winning runs by top-edging Spencer high over the head of wicketkeeper Steve Marsh. As the ball sped to the boundary, the two Glamorgan batsmen ran off, punching the air with sheer delight. It was not long before the champagne corks were popping in the Glamorgan dressing room, while Viv was overcome with emotion, with tears flowing down his cheeks as his adopted county celebrated their first silverware since 1969.

There was a buoyant mood in Glamorgan's ranks at the end-of-year celebrations. The club now had their first one-day title, plus a membership list at record levels and within two years, they were able to start work on their impressive new headquarters in the Welsh captial city.

A delighted Viv Richards lifts the Sunday League trophy at Canterbury in 1993.

TWENTY-FIVE

Champion County 1997

The winter of 1996/97 saw the energetic officials from Glamorgan Cricket take further steps in securing financial support for their ground-development scheme at Sophia Gardens. In addition, moves were taken to develop the on-field activities, especially capturing the services of another high-profile overseas player, who the club believed, would help secure further silverware as Viv Richards had done in 1993.

A top quality overseas bowler was at the top of the club's shopping list and in the autumn of 1996, terms were agreed with Waqar Younis, the experienced Pakistani Test bowler and one of the world's finest exponents of reverse swing. Having played with some success for Surrey between 1990 and 1993, Waqar was very interested in resuming his county career, and despite lucrative offers from other counties, he liked the idea of living and playing away from London and the glare of publicity that it brought.

His signing proved to be a masterstroke, as Matthew Maynard and his team enjoyed a wonderful summer, winning the Championship title for the third time in the club's history, and coming within one wicket of reaching a Lord's final for the second time. Their outstanding form in both the longer and shorter forms of the game dispelled any lingering doubts that Glamorgan were not an ambitious club, with grand plans both on and off the field.

The presence of Waqar meant that there was a real buzz in the club at the start of the season, and a superb double century by Hugh Morris in the opening Championship match, against Warwickshire at Cardiff, was further confirmation of the buoyant mood in the Glamorgan camp. A fortnight later, they recorded their first victory of the summer by beating Kent at Canterbury, before returning to Sophia Gardens at the end of May and completely overwhelming Durham. The carnage began with Steve James hitting a century before lunch and sharing an opening stand of 229 with Hugh Morris, who also made a hundred. Matthew Maynard then applied the coup de grâce with the third century of the innings and laid the foundation for an innings victory.

These early victories saw Glamorgan move to the top of the county table, but ten days later they were given a reality check in their next match at Sophia Gardens, as Middlesex's bowlers bundled out the Welsh batsmen after lunch on the third day for 31 – the fourth-lowest total in Glamorgan's history – with Jamie Hewitt taking a career-best 6-14. But normal service was immediately restored, as in their next Championship match at Liverpool, Lancashire, chasing a target of 273 from 60 overs, were dismissed for 51 in the space of fourteen dramatic overs. Waqar took 7-25, including a hat-trick; the first by a Glamorgan bowler in the Championship for twenty-nine years.

If anyone still had any doubts about Glamorgan's title aspirations, they were quickly erased in the back-to-back Championship matches at Swansea, as Glamorgan defeated Gloucestershire by ten wickets and Sussex by 234 runs, with the latter dismissed for 54. Waqar again took on a starring role as he fully exploited the damp conditions to end with figures of 8-17. By early July, the county were also enjoying a good run in the NatWest Trophy, beating Bedfordshire by seven wickets and then defeating Hampshire by two wickets at Southampton to secure a quarter-final tie with Yorkshire at Cardiff.

It proved to be a real cliffhanger of a match as Glamorgan, chasing a target of 237, had a mid-innings wobble as they lost seven wickets for 69 runs, including captain Maynard who was suffering from chicken-pox. When last man Dean Cosker, the nineteen year old spin bowler, joined Waqar at the crease, 28 runs were still needed, and many thought that Glamorgan's one-day bubble had burst.

Waqar Younis.

But Waqar then had a moment of good fortune as he survived a sharp chance to Michael Vaughan, and, drawing on all of his international experience, the Pakistani farmed the strike against Darren Gough and Craig White, with Cosker showing great maturity as the tenth-wicket pair scrambled the winning runs amid great excitement.

National Westminster Bank Trophy (Quarter-Final)

Glamorgan v. Yorkshire
Sophia Gardens, Cardiff
29 July 1997 (60-over match)
Yorkshire won the toss and decided to bat
Result: Glamorgan won by 1 wicket
Umpires: B. Dudleston, T.E. Jesty

Yorkshire		**first innings**	
M.D. Moxon	c Shaw	b Cosker	34
M.P. Vaughan		b Cosker	22
P.J. Hartley	c Morris	b Cosker	3
*D. Byas	lbw	b Croft	5
D.S. Lehmann	c James	b Waqar	105
C. White	c Shaw	b Watkin	21
A. McGrath	lbw	b Croft	11
+R.J. Blakey		not out	20
D. Gough		b Thomas	4
C.E.W. Silverwood			
R.D. Stemp			
Extras	(6lb, 5w)		11
Total	(8 wickets, 60 overs)		236
FOW:	1-57, 2-61, 3-66, 4-72, 5-127, 6-176, 7-229, 8-236		

Bowling	O	M	R	W
Waqar	12	1	58	1
Watkin	12	2	38	1
Thomas	8	0	44	1
Croft	12	0	45	2
Cosker	12	3	26	3
Cottey	1	0	6	0
Dale	3	0	13	0

Glamorgan		**first innings**	
R.D.B. Croft		b Gough	55
H. Morris	lbw	b Hartley	7
A. Dale	c Byas	b Hartley	6
*M.P. Maynard	c White	b Gough	62
P.A. Cottey		run out	5
S.P. James	lbw	b Gough	0
+A.D. Shaw	lbw	b White	10
S.D. Thomas	lbw	b Vaughan	13
Waqar Younis		not out	34
S.L. Watkin		b Gough	1
D.A. Cosker		not out	3
Extras	(1b, 15lb, 14nb, 11w)		41
Total	(9 wickets, 59 overs)		237
FOW:	1-28, 2-38, 3-140, 4-155, 5-155, 6-174, 7-177, 8-190, 9-209		

Bowling	O	M	R	W
Gough	12	3	36	4
Silverwood	5	0	36	0
Hartley	12	0	49	2
Stemp	12	4	35	0
Vaughan	5	0	17	1
White	12	0	43	1
Lehmann	1	0	5	0

Dean Cosker on 'The Waqar Effect'

Dean Cosker recalls his amazing partnership with Waqar Younis in one of the most thrilling one-day games ever seen at Sophia Gardens:

'This was one of my first big one-day county games. The atmosphere and the crowd were great and I just thrived on the adrenalin out there. I took three wickets when the Yorkies batted – one of these was Martyn Moxon and getting him out gave me great confidence, which I was to need later in the day batting with Waqar.

'I didn't feel too nervous because when you are out there you just rely on your instincts. Waqar was so cool under pressure. He kept talking to me all the time – his words to me were: "Keep taking the run rate down, watch the ball and don't get out." Coming from one of the legends of the game, you try and listen. I survived a shout for lbw off Gough as the ball started reversing a great deal, but when Chris Silverwood bowled a wide, we had won a quite remarkable game!'

Dean Cosker.

Tony Cottey practices on the Sophia Gardens outfield in 1997.

Glamorgan's prize was a semi-final encounter with Essex at Chelmsford – a game that contained much tension and a few sparks of controversy after Steve James anchored the innings with a fine century. Chasing a target of 302, Essex quickly raced to 157-1 at tea and with Stuart Law in imperious form, it looked as if the home team would romp to a comfortable victory. Steve Watkin then dismissed Darren Robinson and Nasser Hussain, before Darren Thomas took 4-14 from 19 balls as Essex's batting disintegrated in the fading light.

Maynard then called Waqar back into the attack, with Essex still needing six runs with two wickets in hand and 42 balls remaining. By now it was 8.10 p.m. and the light was very gloomy, so after just a single delivery from the Pakistani, the umpires took the players off the field. The match then resumed the following morning with Waqar completing his over, before Thomas struck again with his first delivery, leaving Peter Such, the number eleven, to hit the winning runs amid mounting tension.

Glamorgan then got back into winning ways in the Championship with a six-wicket victory over Northamptonshire at Abergavenny. With four games remaining, both Surrey and Kent were in the title hunt along with the Welsh county. Every match and every bonus point became vital as Glamorgan maintained their title quest. The weather then intervened at Leicester, before Glamorgan drew with Surrey at The Oval, a result that extinguished Surrey's title ambitions. Welsh joy was short lived, as news came through that Kent had defeated Gloucestershire to leapfrog Glamorgan and go twelve points clear at the top of the table.

Maynard's team returned to Sophia Gardens knowing that they now needed maximum points and a win in their next match against Essex. Everything seemed to be going to plan,as Essex were forced to follow-on, but Ronnie Irani and Paul Grayson then staged a fightback, leaving Glamorgan a target of 149. The nerve ends were jangling in the Cardiff dressing room as Glamorgan slumped to 26-3, but up stepped Tony Cottey, who shared a defiant and match-winning stand with his captain.

Building work progresses in the autumn of 1998 on the National Cricket Centre.

The new scoreboard and River Stand under construction in the late 1990s.

There was further good news when it was confirmed that Kent had drawn with Yorkshire, leaving the massive crowd at the Cardiff ground to celebrate and plan how they would travel to Taunton the following week to watch the title decider with Somerset. It was a match in which Glamorgan knew that a victory and maximum points would be enough to bring the Championship pennant back to Wales for the first time since 1969. But their plans were hit soon after arriving in Taunton, as Waqar was struck down with a throat infection. Despite feeling ill and having a high temperature, he ventured onto the field and played a role as Somerset were dismissed for 252. Hugh Morris and Matthew Maynard then put on a vintage display of batting, adding 235 in 41 overs, as Glamorgan secured a 275-run lead.

News then filtered through about Kent's healthy progress against Surrey, leaving Glamorgan's bowlers knowing that the ball was in their court to win the county title. Darren Thomas then delivered one of the most important spells of his career and, together with the ever-reliable Steve Watkin, they reduced Somerset to 166-7. Graham Rose and Andy Caddick briefly mounted a rearguard action, but once they were parted, the Somerset innings soon ended, leaving Glamorgan needing 11 runs to win. Steve James and Hugh Morris – in his final innings for the county before joining the E.C.B. – then knocked off the winning runs, leaving the jubilant Glamorgan supporters celebrating another Championship title.

A week or so later, the Glamorgan squad went on an open-top bus tour around the streets of central Cardiff, followed a few days later by both a celebratory party in a specially erected marquee on the outfield at Sophia Gardens and a grand dinner at Cardiff City Hall. At both functions, a minute's silence was observed to mark the passing earlier in the year of Wilf Wooller, the club's *éminence grise* and the spiritual backbone of the county since the Second World War. It was a poignant and fitting tribute to a man who even in his final year, had still popped into the Glamorgan dressing room with a few words of advice on field placing and tactics. No doubt, the great skipper was looking down on Cardiff as the celebrations moved into full swing.

But the club which had meant so much to him were not just celebrating the county title, because a few days earlier, the final paperwork had been completed with the Athletic Club for the takeover of the Sophia Gardens ground. There was further good news when outline planning permission was secured for the ground-development plan, followed by the £4.1 million of funding needed for the first phase, the National Cricket Centre – including a seven-lane indoor school and an administration block on the site of the former scorebox at the Cathedral Road end of the ground.

The lion's share of the funding came from a £3.25 million grant from Sportslot – their first major award to a sporting project in Wales – supplemented by a £250,000 grant from the Sports Ground Initiative to improve spectator seating, plus a Lord's Taverners grant, sponsorship and a generous donation of £100,000 by an anonymous premier member.

Full planning permission then followed in November 1997 from Cardiff City Council, enabling Glamorgan to finalise their agreements with Hyder Consultants and Amey Building Ltd for the building of the National Cricket Centre from May 1998. The new complex, which would be completed in time for the 1999 World Cup, marked the start of a glorious new chapter in Glamorgan's history.

The Opening of the National Cricket Centre

The National Cricket Centre was formally opened on 5 July 1999 by Matthew Maynard and Hugh Morris, who was now the technical director of the E.C.B., and was overseeing the creation of several centres of excellence. The county's former opening batsman was delighted with the new facility:

'This is a fantastic project that not just Glamorgan but the whole of Wales can be proud of. I'm really delighted to see the quality of the new facilities at Cardiff. It makes such a difference to have good practice facilities, both under cover and outdoors.

'I can still remember one of my first days at Glamorgan when West Indian Ezra Moseley began bowling on the artificial wicket that we used to net on out on the edge of the square. Ezra was rather quick and the first ball he pitched on a length went past the nose of the young left-handed opener Mark Davies. You knew then that you were in for a tough time and that was no way to build confidence or improve technique.'

TWENTY-SIX

World Cup Highs and Another Visit to Lord's

1999 saw Glamorgan prepare for the first time in their own indoor centre at the Cardiff ground, and with a centre manager having been appointed, it was not long before a host of coaching programmes began for cricketers of all ages, sexes and backgrounds, as the new complex at Sophia Gardens became a centre of excellence for Welsh cricket.

In the last week of April, the Australian World Cup squad also arrived at Cardiff, where they were scheduled to be based for their warm-up prior to the 1999 competition. A series of special events were also held, including a coaching session for talented players from Cardiff and the Vale of Glamorgan, as well as a grand dinner, which gave Glamorgan the opportunity to say thank you to all of their financial supporters inside the new National Cricket Centre.

Stadium Sophia: a Player's Views on the Ground Development

Darren Thomas was one of many Glamorgan players to pass favourable comments about the new facilities as they prepared for the new season. 'It was lovely to see the club going forward with the development of the ground,' said the all-rounder. 'Back in the mid-1990s, our pre-season preparations used to consist of indoor nets at Neath followed by runs around The Gnoll, but the creation of the National Cricket Centre gave us indoor nets and a multigym. All in all, the development of the ground brought a more professional look to the club on and off the pitch and gone are the days that Glamorgan was considered an old-fashioned club.'

The Australians warm-up programme also included a one-day match with Glamorgan, and with temporary grandstands ringing the boundary, a massive crowd was expected. However, only ten overs were possible before the heavens opened, leaving the umpires the formality of abandoning the match at 2.15 p.m. Fortunately, the weather was set fair two weeks later when the Sophia Gardens ground, and it's impressive new facilities, hosted the World Cup group match between Australia and New Zealand.

The game saw the Kiwis turn the form book upside down as they defeated Australia by five wickets. Only Darren Lehmann and Ricky Ponting looked at ease against a vibrant New Zealand attack for whom Geoff Allott took four wickets to keep the competition favourites in check. Chasing a target of 214 in their 50 overs, New Zealand slipped to 49-4, before Roger Twose and Chris Cairns turned the game on its head with a fifth-wicket stand of 148 to see the Black Caps to a comfortable win, with Twose winning the Man of the Match award for his forthright and unbeaten 80.

ICC World Cup, 1999
Australia v. New Zealand, Group B
Sophia Gardens, Cardiff
20 May 1999 (50-over match)
Australia won the toss and decided to bat
Result: New Zealand won by 5 wickets
Umpires: Javed Akhtar, D.R. Shepherd
Third umpire: R.E. Koertzen
Referee: R. Subba Row
Man of the match: R.G. Twose

Australia		**first innings**	
M.E. Waugh	lbw	b Allott	2
+A.C. Gilchrist	c Astle	b Allott	14
R.T. Ponting	c Harris	b Astle	47
D.S. Lehmann	c Astle	b Harris	76
*S.R. Waugh	c Astle	b Harris	7
M.G. Bevan		b Allott	21
S. Lee		run out (Nash)	2
S.K. Warne		b Allott	15
D.W. Fleming		not out	8
A.C. Dale		not out	3
G.D. McGrath			
Extras	(10lb, 3nb, 5w)		18
Total	(8 wickets, 50 overs)		213
FOW:	1-7, 2-32, 3-126, 4-149, 5-172, 6-175, 7-192, 8-204		

Bowling	O	M	R	W
Allott	10	0	37	4
Nash	8	1	30	0
Cairns	7	0	44	0
Larsen	10	2	26	0
Harris	10	0	50	2
Astle	5	0	16	1

New Zealand		**first innings**	
M.J. Horne	c Gilchrist	b Dale	5
N.J. Astle	c Ponting	b Fleming	4
C.D. McMillan	c Fleming	b Warne	29
*S.P. Fleming		b McGrath	9
R.G. Twose		not out	80
C.L. Cairns	c Dale	b Fleming	60
+A.C. Parore		not out	10
C.Z. Harris			
D.J. Nash			
G.R. Larsen			
G.I. Allott			
Extras	(2lb, 4nb, 11w)		17
Total	(5 wickets)		214
FOW:	1-5, 2-21, 3-47, 4-49, 5-197		

Bowling	O	M	R	W
Fleming	8.2	1	43	2
Dale	5	1	18	1
McGrath	9	0	43	1
Lee	6	0	24	0
Warne	10	1	44	1
S.R. Waugh	4	0	25	0
Bevan	3	0	15	0

Inside the National Cricket Centre as it nears completion in the late summer of 1998.

Building work continues on the National Cricket Centre at the end of the 1998 summer.

It was the turn of Cardiff to play host to the Rugby World Cup six months later, as during October and November the W.R.U. staged the world's premier competition, with the final being played at the impressively redeveloped Millennium Stadium. It came about following the rebuilding of the National Stadium and the creation of the massive indoor stadium – at the time the world's largest with 74,500 seats – which was established on the site of the former Arms Park rugby ground.

The Millennium Stadium

Having won the right to host the Rugby World Cup in 1999, the W.R.U. took the bold decision to update the National Stadium, which could only accommodate 53,000 and create a modern, multi-purpose, state-of-the-art building with a portable pitch under a retractable roof – the first in a British sporting stadium.

The scheme cost £126 million, funded by the National Lottery, ticket debentures and loans. Demolition work began immediately after the last game in the old stadium on 26 April 1997 as Cardiff defeated Swansea in the SWALEC W.R.U. Cup, and just over two years later, the first match at the new sporting venue took place on 26 June 1999, when Wales recorded their first-ever victory over South Africa, in a partially completed stadium. By October 1999, the Millennium Stadium was ready in time for the launch of Rugby World Cup, and with the redeveloped of Wembley Stadium, a series of F.A. Cup Finals were allocated to Cardiff's new stadium from 2001.

In addition, to rugby and football, the Millennium Stadium has also played host to other major sporting events including the Rugby League Challenge Cup final, Grand Prix speedway, World Rally Championships, World Championship boxing and indoor cricket, as well as a variety of musical events and concerts. The stadium, situated in the heart of the thriving city, acts as a highly visible statement about the importance of sport in the life of Cardiff and Wales.

The Millennium Stadium, seen from the western bank of the River Taff.

The tented village across the outfield during the 1999 Rugby World Cup.

The square recovers during the spring of 2000 after being under cover for the previous autumn's Rugby World Cup.

After lengthy negotiations, Sophia Gardens was also used for 1999 Rugby World Cup, with a huge tented village laid out over the square and the immediate surrounds so that the competition's sponsors could entertain their many corporate guests. Precautions were taken to protect the cricket pitch but, as Len Smith, Glamorgan's groundsman, and his team started their preparations for the 2000 season, they found, to their horror, that the huge marquee had caused the grass to wither.

For a while it looked as if lasting damage had been caused to the pitch, which Smith and his team had taken great efforts to improve – work which had been recognised by the E.C.B. with several awards. The groundstaff's work had significantly improved the Cardiff wickets, for so long described as slow and low. However, as Allott's performance in the World Cup fixture had shown, there was now decent pace and carry in the surface.

As the Glamorgan players and their new coach Jeff Hammond gathered at Cardiff for their pre-season training, it looked as if the club had been dealt another hammer blow, even before the first ball had been bowled. But after the removal of the deadgrass and roots, the whole square was re-seeded, while compacted areas of soil were removed. This significantly improved the aeration of the square and thanks to the hard work of the ground staff, the damage was repaired and the wickets were ready by the time Matthew Maynard and his team began their season in the resurrected zonal rounds of the Benson & Hedges Cup.

They began with a rain-affected contest against Gloucestershire, and despite being shortened to 25 overs, this game set the pattern and established the tactics upon which Glamorgan reached Lord's for the first time since 1977. After Gloucestershire had been restricted to 148-6, Robert Croft and Matthew Elliott launched the Welsh reply with a brisk opening partnership of 59, with Croft acting as a pinch-hitter and exploiting the early fielding restrictions.

Further victories saw Glamorgan finish on top of their group, and gain a home quarter-final tie with Hampshire. Much was made in the media in the days leading up to the match at Cardiff about the damage caused by the rugby marquee. After winning the toss, visiting captain Robin Smith seemed to be wary of batting first on the surface, and asked Glamorgan to bat hoping that his bowlers could exploit the overcast conditions and any gremlins in the wicket. Peter Hartley and Dimitri Mascarenhas then reduced Glamorgan to 31-3, but Adrian Dale and Keith Newell counter-attacked with a partnership of 99 to take Glamorgan to 182-6.

The Glamorgan bowlers then ripped through the visitor's top order with Steve Watkin and Owen Parkin bowling a superb spell with the new ball, both men giving the Hampshire batsmen little width and forcing them to take chances in order to score runs. The visitors subsided to 15-5 as Parkin finished with figures of 8-4-16-3, while Watkin had the remarkable analysis of 7-5-3-2 as Glamorgan completed a comprehensive victory by 113 runs.

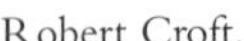
Robert Croft.

Owen Parkin.

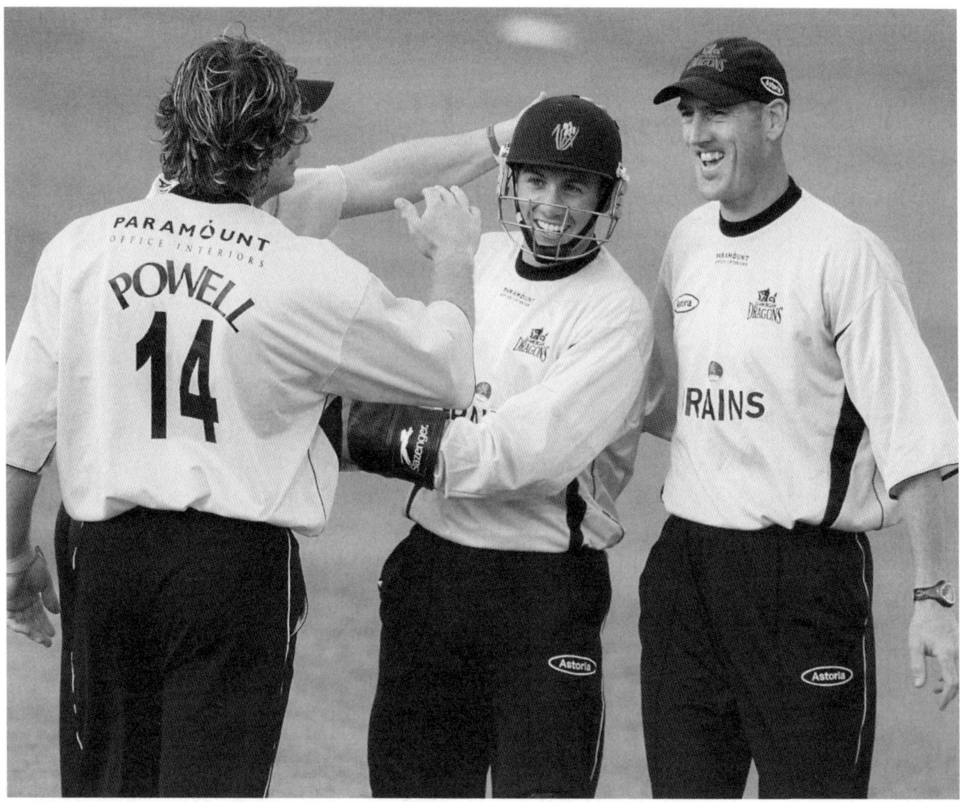

Matthew Elliott *(right)* joins in with the congratulations to Mark Wallace with Mike Powell and Ian Thomas.

The Mighty Daffodil!

As the crowd assembled under the pavilion balcony at Sophia Gardens after the quarter-final victory over Hampshire, the victorious Glamorgan team gathered in their dressing room and gave a loud rendition of their new team song – a concept introduced by Matthew Elliott with the lyrics penned by Owen Parkin to the tune of *Glory Glory Man United* sung by the football supporters at Old Trafford:

Over the Severn and down to the Taff,
like lambs to the slaughter, they take on the Daff.
Now do they know how hard the Welsh we fight,
as they trudge back to England beaten out of sight!

We are Glamorgan, dragons you and me,
together we stand as the pride of Cymru,
We play to conquer , we play to thrill,
We play for the glory of the mighty daffodil.'

Glamorgan's reward was their first semi-final in the competition for twelve years, and a home tie with Surrey. With ten international cricketers in their ranks, the visitors were the firm favourites before the start of the contest, but Matthew Maynard's team turned the tables on their illustrious opponents with another confident all-round display, and another superlative display of batting by the Welsh county's leader.

Benson & Hedges Cup Semi-Final

Glamorgan v. Surrey
Sophia Gardens, Cardiff
27, 28 May 2000

Glamorgan won the toss and batted
Umpires: D.J. Constant and J.W. Holder
TV Umpire: V.A. Holder
Man of the Match: M.P. Maynard
Result: Glamorgan won by 32 runs (D/L Method)

Glamorgan		**first innings**	
R.D.B. Croft	c and	b Tudor	1
M.T.G. Elliott		b Bicknell	6
M.J. Powell		b Tudor	67
*M.P. Maynard	c Salisbury	b A.J. Hollioake	109
A. Dale		run out	25
S.P. James		not out	10
K. Newell		b A.J. Hollioake	6
A.G. Wharf		run out	0
+A.D. Shaw		b. A.J. Hollioake	0
S.L. Watkin		run out	1
O.T. Parkin		run out	0
Extras	(lb14, w10, nb2)		26
Total	(all out)		251
FOW:	1-3, 2-27,3-160, 4-226,5-231, 6-241, 7-250, 8-250, 9-251		

Bowling	O	M	R	W
Bicknell	10	0	40	1
Tudor	10	2	46	2
B.C. Hollioake	7.1	0	49	0
Ratcliffe	7	0	26	0
Salisbury	8	0	40	0
A.J. Hollioake	7	0	36	3

Surrey		**first innings**	
M.A. Butcher	st Shaw	b Croft	32
A.D. Brown	c Elliott	b Parkin	0
A.J. Tudor	lbw	b Parkin	0
+A.J. Stewart	c James	b Parkin	85
G.P. Thorpe		b Wharf	21
*A.J. Hollioake	lbw	b Wharf	1
B.C. Hollioake	c Newell	b Wharf	4
I.J. Ward		b Croft	2
J.D. Ratcliffe	c Dale	b Croft	24
M.P. Bicknell	c James	b Parkin	25
I.D.K. Salisbury		not out	0
Extras	(lb 13, w 5)		18
Total	(all out)		212
FOW:	1-11, 2-11, 3-65, 4-101, 5-105, 6-121, 7-125, 8-170, 9-201		

Bowling	O	M	R	W
Parkin	8	0	60	4
Watkin	9	0	30	0
Wharf	9	0	37	3
Dale	7	0	30	0
Croft	10	0	42	3

Persistent rain during the build-up to the game, and then again on the Saturday morning, meant that play was delayed until 4 p.m., and in the 24.1 overs that were possible, Glamorgan reached 99-2 when play was called off for the day. The following day, Maynard and Mike Powell resumed their partnership with both men playing responsibly, adding 133 in 27 overs before the Glamorgan captain was dismissed for 109. The value of his innings was then highlighted as his side collapsed, losing their last six wickets for 25 runs.

With Surrey's impressive line-up, it seemed as if the hard work of Powell and Maynard might have all been in vain, but Owen Parkin once again made early breakthroughs, dismissing Alistair Brown and Alex Tudor. Mark Butcher and Alec Stewart then restored Surrey's fortunes before Butcher fell to a superb stumping by Adrian Shaw off Robert Croft's clever spin bowling – a feat the Glamorgan wicketkeeper was to repeat a few days later in Glamorgan's tourist match against the West Indians when Shaw stumped the illustrious Brian Lara.

Alex Wharf then bowled perhaps the most decisive spell of the contest, ripping the heart out of Surrey's middle-order by dismissing Adam and Ben, the Hollioake brothers, as well as Graham Thorpe, the England middle-order batsman. After another interruption for rain, Alec Stewart and the tail tried to engineer a late rally, but Parkin still had three overs up his sleeve and he returned to finish things off.

Mike Powell who shared a vital partnership with Matthew Maynard in the semi-final against Surrey.

Alex Wharf.

When Steve James held onto a lobbed drive from Martin Bicknell, Glamorgan had won by 32 runs under the Duckworth-Lewis method, and their victory was accompanied by scenes of sheer euphoria as the players gathered on the balcony of the Cardiff pavilion, while below their ecstatic supporters celebrated as if the cup had been lifted.

For the next few weeks, cricket enthusiasts and sports fans all over South Wales started to make their arrangements for 12 June and the match against Gloucestershire. 'Daffodil Day' duly saw over 15,000 Welsh supporters descend from far and wide as Lord's became more like Cardiff Arms Park for a rugby international. All were hopeful that this would be the day when Matthew Maynard would take a piece of silverware back to Wales, from the very heart of English cricket, and it seemed as if the script was going according to plan as Maynard won the toss and then scored a superb century – the first man to score a hundred in both the semi-final and final of a knockout competition.

But once again, apart from Michael Powell, none of the other Glamorgan batsmen were able to give Maynard further support, as their innings fell away with the bowling of Australian all-rounder Ian Harvey strangling the lower order. Maynard was run out in the final over with Glamorgan finishing on 225.

Even Glamorgan's most fervent supporters knew in their heart of hearts that their side had finished twenty or thirty runs short of a decent score, and so it proved as after a rollicking first wicket stand by Gloucestershire's openers, captain Mark Alleyne and Matt Windows shared a brisk partnership of 95 in 17 overs to see their side to victory by seven wickets – their third successive win in a one-day final. However, it was Maynard who was the unanimous choice as Man of the Match after his vintage display of cultured strokeplay, though the Glamorgan captain would have been delighted to have swapped 99 or so of his runs for a Glamorgan victory and a piece of silverware. However, it was not long before the gifted batsman was helping Glamorgan to win a one-day title and starting to stock the trophy cabinet at the club's newly developed ground at Cardiff.

TWENTY-SEVEN

More Titles, Plus a Victory for Wales

2001 and 2002 saw Glamorgan achieve a unique feat by firstly winning the Second Division of the Norwich Union League, and then securing the First Division title of the one-day league with a number of thrilling one-day contests being staged by the Welsh county at Sophia Gardens, with the side being led by Steve James, who had taken over the captaincy from Matthew Maynard.

The acquisition of Jimmy Maher, the captain of Queensland, had given the Welsh county another forthright top-order batsman, and the Australian displayed his skills with an assertive 94 from just 76 balls as Glamorgan posted a mammoth total of 305-6, their highest-ever score in one-day cricket, in the contest with Worcestershire at Sophia Gardens. With Robert Croft in canny mode with the ball, the visiting batsmen were never in the hunt, as Glamorgan recorded a morale-boosting win by 111 runs to consolidate their promotion bid.

In mid-August the Glamorgan Dragons added the scalps of the Essex Eagles to their tally on a perfect batting wicket at Cardiff. Keith Newell (who had joined the Welsh county from Sussex) and Robert Croft were both in awesome form with the bat, with both batsmen scoring attractive half-centuries. After a late flurry from Mike Powell, Glamorgan reached 289-6, before Andrew Davies tore into the heart of the Eagles batting, with the young swing bowler taking 5-39 to set up a comprehensive victory by 178 runs, keeping James's team in the top three of the table.

At the end of the month, the Dragons took on the Durham Dynamos, who were top of the table, in another exciting match at Sophia Gardens. For the fifth time in the summer, the Dragons batsmen topped 250, with Maher and Maynard sharing a quick-fire stand of 71 for the fifth wicket. Nicky Peng, the young Durham opener, then took the attack to the Glamorgan bowlers, but he received limited support, and when Peng was caught by Maher off Dean Cosker for 92, Durham's run chase ended as Glamorgan gained a vital win to take them to the top of the Division Two table.

Two days later, Glamorgan secured promotion into Division One after another vintage display of batting from Matthew Maynard in the day-night encounter against the Hampshire Hawks at Cardiff. Floodlit cricket had been a popular innovation at the Cardiff ground in 2000, with the inaugural match against Essex being played in front of a full house at the club's headquarters. The prospect of seeing the Dragons gain promotion attracted another capacity crowd to Sophia Gardens for the match against the Hawks. Maynard duly responded to the packed stands with an audacious century, reviving memories of his batting at Lord's the previous year – and all after the side had slipped to 55-4.

Maynard took the game by the scruff of the neck as he struck an unbeaten 116 – his fourteenth one-day century for the county and a new Glamorgan record – and shared a 92-run partnership in just 12 overs with Adrian Dale, which put Glamorgan back into the ascendancy. Robert Croft then claimed 4-33 as the Hawks tried to chase the target of 245. Once Croft had removed Neil Johnson, their overseas batsman, the target was out of the Hawks' reach, and Glamorgan cruised to a 51-run victory. This win took the side four points clear of both Durham and Worcestershire at the top of the table.

It proved to be a decisive victory as the next week Durham defeated Worcestershire to end their title aspirations and – despite the Dragons losing to the Sussex Sharks at Hove – Glamorgan were confirmed as champions of Division Two. The following week, the Dragons were formally presented with their trophy after their match at Sophia Gardens with the Middlesex Crusaders.

Keith Newell hits the ball for four.

Andrew Davies dismisses Hampshire's Sean Ervine in a floodlit match at Sophia Gardens in 2004.

The match with Middlesex was also the final appearance in Glamorgan's colours of Steve Watkin who had been appointed as director of the newly created cricket academy, based at the National Cricket Centre at the Sophia Gardens ground, and it brought an end to a season which had also seen Glamorgan stage their second one-day international, with Australia playing Pakistan in a NatWest Series match on 9 June.

Byron Denning: the Greatest Scorer at Sophia Gardens

Tragically, the match against Middlesex at Sophia Gardens was the final game for another vital member of Glamorgan's set-up: their loyal and popular scorer Byron Denning died just six weeks later after a short illness. 'Dasher' had become part and parcel of the side since becoming the club's scorer in 1983, and although he always remained totally impartial in the scorebox, he took great pride and satisfaction in being part of one the most successful Glamorgan teams on record.

As part of his match-day duties, Byron had also been the voice heard over the public-address system, as he combined scoring with announcing. Byron's gentle and mischievous humour over the tannoy enlightened many a dull day at Cardiff and Glamorgan's other home venues. Indeed, it was he, as befitted a proud grandfather, who once told the ladies in the crowd to put their hands over the ears of any small children, in case they were distressed as he read out Glamorgan's bowling figures after they had been on the receiving end of a mauling by the visiting Worcestershire batsmen.

Another gem took place at Pentyrch in 1993, when Glamorgan visited the small club ground north of Cardiff. The ground, set in open countryside, had virtually no distinguishing features apart from a small pavilion, but 'Dasher' was in his element as on the horizon he could just about spy the Severn Estuary, some ten miles away, and the southern end was duly christened 'The Sea End'!

Again, there was a massive crowd at Cardiff to see some high-quality batting on a true and quite pacy wicket, on which Glenn McGrath and Shane Warne delighted the capacity crowd with some fine seam and spin bowling as Pakistan slipped to 85-6. However, Yousuf Youhana and Rashid Latif then added 124 for the seventh wicket, with both men scoring combative half-centuries as Pakistan were eventually dismissed for 257 with just one delivery remaining of the fiftieth and final over.

After the early loss of Adam Gilchrist, Mark Waugh and Ricky Ponting then took the score to 112 in the eighteenth over when Waugh fell three short of his fifty. Thirty runs later, Ponting was dismissed by Saqlain Mushtaq for 70, but Michael Bevan and Steve Waugh then shared an unbroken stand of 116 in 22 overs to see Australia to an emphatic seven-wicket victory, which consolidated their position as the world's leading side in one-day cricket.

The Wooller Gates

The ground redevelopment at Cardiff has seen the creation of three major entry points into the ground – each named after the men who led Glamorgan to their Championship titles in 1948, 1969 and 1997.

The first set of gates – the Wooller Gates – pre-date the major construction phase and result from fund-raising efforts during the Millennium year when Glamorgan officials, notably honorary librarian David Irving, considered ways of creating a permanent tribute to the county's former captain and secretary. By the end of 2000 sufficient capital had been secured to allow Kenfig Ironcraft to commence work on the creation of the gates.

On 29 June 2001 – the first day of the county's Championship match against Northamptonshire – the official opening took place, with the honours being done by club president Tony Lewis, plus Tom Graveney, the former England Test batsman, and Enid Wooller, Wilf's widow. Many members of the Wooller clan were also present, including Wilf and Enid's grandchildren, along with a host of former county stars as the opening of the Wooller Gates coincided with the annual reunion of the Glamorgan Former Players Association. In 2008 the entrance into the area at the rear of the Really Welsh Pavilion at the SWALEC Stadium became the Lewis Gates, while the entrance adjacent to the scoreboard and the rear of the Grandstand became the Maynard Gates.

The official party for the formal opening of the Wooller Gates in 2001. From left to right: Tom Graveney, Enid Wooller, Gerard Elias, Tony Lewis, Steve James, Mike Fatkin and David Irving, who oversaw the fund-raising campaign for their erection.

2002 saw Glamorgan win another title, as Steve James's side won the Division One prize in the National League with their title success coming in a cliffhanger of a match against Kent at Canterbury. Many comparisons were made with Glamorgan's pilgrimage to the St Lawrence ground in 1993 but the Canterbury tale of 2002 had important differences, not least that the club had opted for an overseas bowler rather than a batsman, with Michael Kasprowicz, the thirty year old seam bowler from Queensland filling the overseas berth.

'Kasper' soon made his presence felt in Glamorgan's opening National League game at Cardiff against the Durham Dynamos. The Australian produced a lively opening spell of 3-18 in seven overs as the Dragons opened their account with a 20-run victory. He then featured in a thrilling tie – the first ever in a one-day game at Sophia Gardens – as Glamorgan ended all-square with the Kent Spitfires in a contest reduced to 23 overs per side. Chasing a target of 155, the visitors looked the likely winners at the start of the final over, needing six runs with four wickets intact. But after failing to score from Adrian Dale's first delivery, Geraint Jones was caught off the next ball, and when Mark Ealham was out to the fourth, Kent still needed six runs to win. James Golding struck the fifth ball for a boundary, but could only scramble a single from the final delivery to leave the game tied.

Further victories in the course of the next six weeks maintained the Dragons title quest. By mid-August, there were just three games remaining, including a game at Canterbury, and there was plenty of talk in the media about Glamorgan repeating their pilgrimage down to Kent in 1993 and winning the title. The scriptwriters were kept busy as Matthew Maynard then produced another masterclass of batting at Sophia Gardens; the thirty-six year old rolled back the years, with a scintillating display in the day-night encounter with their nearest rivals, the Worcestershire Royals.

Both teams knew the importance of this game, and a capacity crowd thronged into Sophia Gardens to watch the encounter that, in effect, would decide the outcome of the Division One title. The Royals made the better start as the Dragons slumped to 24-2, but then Mike Powell and Matthew Maynard revived memories of their efforts in the 2000 season by sharing a stand of 133 in 19 overs. This time, it was Powell who was the more assertive early on, with the twenty-five year old unleashing some powerful drives as Maynard quietly pushed the ball around.

'Kasper'.

Robert Croft is mobbed by his teammates during Wales' victory over England at Sophia Gardens in 2002.

After Powell departed for 71, Maynard took the attack to the Worcestershire bowlers, and on 87 he seemed on course for his second-successive century in floodlit games at Cardiff when he gave Gareth Batty a return catch. Maynard's awesome innings had given his side a spur, and Worcestershire never looked like scoring the 281 runs they needed against the Dragons attack, as the Welsh county cruised to a 103 run win.

The demolition of Worcestershire meant that a win, or two points, on 15 September against Kent at Canterbury would guarantee the Welsh county the First Division title. As in 1993, there was an exodus of Welsh sporting fans down to the St Lawrence ground. They were treated to a wonderful and dramatic game of cricket, the script of which even Geoffrey Chaucer would have been hard-pressed to match. But, for all of the Dragon's supporters who had made the long journey down to Canterbury, what mattered most was that at the end of the day, the character and fortitude of the Welsh side showed through as they duly won the game to lift the Division One title. Once again, the backbone of the Dragons innings was provided by Mike Powell, whose composed innings of 74 from 83 balls set Glamorgan on course for a decent score. Their bowlers then claimed wickets at vital times, none more so than Andrew Davies, who claimed the vital scalp of Australian Steve Waugh. Some smart fielding then thwarted the Spitfires middle and lower order, and as the game went down to the wire, Kasprowicz held his nerve in the final over to stifle a late rally from the home batsmen as the Dragons won by four runs.

The Honours Board at Sophia Gardens

To celebrate Glamorgan's success in reaching the final of the Benson & Hedges Cup in 2000, a series of honours boards were installed on the walls of the dressing rooms at Sophia Gardens. Seeing the names of some of the great players in the club's history had been an uplifting experience for several of the young players, whose names were now added to these boards after their fine efforts in winning the one-day titles.

'When I've looked up at these boards, it's shown me what the game is all about,' said wicketkeeper Mark Wallace. 'Now we'll have another board put up with the names of the 2001 and 2002 teams, and I'll be able to look up at that and take a great deal of pride from having been involved.'

'Being part of the team at Canterbury was one of the most emotional moments I experienced in cricket,' said opening batsman Ian Thomas. 'After the victory everybody sat down to have a say about what winning the title meant to them and how they really felt about it. It showed the pride and honour the boys have in playing and winning for Glamorgan, and Wales! I felt very proud to see the names added to the honours board, and it brought back very happy memories of that wonderful day in Kent.'

2002 also saw Wales defeat England at Sophia Gardens as the Cardiff ground hosted a friendly one-day international game as the English limited-overs team warmed up for their forthcoming international triangular series with India and Sri Lanka. It was a ground-breaking 'home international', with Somerset's Steffan Jones, Sussex's Tony Cottey and South African Jacques Kallis joining the bulk of the Glamorgan squad for the 50-over friendly.

Like other Wales–England encounters, there was a special edge to the atmosphere as the players practised at Sophia Gardens ahead of the game, with the Welsh side eager to beat the English team. This was evident as a fired-up performance in the field restricted the English side to 189-9 after they had been put in. Right from the start, Wales were the superior team, as firstly Jacques Kallis and Andrew Davies bowled accurate opening spells, before Steffan Jones and Darren Thomas ripped the heart out of the English middle order as three wickets fell for 16 runs in a nine-over spell from the two Welshmen.

Robert Croft then delivered an exemplary spell of off-spin as the English lower order tried to step up the run rate, but the damage had already been done. Croft then put the English bowlers to the sword as he gave his side a flying start with Matthew Hoggard bowling eight wides and two no-balls in a seven-over spell which yielded 63 runs. Steve James and David Hemp shared a partnership of 132 for the second wicket, as the Welsh side strolled to an eight-wicket win.

The game had been a great victory for the Welsh team, and for Welsh cricket as well, and their success in this game, coupled with the outstanding win in the National League gave further impetus to the campaign for the ground development at Sophia Gardens and the creation of a national cricket stadium.

TWENTY-EIGHT

Twenty20 Visions

After the success of the Wales-England fixture in 2002, further 'home internationals' were staged at Cardiff in 2003 and 2004 as part of a three-match NatWest Bank Challenge, in addition to providing a competitive practice match for the England one-day players as the national team warmed up for their matches in the triangular series.

The England team duly got their revenge in the next contest, on 14 June 2003, against a Wales side boasting Steffan Jones and all of the regular Glamorgan one-day team, including Michael Kasprowicz. Indeed, the Queenslander filleted England's middle order, removing debutant Jim Troughton and Andrew Flintoff for ducks as England slipped to 44-4. Their position was restored by half-centuries from Marcus Trescothick and Anthony McGrath, as England ended on 235-8.

Skipper Robert Croft launched the innings with a forthright fifty, but the two big guns in the middle-order – Maynard and Powell – were dismissed for 9 and 7 respectively, and with the England bowlers giving little away, wickets fell at regular intervals as the Welsh side were dismissed for 227 in the forty-ninth over, leaving England the victors by eight runs.

The following year, England clinched the series as they won again, although this time it was by the more convincing margin of six wickets, and with over ten overs to spare. Only David Hemp offered any lengthy resistance to the English bowlers, before Rob Key struck a forthright 83 and Andrew Strauss weighed in with an unbeaten 92 to see England record a comfortable victory.

South Africa had also recorded a comfortable win at Cardiff in their NatWest Series One-Day International in July 2003 against Zimbabwe. Only Heath Streak, with 54, came to terms with the Proteas attack, for whom Jacques Kallis celebrated his return to Welsh soil with three wickets. Graeme Smith and Herschelle Gibbs then dominated the Zimbabwean attack, with Gibbs making an unbeaten 93 as his side strolled to a nine-wicket victory.

The One-Day International at Cardiff in 2004 was a more closely contested affair as the West Indies met New Zealand at Sophia Gardens in the first week of July. After being put in to bat, Brian Lara delighted the crowd with 58 in even time with 9 fours and a massive six, but he became one of three wickets to fall to Chris Cairns as the Caribbean team ended on 216. Dwayne Bravo and Jerome Lawson soon got among the Kiwi batsmen, but Hamish Marshall played a resolute innings, with his patient 75* guiding his side to victory by five wickets.

2004 was another very successful season for Glamorgan as Robert Croft's team lifted the National League title, winning eleven of their sixteen matches in the competition, which now involved innings with a maximum of 45 overs. The Glamorgan Dragons won their first four matches at Sophia Gardens, all by comprehensive margins, and although they lost the final two games at Cardiff in late August, these defeats did not matter a jot as the outcome of the title had already been decided when Croft's team defeated Lancashire by five wickets at Colwyn Bay on 22 August. The Dragons' captain scored a blistering 106 to seal victory with four overs in hand.

The rest of the Dragons side had also enjoyed themselves in their league matches at Sophia Gardens, with the two Matthew's – Elliott and Maynard – demolishing Northamptonshire in the first week of May with an unbroken stand of 169 for the fourth wicket. The Australian scored a superb century as Glamorgan, chasing a target of 233, eased to a seven-wicket victory with over six overs in hand.

A fortnight later it was the turn of the Dragons bowlers to make hay at Sophia Gardens as the Essex Eagles were restricted to 162-9 with both Alex Wharf and Andrew Davies claiming three wickets. Wharf, batting at number three in the order, then bludgeoned 41 in quick time as the Dragons won by six wickets.

David Hemp strikes a boundary during Glamorgan's match at Cardiff in 2002 against Gloucestershire.

The Dragons then confirmed their title aspirations in the last week of June, with a nine-wicket thrashing of the Surrey Brown Caps in a rain-affected contest at Cardiff. Once again, Davies proved to be a handful with the white ball, taking 3-36, while Croft chipped in with a miserly 3-34 in his nine-over quota. But the captain's work was not over for the day, as after a rain delay had seen a readjusted target of 94 in 15 overs, Croft and his opening partner Ian Thomas blasted thirteen boundaries as the Dragons reached their target in just 8.2 overs.

A month later, it was the turn of the Hampshire Hawks to be comprehensively beaten at Cardiff, with Davies (4-30) and Croft (3-30) once again starring with the ball in the day-night contest. Matthew Elliott then played another turbo-charged innings with his unbeaten 81 containing 9 fours and 2 sixes as, to the delight of another full-house crowd, the Dragons strolled to a seven-wicket victory with ten overs to spare.

By this time, the Dragons had also enjoyed a fine run in the Twenty20 Cup, the new competition which had been introduced into the county calendar the previous year. It proved to be an instant hit all across the country, with thousands of people, watching the all-action contests, which were played in early evening in high summer.

The Glamorgan Dragons made a modest start in the inaugural season, recording just one win in their zonal matches, with their solitary victory coming at Cardiff as they defeated the Worcestershire Royals by 56 runs. It was a completely different story in 2004, as they began with a morale-boosting win at Northampton, followed by an eight-wicket victory over the Somerset Sabres at Taunton as Ian Thomas became the first Glamorgan batsman to score a century in the new competition.

Three days later, the Dragons lost to the Warwickshire Bears at Cardiff, but the following week, Robert Croft's team bounced back at the same ground by defeating the Gloucestershire Gladiators by 32 runs with Alex Wharf taking 3-23 and Andrew Davies, Darren Thomas and Adrian Dale all claiming a couple of victims. The next night, the Dragons won again, at New Road, Worcester, to clinch a quarter-final tie and a home draw.

The Dragons' opponents were the Bears, who a fortnight before had won by 26 runs at Sophia Gardens, after a fine performance by their Australian all-rounder Brad Hogg. The quarter-final saw the Dragons turn the tables on the Bears in front of a massive crowd of 8,500 at the Cardiff ground. The visiting batsmen stuttered against a waspish spell of 3-32 from Darren Thomas and a vibrant performance in the field by the lithe Dragons fielders.

Twenty20 Cup, Quarter-Final
Glamorgan v. Warwickshire
Sophia Gardens, Cardiff
19 July 2004 (20-over match)
Warwickshire won the toss and decided to bat
Result: Glamorgan won by 5 wickets
Umpires: P.J. Hartley, R. Palmer

Warwickshire		**first innings**	
N.M. Carter	c Croft	b S.D. Thomas	17
M.A. Wagh	c Wallace	b S.D. Thomas	9
*N.V. Knight	c I.J. Thomas	b Wharf	14
G.B. Hogg	c I.J. Thomas	b Wharf	54
D.P. Ostler	st Wallace	b Croft	13
J.O. Troughton		b Dale	1
D.R. Brown	c Hemp	b S.D. Thomas	19
G.G. Wagg		not out	21
I.R. Bell		not out	1
+T. Frost			
A. Richardson			
Extras	(4b, 2lb, 3w)		9
Total	(7 wickets, 20 overs)		158
FOW	1-17, 2-34, 3-51, 4-81, 5-84, 6-122, 7-157		

Bowling	O	M	R	W
Davies	4	0	31	0
S.D. Thomas	3	0	32	3
Wharf	4	0	28	2
Dale	4	0	20	1
Croft	4	0	22	1
Cosker	1	0	19	0

Glamorgan		**first innings**	
M.P. Maynard	c Frost	b Brown	0
I.J. Thomas		b Carter	0
M.T.G. Elliott	lbw	b Brown	48
D.L. Hemp	c Carter	b Hogg	74
S.D. Thomas	c Knight	b Carter	7
+M.A. Wallace		not out	20
A. Dale		not out	8
*R.D.B. Croft			
A.G. Wharf			
A.P. Davies			
D.A. Cosker			
Extras	(4lb)		4
Total	(5 wickets, 19 overs)		161
FOW	1-0, 2-2, 3-120, 4-128, 5-150		

Bowling	O	M	R	W
Brown	4	1	28	2
Carter	4	0	25	2
Bell	2	0	19	0
Hogg	4	0	36	1
Richardson	2	0	17	0
Wagh	2	0	17	0
Troughton	1	0	15	0

Chasing a target of 159, the Dragons made a poor start, slumping to 2-2 with both Matthew Maynard and Ian Thomas back in the dugout as it looked like the Bears would clinch a place in the Finals Day at their home ground. But David Hemp and Matthew Elliott had other ideas, as they shared a partnership of 118 for the third wicket to turn the game in the Dragons favour.

Mark Wallace drives a ball to the boundary during Glamorgan's match against Northamptonshire at Cardiff in 2006.

Both batsmen departed with 23 runs still needed in the final four overs, and after their dramatic collapse against Brad Hogg's wrist-spin in the previous encounter, a few flutters went through the home camp. But the jaunty Mark Wallace quelled any anxiety as with a mix of the orthodox and the audacious, he saw the Dragons home with an over to spare and a place at Finals Day on 7 August.

By their own admission, the Dragons didn't fire on all cylinders on the big day, as in the semi-final against the Leicestershire Foxes, Darren Maddy blitzed a quickfire 72 from 40 balls to see his side to a decent total of 165-5 from their 20 overs. The Dragons top-order then departed in the first six overs, and it was left to David Hemp and Mark Wallace to get the scoreboard ticking over. But once they were both out, the Bears regained the upper hand, with Mark Cleary and Claude Henderson each taking three wickets as the Foxes reached the final.

Matthew and Son

Not many professional cricketers get the chance to play in a proper match alongside their sons, but this feat was achieved by Matthew Maynard; on 15 August 2005 he played alongside his sixteen year old son Tom in a match, as part of his testimonial year, against a star-studded Lashings World XI at Sophia Gardens.

The 30-overs-a-side contest, won by Maynard's Welsh XI, rounded of his illustrious county career, having announced his retirement the previous year as he became England's assistant coach. Matthew bowed out with a typically forthright innings of 46, before he was run out by Vasbert Drakes. The thirty-nine year old departed to a standing ovation from the enraptured Cardiff crowd, and was replaced at the crease by his sixteen year old son in a most tangible changing of the guard.

It was rather fitting that Matthew should play his final innings for Glamorgan at the Cardiff ground, as it was at Sophia Gardens where he had played some of his finest innings, including his maiden double-hundred against Nottinghamshire in 1991, plus an innings of 114 against Leicestershire in 2004, his fifty-third first-class century for the club, breaking the county record jointly held by Hugh Morris and Alan Jones.

Despite their failure in the semi-final, the Dragons' success in the Twenty20 competition in 2004 had an important bearing on the ground development at Sophia Gardens. The floodlit contests in the competition, as well as the day-night contests in the National League, had attracted bumper crowds to the Cardiff ground, with huge temporary stands, normally only required for the One-Day Internationals, installed at the Pontcanna End of the ground.

Glamorgan were not alone as every county club reported a further rise in attendances in 2004 and more sell-out matches in the Twenty20 competition. With the hospitality suites also packed out for these enjoyable contests, it was a clear sign that the installation of permanent floodlights at the Cardiff ground would be a shrewd investment. The Glamorgan officials duly secured the finance needed for their installation, and applied for planning permission for the erection of four stacks, plus a small sub-station adjacent to the Wooller Gates.

Installation took place during the spring of 2005 and on 22 April 2005 they were formally switched on by David Morgan, now the chairman of the E.C.B. who, when chairman of Glamorgan in the mid-1990s, had done so much to progress the stadium development scheme and the acquisition of the lease from Cardiff Athletic Club. Even though the day-night contest against the Essex Eagles was washed out, the glow of the lights over the Cardiff ground marked the dawn of the final phase of the ground development and the acquisition of the greatest prize of all: Test cricket.

Ian Thomas, Glamorgan's first centurion in Twenty20 cricket with a century against Somerset at Taunton in 2004

An aerial view of the Cardiff ground in 2005.

The arrival of the permanent floodlights at Cardiff in 2005.

TWENTY-NINE

A Test for Wales

Glamorgan's National League success in both 2002 and 2004, plus their success in Twenty20 cricket, led the committee, now under the dynamic chairmanship of R. Paul Russell, to press ahead with stages two and three of the ground-development project at the Cardiff ground.

Limited finances had previously prevented the club from progressing their schemes beyond stage one, so midway during 2003 a group – under the chairmanship of Gareth Williams – comprising committee members, sponsors and other volunteers planned a Ground Appeal Year for 2004. With the name of 'The National Cricket Stadium for Wales Appeal' it further promoted Glamorgan Cricket as the stewards of Welsh cricket, and the Sophia Gardens ground as a centre of excellence for Wales. Without a player beneficiary in 2004, the appeal sought to kick-start the fund-raising for the ground development by spending the year highlighting the grand plans and eliciting the support of the Welsh public to help bring these plans to fruition.

Test Cricket for Wales!

The National Cricket Stadium for Wales Appeal championed the notion of Cardiff becoming a Test Match ground: 'We believe that there is a very strong case for Test cricket in Wales,' announced Appeal Year Chairman Gareth Williams in the glossy promotional literature. 'Like Durham, we have a powerful geographical argument. We have to make a case though, based on improving the facilities and selling out the matches that we're allocated.

'We believe it's more realistic to be aiming for the interim step of staging regular one-day international matches involving England than to seek a full Test match from the outset. That being said, we would certainly like to think that successfully staging these, along with the quality of facilities the development will bring about, is a very good argument for a Test match being played in Wales for the first time.'

The Appeal Year events were launched at an illustrious Hall of Fame dinner at the Marriott Hotel in Cardiff on 17 April: the first eleven inductees into the club's Hall of Fame were announced, while race nights, golf days, cricket matches and a grand ball in the National Cricket Centre all helped to raise capital and increase public awareness of the club's grand schemes.

The installation of permanent floodlights was one of four important changes that were introduced to the plans during 2005, compared with those originally proposed in 1996, and given planning approval in 1999. The others were the creation of a pavilion complex at the northern end of the ground, rather than at the Cathedral Road End, the erection of a massive new grandstand on the site of the former pavilion and creating another large enclosure at the Cathedral Road End, below a state-of-the-art media centre, thereby increasing seating capacity over the base level for Test matches set at 15,000 by the E.C.B.

There was also an important change to the pavilion complex at the Pontcanna End, with the changes stemming from conversations with Cardiff Council. They were seeking a temporary home for the Cardiff Devils ice hockey team, whose stadium in the centre of Cardiff was poised to be demolished as part of the St Davids 2 development.

The only fly in the ointment was the timescale, with the National Ice Rink being earmarked for demolition in September 2006, leaving the city planners needing to find a temporary home

Above and below: A bumper crowd at the Twenty20 quarter-final in 2004 as the Glamorgan Dragons defeat the Warwickshire Bears.

before the new site in Cardiff Bay was ready. At the Council's suggestion, a scheme was therefore drawn up during 2005 whereby an indoor arena was added to the ground-development scheme at Sophia Gardens, with the new 'Icehouse' adjoining an enlarged pavilion on the northern side of the cricket ground.

The Welsh National Ice Rink

Opened in 1986, the grandly titled Wales National Ice Rink in Hayes Bridge Road had witnessed many thrilling games and it was seen by the city planners as an integral part of the much-vaunted Sports Village complex in Cardiff Bay. While delays had taken place with the creation of the village, steady headway had been made with the St David's retail development in the heart of the city centre. With anchor stores agreeing to be part of the new mall complex, the Council therefore drew up plans for the demolition of the existing buildings in this area, which included the ice rink, and the construction of the new shopping complex called St David's 2.

The Glamorgan officials were delighted to consider an indoor arena in their scheme, as it would significantly add to the portfolio of facilities at their ground, and if Glamorgan – as the project literature had trumpeted – was to host a Test match, this was an ideal opportunity to make a bid.

It all seemed too good an offer for Glamorgan to ignore, and plans were duly submitted to the Council for the new pavilion complex. However, local residents lodged objections, with fears being raised about the impact the new complex – especially the ice rink – would have on the surrounding area and the historic parklands.

Several public meetings were held during 2005 where Glamorgan officials and representatives from the Cardiff Devils tried to appease local residents about their worries. An alternative scheme was also put forward by the Council involving a temporary home in the Bay. With CADW also objecting to the new pavilion at the Sophia Gardens ground, time was running out for the Cardiff Devils to find a new home. In November 2005 their management withdrew their strong objections to the temporary base, and in January 2006 Cardiff City Council decided to build a temporary ice facility in the bay.

Glamorgan's officials were naturally disappointed at the decision, as they believed that the Sophia Gardens scheme was far superior. The Devils opening game in December 2006 had to be postponed at the last minute because the ice was not up to standard while the decision in February 2007 to deny Cardiff a 'super casino' has also further delayed development, and the upshot is that the Devils seem likely to remain in their 'temporary' home for some years to come.

The debate over the indoor arena also brought a lot of criticism towards Glamorgan Cricket. Much of this was unfairly directed at a club which had already successfully obtained planning permission to develop its property, and one that, throughout its occupancy of Sophia Gardens, had enjoyed a good relationship with local residents. With the indoor arena being dropped from the proposals, a revised plan for the pavilion was drawn up. Contact was also made with officials from CADW, who had previously objected to the ice-house development, and a suitable design was agreed for the new, three-storey complex, combining glass and timber, and having a landscaped lawn plus car parking bays in front of the pavilion.

After a year of often quite heated debate with local residents and other interested parties, the Glamorgan officials were naturally keen to continue their dialogue with the City Council. The success of the 2005 Ashes series, and the massive benefits the England-Australia games had brought to the grounds and cities staging games helped to focus discussions with the city fathers. The Millennium Stadium had brought immense benefits to the city, and following the closure of Wembley Stadium for redevelopment, the staging of the F.A. Cup final and other major sporting events at the Millennium Stadium had all brought a wealth of economic benefits for the City of Cardiff.

Bangladesh Defeat Australia

After Bangladesh recorded a famous victory in their NatWest Series One-Day International at Sophia Gardens on 18 June 2005 it caused shockwaves around the cricketing world. 'Bangladesh produce the biggest shock in cricket history,' proclaimed one newspaper in Pakistan, while *The Sydney Morning Herald* and *The Melbourne Age* both called it 'the greatest shock in Australian sporting history.'

Before the match, Bangladesh had only recorded three wins against Test-playing opposition in over a hundred one-day internationals, and after being humbled by ten wickets a couple of days before by England, it still looked a one-horse race with Australia – despite defeats earlier in the week to England in a Twenty20 game and Somerset in a warm-up match at Taunton – quoted by one bookmaker as favourites at 250/1 on but even when Australia slumped to 9-2 in the face of exemplary new-ball bowling in overcast and muggy conditions, few eyebrows were raised, and Australia still looked to be in total control as a fourth-wicket partnership of 108 between Damien Martyn and Michael Clarke saw their side to 249-5. Bangladesh slipped to 72-3 but, within a couple of hours, the stuff of fairytales had taken place at Sophia Gardens, and sporting journalists all over the globe were filing copy about one of the greatest shocks in world sport, after Mohammad Ashraful and Habibul Bashar had turned the game, and the form book, on its head with an audacious match-winning partnership of 130 in 24 overs.

After Bangladesh scored the winning run, with four balls in hand, there were jubilant scenes, both at Sophia Gardens and on the streets of Dhaka where celebrations went on long into the night. The following morning, the Bangladeshi parliament convened for a special meeting so that their president could send a congratulatory message to Habibul Bashar's young team, with the message ending by saying that, 'Cardiff now has a very special place in Bangladesh history.'

4,500 people were present at Glamorgan's headquarters to watch this moment of sporting history, and in the words of the county's chief executive, 'I think in five years time, it will be more of a case of half a million people claiming that they were there. The crowd saw 500 runs and a piece of cricket history and it's great to know that those pictures of a sun-kissed Sophia Gardens have gone around the world.'

The NatWest Series

Australia v. Bangladesh
Sophia Gardens, Cardiff
18 June 2005
Bangladesh won by 5 wickets
Australia won the toss and decided to bat
Umpires: B.F. Bowden and D.R. Shepherd
Scorers: B. Jones and B. Young

Australia		**first innings**	
+A.C. Gilchrist	lbw	b Mortaza	0
M.L. Hayden		b Hossain	37
*R.T. Ponting	lbw	b Baisya	1
D.R. Martyn	c Iqbal	b Baisya	77
M.J. Clarke	c Mortaza	b Baisya	54
M.E.K. Hussey		not out	31
S.M. Katich		not out	36
G.B. Hogg			
J.N. Gillespie			
M.S. Kasprowicz			
G.D. McGrath			
Extras	(3lb,2w,8nb)		13
Total	(5 Wickets,50 Overs)		249
FOW	1-0,2-9,3-57,4-165,5-183		

Bowling	O	M	R	W	w	nb
Mashrafe Mortaza	10	2	33	1	1	0
Tapesh Baisya	10	1	69	3	0	8
Nazmul Hossain	10	2	65	1	0	0
Mohammad Rafique	10	0	31	0	1	0
Aftab Ahmed	10	0	48	0	0	0

Bangladesh		**first innings**	
Javed Omar	c Hayden	b Kasprowicz	19
Nafees Iqbal	c Gilchrist	b Gillespie	8
Tushar Imran	c Katich	b Hogg	24
Mohammad Ashraful	c Hogg	b Gillespie	100
*Habibul Bashar		run out	47
Aftab Ahmed		not out	21
Mohammad Rafique		not out	9
+Khaled Mashud			
Mashrafe Mortaza			
Tapesh Baisya			
Nazmul Hossain			
Extras	(1b, 11lb, 6w, 4nb)		22
Total	(5Wickets,49.2 overs)		250
FOW:	1-17,2-51,3-72,4-202,5-227		

Bowling	O	M	R	W	w	nb
McGrath	10	1	43	0	0	2
Gillespie	9.2	1	41	2	2	0
Kasprowicz	10	0	40	1	0	2
Hogg	9	0	52	1	1	0
Clarke	6	0	38	0	1	0
Hussey	5	0	24	0	0	0

With Wembley Stadium nearing completion, the City Council were keen to find other high-profile sporting events which would keep the name of Cardiff on the world stage. After England's magnificent success in the 2005 Ashes, what better than an Ashes Test being allocated to Sophia Gardens? International Test match cricket would join rugby and soccer as regular features of the capital city's sporting calendar, especially when research commissioned by UK Sport had shown that Test cricket can boost a local economy by over £1 million a day.

During 2005/06, a bid was formulated, with the support of Cardiff Council, the Chamber of Commerce and the Welsh Assembly Government for Glamorgan to make a bid to stage an Ashes Test match in 2009. A revised ground-development plan was also submitted to the City Council, with the plans entirely in keeping with the parkland setting and enhancing the vista of the immediate locality. With the projected capacity exceeding 16,000, Glamorgan were also able to confirm their bid to the E.C.B. for the Category 'A' ground status required for Test match cricket.

One good piece of news had already reached Glamorgan, as in the first week of January 2006, they received confirmation from the E.C.B. that the whole process for allocating major international matches was to change. A new body called the Major Match Group, under the chairmanship of Lord Bill Morris, the well-known cricket lover and former trade union leader, would make recommendations. No longer would there be long-term staging agreements, and instead there would be a whole new process: any county could bid for any match provided they complied with new criteria and submitted an acceptable bid against something called 'the balanced scorecard', which earmarked proportions of a total 100 per cent mark to specific areas such as financial bids, quality of pitch and practice facilities, location, ticket prices, security and the like.

In the words of chief executive Mike Fatkin:

> Whereas before we had no inkling of what we were being examined against, we now had the exam questions set out for us. I well recall the discussion I had with the chairman when we received the letter. When asked by him about the chances of staging an Ashes Test match in 2009, I have to confess my first reaction was to laugh. Only to realize he was serious. And when I stopped to think about it, his simple question – why not? – was, in fact, a very apposite one. Why not indeed? The E.C.B. was setting out for us the criteria we would need to meet in order to be considered. What was there to prevent us putting in a bid?

At the end of March 2006, a visit was made to Sophia Gardens by the newly instigated Major Match Group (M.M.G.). The group listened to various presentations from Glamorgan officials, and others from the Assembly Government and Council, as the county club adopted a 'Team Wales' approach to demonstrate to the M.M.G. that they were more than capable of staging both one-day international and five-day Test matches on a regular basis in Cardiff.

After another poor season on the field, and a financial loss, a small minority of Glamorgan members suggested that the club were forgetting the performances of the team, and focussing too much on the pursuit of Test cricket. These claims were completely dispelled at the club's A.G.M. on 30 March 2006 as, in a wide-ranging and upbeat speech, Mike Fatkin stressed the importance of Test cricket to both Glamorgan's future success and the development of cricket in Wales, and at the end of the meeting, the 180 or so members who had attended the meeting were able to watch the short video presentation which the club had shown the M.M.G.

Several also had a look at the ground model and the other plans on display, and the warm comments made were testament that the rank-and-file members were fully behind the club as they waited both for a decision from the planners at Cardiff Council and also from the M.M.G. As it turned out they didn't have to wait too long before getting the champagne out!

Why Test Cricket is Good for Glamorgan Cricket

In his speech at the Glamorgan A.G.M. in March 2006, Mike Fatkin emphasised that Glamorgan had to move forward in order to provide the quality cricket that all of the county's fans want to see in the future.

'Cricket is changing, and it is no accident that all the counties with Test grounds make an operating profit, while most of the others make a loss. Test cricket will allow Glamorgan not only to compete with the best, but it will also allow the county to further develop the tremendous cricketing talent we have in Wales.'

'Glamorgan's academy system has already seen four of the county's homegrown youngsters being selected for the England Under-19s (Ben Wright, Mike O'Shea, Aaron Shingler and Adam Harrison), and the club's ambition is to see more Welsh youngsters join Simon Jones and represent England at the highest level.

'With the change in the way the E.C.B. will allocate future Test cricket, Glamorgan has for the first time an opportunity to bring Test cricket on a regular basis to Wales. It is an opportunity that Glamorgan Cricket does not intend to miss. It is the key to ensuring that Glamorgan will always be in the group of county sides challenging for major honours each season.'

The delighted Bangladesh team celebrate at Cardiff after their historic victory over Australia in 2005.

THIRTY

The Dream Becomes a Reality

Thursday 20 April 2006 will go down in Glamorgan's history as a date of great significance because that was when the E.C.B. announced that Glamorgan Cricket had been given the right to host an npower Ashes Test against Australia in 2009.

It was a decision that was greeted with sheer delight by Welsh cricket fans throughout the world, with Glamorgan chairman Paul Russell echoing their sentiments by saying, 'This is a great day not only for Welsh cricket but for Wales. Looking at the E.C.B. website and seeing "npower Test matches *v.* Australia 2009 – The Brit Oval, Cardiff, Edgbaston, Headingley and Lord's" fills me with great pride both as a Glamorgan member and as a Welshman.'

Glamorgan's captain Robert Croft could not contain his excitement when he heard the news, as the team were preparing for their Championship match against Derbyshire at Sophia Gardens:

> I know that this news will provide cricket in Wales and Glamorgan in particular with a massive boost. I can still remember the day I made my debut as a full England Test cricketer. I know that throughout Wales this will inspire young cricketers to join Simon Jones and become the Test cricketers of the future. I am delighted for all cricket fans in Wales and on their behalf I pay tribute to all of those who have worked so hard to make what was once a dream for so many of us a reality.

The Chairman Pays Tribute to His Team

The news in April 2006 that Sophia Gardens had been awarded Category A status was met with delight by Glamorgan Chairman, R. Paul Russell, who, quite fittingly, praised the efforts of his team of officials at Sophia Gardens, as well as the other organisations who had backed the bid:

'This result could not have been achieved without the fantastic support Glamorgan has received from so many organisations. When the Major Match Group's inspection team visited Glamorgan at the end of March they were literally bowled over by the sheer enthusiasm of so many people to bring Test cricket to Wales.

'Without this "Team Wales" approach bringing together the Assembly, the City Council, the Cardiff Business community and the tourist industry, we would not have been successful. We were also fortunate to be able to build on the worldwide international reputation gained by Cardiff in hosting major world-class sporting events at the Millennium Stadium.

'The newly redeveloped Sophia Gardens will allow Cardiff to become one of the few major cities in the world to host world-class events in three major sports: cricket, football and rugby.'

The reaction from others was equally impressive, with the First Minister Rhodri Morgan describing it as mouth-watering. However, there was still one hurdle to be jumped, namely the meeting on 10 May of Cardiff Council's Planning Committee. With the prospect of so many benefits coming into the City, and to Wales as a whole, they approved Glamorgan's plans, and during the second half of the 2006 season work began preparing the ground for the major building phase, as well as the One-Day International on 30 August between England and Pakistan. Among the first areas to disappear in late July were the old office block – now doing service as a hospitality block – and the enclosures either side of the pavilion. In their place new, temporary grandstands were erected to host the 15,000 crowd.

Paul Russell, the Chairman of Glamorgan Cricket, who has masterminded the impressive stadium development.

By early August 2006 a new double-deck media centre was also in place at the River End with the former single-storey Turnbull Suite being demolished and replaced by four Portakabins, thereby providing sufficient seating for the England match. State-of-the-art facilities were also installed including Wi-Fi access for the journalists and broadcasters covering the match.

Steve James on England's first-ever One-Day International at Sophia Gardens

It would be easy to bemoan the fact that Cardiff's first staging of a full England one-day international ended in an abandonment, but the truth is that we were lucky to have any cricket at all. The more pessimistic weather forecasts predicted rain reaching Cardiff at about 2.30 p.m., just in time for the start of this floodlit encounter. So for 56.2 overs to be played – and final confirmation of the game's end not coming until my normal cocoa-time at 9.37 p.m. – was some achievement.

Not that everyone was happy that England should have to field for seven overs of Pakistan's reply to their 202 all out. Recalled fast bowler Darren Gough went onto the field shaking his head at the damp conditions (groundsman Len Smith and his merry men could have done no more, mind) and continued to do so throughout, his mood darkened further when Ian Bell slipped at mid-off and could not stop the innings' first ball.

The prevailing gloom and dampness meant Smith's beloved pitch seamed more than usual – justifying Inzamam-ul-Haq's insertion of England – but it was of a decent enough pace and further proof, if any were needed, that the quality of the pitch will not be a problem come the Ashes Test in 2009.

Of course that forthcoming event meant all eyes of the national media were on the off-field organisation of this match, even if that was palpably unfair because it will be a very different stadium which hosts the Test. Yes, there were some minor problems, such as many spectators still being outside when the match started. And the curmudgeonly cynical side of me which sits so well amid the national cricket media feared especially when the Wi-Fi internet access, which most journalists rely slavishly on these days, failed (not because, apparently, of any fault at Glamorgan, but because of a cabling fault elsewhere in Cardiff following the previous night's Rolling Stones concert in the Millennium Stadium). But even that passed without next-day reference. That for me sealed it: the day – and long night – must have been a success. Cardiff had passed its first 'test'.

NatWest Series
England v. Pakistan
Sophia Gardens, Cardiff
30 August 2006 (50-over day/night match)
Pakistan won the toss and decided to field
Result: No result
Umpires: B.R. Doctrove, I.J. Gould
Third umpire: M.R. Benson
Fourth Official: P.J. Hartley
Referee: M.J. Procter
Scorers: B. Jones and B. Young
Man of the Match: No award made

England		**first innings**	
M.E. Trescothick	c Kamran Akmal	b Mohammad Asif	16
*A.J. Strauss	c Shahid Afridi	b Mohammad Asif	2
I.R. Bell		run out (Shahid Afridi)	88
K.P. Pietersen	c Kamran Akmal	b Mohammad Asif	2
P.D. Collingwood	lbw	b Shahid Afridi	14
J.W.M. Dalrymple		b Shoaib Akhtar	27
R. Clarke	c Shoaib Malik	b Shoaib Akhtar	6
+C.M.W. Read	c and	b Mohammad Hafeez	0
S.I. Mahmood		b Shoaib Akhtar	1
D. Gough	c Shoaib Malik	b Shahid Afridi	8
S.C.J. Broad		not out	8
Extras	(5lb, 5nb, 10w)		20
Total	(all out, 49.2 overs)		202
FOW:	1-14, 2-35, 3-51, 4-98, 5-166, 6-166, 7-167, 8-173, 9-173, 10-202		

Bowling	O	M	R	W
Shoaib Akhtar	10	1	45	3
Mohammad Asif	10	3	28	3
Naved-ul-Hasan	7	0	43	0
Abdul Razzaq	4	1	10	0
Shahid Afridi	8.2	0	38	2
Mohammad Hafeez	10	0	33	1

Pakistan		**first innings**	
Shoaib Malik	lbw	b Broad	5
Mohammad Hafeez		not out	18
Younus Khan		not out	12
Mohammad Yousuf			
*Inzamam-ul-Haq			
Abdul Razzaq			
Shahid Afridi			
+Kamran Akmal			
Naved-ul-Hasan			
Shoaib Akhtar			
Mohammad Asif			
Extras	(4lb, 7w)		11
Total	(1 wicket, 7 overs)		46
FOW:	1-12		

Bowling	O	M	R	W
Gough	4	0	28	0
Broad	3	0	14	1

The media centre at the River End is upgraded to a double-deck structure, ready for the international match between England and Pakistan in 2006.

The match with Pakistan was the first full international played by England in Cardiff, and their first in Wales since 1973 when they played a Prudential Cup match at Swansea against New Zealand. The game was also the first full international under the newly installed floodlights at Cardiff, and after weeks of hard effort, everything that could have been done off the field was set in place, only for the weather to intervene and force the abandonment of the game as Pakistan, in reply to England's meagre total of 202 were 46–1 in the seventh over.

In mid-September, the old Cardiff pavilion was used for the final time for Glamorgan's Championship match against Gloucestershire and, during the autumn, further demolition work took place including removal of the scoreboard at the River End. The large grandstands at the Cathedral Road End were also dismantled. Other key elements were set in place as finance was secured from Allied Irish Bank, while a series of detailed meetings took place with HLN Architects, Arup, Davis Langdon and Boyer Planning over the details of the building phase.

Carillion Regional Building were also appointed as the major contractors and as the demolition crew from Cuddy worked on the southern side of the ground, either side of Christmas 2006, clearing away the old pavilion, staff from Carillion – under the direction of Project Manager Mike Baynham – began their preparatory work on the northern side.

The first few weeks of 2007 saw the foundations being laid for the new pavilion complex, as well as those for the new grandstand on the site of the former pavilion. The work also began in earnest upon new enclosures at the River End, the media centre complex at the Cathedral Road End and the entrance stand that was occupying the area near the Wooller Gates where the leisure complex had previously been earmarked.

In February 2007, work began on erecting the shell of the new pavilion, with giant cranes lifting and swiftly fixing in place the girders and scaffolding for the new structure. This was followed by the assembly of the seating areas on the pitch-facing side of the lavish new complex, as well as the new enclosures at the River End. At the start of May 2007, work began erecting the super-structure for the massive new grandstand, as well as the media centre and seating areas at the Cathedral Road End. By mid-June these other structures were complete, and Glamorgan – who had led a peripatetic existence in the first half of the season – played their four home Twenty20 matches under the floodlights at their emerging new stadium.

The Glamorgan and Gloucestershire teams line up in front of the old pavilion at Cardiff during the final Championship match prior to the start of the redevelopment scheme in September 2006.

The old office block at Sophia Gardens in June 2006, shortly before its demolition and replacement with a temporary stand for the One-Day International between England and Pakistan.

The Vice-Presidents' Enclosure in September 2006.

Although the players had to use the changing rooms in the National Cricket Centre, everyone was most impressed with the new facilities, and the excellent progress made by the Carillion staff meant that an additional 700 seats were available for the county's supporters, taking the seating capacity for these matches in 2007 to nearly 4,000.

From mid-July, seats were installed on the new grandstand and Cathedral Road enclosure, while work began on the internal structure and fit-out of the new buildings as Glamorgan returned to Cardiff in the second week of August for the first of three Championship matches in their new stadium.

On 3 August, the M.M.G. also made an inspection of the new ground at Sophia Gardens, primarily to ensure that everything was proceeding satisfactorily, and to the delight of the Glamorgan officials, Lord Morris was fulsome in his praise:

> As you visit cricket grounds all over the world, you hear the scenery being described and I only have one regret that the late John Arlott won't be here on that very first morning when England play in Cardiff to give the poetic description of what will become a very important landmark for cricket. I was here when England played Pakistan in August 2007, and the project was then described to me. It has since exceeded my expectations and it is absolutely fabulous in terms of facilities, yet maintaining the aesthetic value it has.

The M.M.G. leader and his party also had a chance to view the new facilities, including the Glamorgan Cricket Heritage Gallery in the National Cricket Centre completed with the generous support of a £50,000 grant from the Heritage Lottery Fund. Comprising over forty display panels and a series of plasma screens, it was formally opened on 28 June by R. Paul Russell and Dan Clayton-Jones, the chairman of the Heritage Lottery in Wales, who said:

> Wales has a proud sporting heritage, and while rugby might grab more headlines, Glamorgan Cricket has made an enormous contribution to our sense of pride and sporting achievement as Wales' sole

> representative in the English County Championship. Many more people will now be able to learn all about the club's fascinating past, and I'm sure that a whole new generation of players and fans across the country will be inspired to pick up a bat and play.

By mid-December, most of the construction work at the Cardiff ground was complete, with the bulk of the work after the Christmas holidays focussing on the fit-out of the new buildings. The county club were also able to announce several deals with sponsors for the new facilities, including the superb new pavilion, now known as The Really Welsh Pavilion following sponsorship from the company who are the leading producers of flowers, vegetables and other market garden produce in Wales.

The spacious room, hosting the Business Club on the first floor of the pavilion, was sponsored by Morgan Cole Solicitors, while the Pavilion Members' Lounge became known as the Procopy Lounge following a deal with the Cardiff-based firm who are South Wales' leading office and technology company.

On 4 March 2008 it was also announced that the magnificent new ground would hereafter be known as The SWALEC Stadium following a ten-year partnership with SWALEC, the leading energy supplier in Wales, as part of the biggest single sponsorship by a county cricket club, and the biggest naming rights agreement ever entered into in Wales, worth in excess of £1.5 million.

In announcing the record-breaking deal, R. Paul Russell, the chairman of Glamorgan Cricket, stated:

> The new SWALEC Stadium is an iconic statement of the new 'can do' attitude of the new Wales. With our partners in the Welsh Assembly Government and the City Council, we saw this new national stadium as an opportunity to show the world what can be achieved by Team Wales. The SWALEC Stadium is already a tribute to the skill and energy of the Welsh construction industry. SWALEC is associated with excellence in the energy sector in much the same way as the new SWALEC Stadium will be associated with the best that modern cricket can offer. I'm sure that when cricket fans throughout the world are asked to name a Test stadium in the UK, the SWALEC Stadium will soon rank alongside that of Lord's, the Brit Oval and Australia's top ground, the MCG.

A fortnight after this announcement, the SWALEC Stadium was formally handed over to Glamorgan Cricket by Carillion who had undertaken – on time and to budget – the construction work. After a short presentation in the Morgan Cole Lounge, sponsors and others connected with the redevelopment were given a short tour of The Really Welsh Pavilion. In April 2008, Glamorgan members and season ticket holders also went on the tours of the SWALEC Stadium that are now provided – on a pre-booked basis - by the cricket club .

On 11 April 2008 confirmation came through from the E.C.B. that the Cardiff ground would also host the first npower Test between England and Australia in July 2009 – a decision greeted with great delight by all cricket fans in Wales, as well as those in the West Country for whom the SWALEC Stadium now becomes their nearest Test match venue. There was further good news for the forward-thinking Glamorgan officials, as the SWALEC Stadium was also allocated a One-Day International between England and Australia in 2010, followed in 2011 by another Test match, between England and Sri Lanka, and a further One-Day International between England and India.

In the words of Paul Russell:

> Hosting the first Ashes Test in 2009 is really a great honour for any new ground. For such a prestigious game to be the first-ever Test match at a new stadium must be a first in world cricket. It is boy's own stuff, and the eyes of the world are going to be on Cardiff, Glamorgan and the SWALEC Stadium. That puts a great responsibility to make sure they see something good, and that is precisely what we intend to do. There were some doubters questioning whether we could achieve it, but I am really pleased we finally have and I am so proud of this fantastic stadium.
>
> Some people have written about the shock decision to stage an Ashes Test in Cardiff, but they obviously have not been down here and seen what we have achieved. One pundit described the decision to host the game as a joke, but I don't think there are many people laughing when they have seen the transformation to this stadium.

September 2006 and contsruction work commences on the new pavilion.

June 2007 and the shell of the Media Centre is in place as Glamorgan commence their Twenty20 campaign.

The builders put the finishing touches to the Really Welsh Pavilion in January 2008.

Glamorgan's first fixture at The SWALEC Stadium took place at the Cardiff ground on 9 May 2008, with the Welsh county staging a Friends Provident Trophy match against Gloucestershire. Given the efforts in the early 1900s by Bristol-born Joseph Brain to bring Test cricket to Cardiff, the West Country side were most worthy visitors to the new Stadium.

On 3 September 2008 England played South Africa in a floodlit One-Day International, just a few days after the sixtieth anniversary of Glamorgan's first ever Championship success. That victory, at Bournemouth, was the greatest event in Glamorgan's history during the twentieth century, with the club shedding its previous tag of being a Cinderella county on the field. Sixty years on, the game against South Africa was the first in a series of major international matches, including Tests, at Cardiff as Glamorgan Cricket entered the twenty-first century with a stadium, and other off-field facilities, of which Wales can be proud.

Sadly, the weather in South Wales was far from being celebratory, with a series of deluges affecting all of the region in the last fortnight of August and the first week of September. Under the circumstances, it was quite an achievement to get some play, but after a couple of overs, the rains returned and the contest was abandoned. Nevertheless, over 15,000 fans had safely, and swiftly, made their way to and from the ground and, as a dress rehearsal for the Test matches, it had been a good dry run – if that is the correct word!

The match had also given the hundreds of corporate guests and sundry VIPs a chance to enjoy the excellent hospitality and corporate facilities. Indeed, the SWALEC Stadium now boasts a thriving Conference and Banqueting department, with Phase two works in 2008/9 adding to the range of first-class facilities, now capable of hosting over 2,000 guests and delegates, right in the heart of Wales' capital city. Phase two works have seen the addition of a new upper storey to the National Cricket Centre, while reconfiguration works have seen the creation of two new conference suites and a row of new hospitality boxes. On the outfield, the Autumn of 2008 saw the removal of the old turf, followed by the installation of a new drainage system, plus the laying of fast-drying turf, thanks to a grant of £750,000 from the ECB.

By the Spring of 2009, everything was in place for the start of the new season, with everyone looking forward to the first npower Ashes Test, starting on 8 July, as Glamorgan Cricket took its place on the international stage with a stadium boasting all of the facilities now required of a major ground, allowing Cardiff to become a Test Match ground, almost 200 years after the first record of a game of cricket in the city.

2008 and the Really Welsh Pavilion is completed.

The view from the Cathedral Road End as the Glamorgan Dragons play the Gloucestershire Gladiators in a Friends Provident Trophy match at the SWALEC Stadium in May 2008 – the first match at the Dragon's redeveloped headquarters.

The SWALEC Stadium as seen from the Really Welsh Pavilion.

Acknowledgements

The compilation of this book and the reproduction of the images, telling the fascinating story of the Cardiff ground, would not have been possible without the help and support of the following people and organisations – Dennis Morgan, Brian Lee, Katrina Coopey, Gwyn Prescott, Bryn Jones, Matthew Williams, Stewart Williams, Howard Evans, John Billot, Grahame Lloyd, David Smith, Richard Shepherd, Andrew Weltch, Gareth Goldsworthy, John Jenkins, Duncan Pierce, Huw John, Phil Blanche, Lawrence Hourahane, Jim Pleass, Katy Thomas, Barry Milton, the staff of the Glamorgan Record Office, Cardiff Central Library, Media Wales, the *South Wales Evening Post*, the National Library of Wales plus all my colleagues at Glamorgan Cricket.

The SWALEC Stadium.